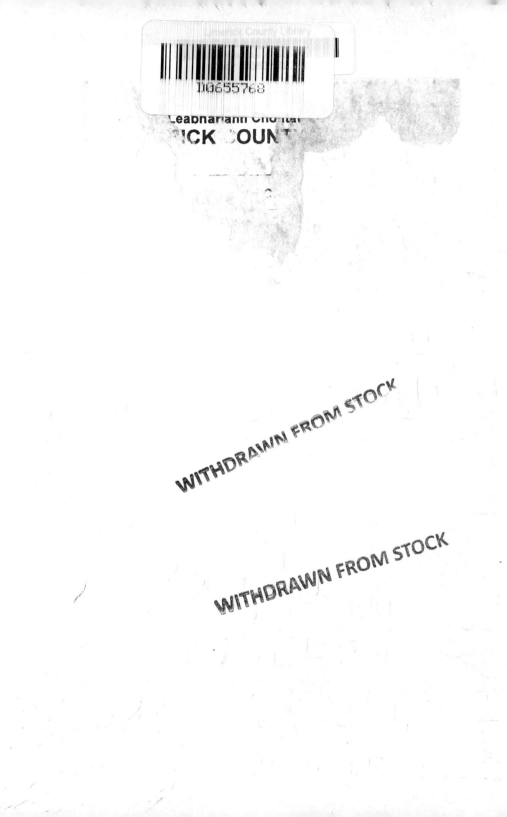

EVERY WOMAN'S LUCK BOOK

This edition published in the UK in 2003 by
Icon Books Ltd., Grange Road, Duxford, Cambridge CB2 4QF
e-mail: info@iconbooks.co.uk   www.iconbooks.co.uk

Originally published in the 1930s by The Amalgamated Press Ltd., London
(Original publication date unknown.) Every effort has been made to trace
the copyright holder of the material reproduced in this book. If notified, the
publisher will be pleased to acknowledge the use of any copyright material.

Sold in the UK, Europe, South Africa and Asia by Faber and Faber Ltd.,
3 Queen Square, London WC1N 3AU or their agents. Distributed in
the UK, Europe, South Africa and Asia by TBS Ltd., Frating Distribution
Centre, Colchester Road, CO7 7DW. Published in Australia in 2003
by Allen & Unwin Pty. Ltd., PO Box 8500, 83 Alexander Street, Crows
Nest, NSW 2065. Distributed in Canada by Penguin Books Canada,
10 Alcorn Avenue, Suite 300, Toronto, Ontario M4V 3B2. Published in the
USA in 2003 by Totem Books. Inquiries to Icon Books, UK, as above.
Distributed to the trade in the USA by National Book Network Inc., 4720
Boston Way, Lanham, Maryland 20706.

This edition copyright © 2003 by Icon Books Ltd.

ISBN 1 84046 518 2

Printed and bound in the UK by Mackays of Chatham plc.

CONTENTS

Chapter	I	What Does the Future Hold ?	Page	3
,,	II	The Stars Foretell your Destiny	,,	5
		The " Postman's Knock " Game	,,	30
,,	III	Find Fortune in the Cards	,,	31
,,	IV	Tell-tale Tea-leaves	,,	42
,,	V	Features and Fate	,,	49
,,	VI	Luck in Marriage	,,	57
,,	VII	Hands of Destiny	,,	67
		The " Colour and Destiny " Game	,,	96
,,	VIII	Lucky Stones	,,	97
,,	IX	Reading " His " Writing	,,	101
,,	X	Say it with Flowers	,,	109
,,	XI	" Bumps " that Betray	,,	119
,,	XII	Luck in Love	,,	126
		The " Road of Life " Game	,,	133
,,	XIII	" Confessions "	,,	134
,,	XIV	Improve your Luck	,,	146
,,	XV	Lucky Birthday Forecasts	,,	151
		The " Maze " Game	,,	166
,,	XVI	Your Lucky Number	,,	167
,	XVII	The Lucky Dream-book	,,	172
		Key to Plates	,,	192

LIST OF PLATES

Plate	1	Character in Eyes	Facing Page	32
,,	2	,, ,,		
,,	3	,, ,,		
,,	4	,, ,,	,,	33
,,	5	,, ,,	,,	64
,,	6	,, ,,		
,,	7	,, ,,		
,,	8	,, ,,	,,	65
,,	9	Character in Mouths	,,	128
,,	10	,, ,,		
,,	11	Character in Noses		
,,	12	,, ,,	,,	129
,,	13	Character in Chins	,,	160
,,	14	,, ,,		
,,	15	Character in Ears		
,,	16	Character in Hands	,,	161

CHAPTER I

What Does the Future Hold?

We all believe in luck—Good fortune can be won—The purpose of this book—Peering into the future by various methods—Character shapes destiny—How to be popular.

EVERYBODY believes in luck in their heart of hearts, even those who declare that there is "no such thing." None of us can completely control our fate ; try as we will, we cannot shape the course of events to please ourselves. Things happen — sometimes things that have a decisive effect on the whole course of our lives—that we cannot possibly control. To us, these things are luck, good or bad.

But if Fate cannot be ordered, at least good luck can often be won, and bad luck avoided, to some extent. From the very earliest times wise men have believed that to do certain things brings good luck, and to do others is unlucky. In this little book you will find several chapters telling you of ways to win good fortune and avert evil ; telling you, too, how by your own outlook on life you can attract good luck to yourself and make Dame Fortune smile upon you. And in the Dream Book at the end you will find the portent of almost any dream you may have—and many an indication of the future, many a timely warning of impending danger, has been given in dreams.

Trying to peer into the future, too, is irresistibly fascinating to everyone, even the scoffers. It is not given to all of us to pierce the veil, but the various expert writers who have contributed to this book tell you, in the chapters on Astrology, Palmistry, and Numbers, and those on Fortune-telling by means of Cards, Tea-leaves and so on, various interesting ways of forecasting what life may hold for yourself and your friends.

Character shapes Destiny, and to know yourself, and to be able to form a true judgment of others helps you on every step along Life's pathway. And so in other chapters you will find valuable information on judging Character from Appearances, from Handwriting, by Phrenology and in other ways.

Apart from its value as a guide through life, this book will help you to be an entertaining companion socially, for everyone loves to be told about themselves and their future, and a girl who can tell fortunes by Palmistry, by Cards, or in any other way will be welcome wherever she goes. A little study of the subject is well worth while, and a pleasant way of passing many an idle hour.

May this book bring you luck, and help you on to good fortune and lifelong happiness.

CHAPTER II

The Stars Foretell Your Destiny

*Horoscopes for everyone—Your characteristics—Career—
Mr. " Right "—Lucky engagement ring—Lucky wedding date
—Lucky colour, etc.*

THOSE who have made a study of Astrology, the science of foretelling the future from the stars, base their prophecies upon the Zodiac, an imaginary belt in the heavens through which the sun passes in the course of each year. The Zodiac has twelve divisions, and according to the division in which the sun was at the hour of your birth, so your character and destiny are influenced. Each division is given a name and a sign, from a constellation of stars that lies in it; the twelve signs of the Zodiac, and approximately the periods of the year they govern, are as follows :

ARIES, the Ram—March 21st to April 20th.
TAURUS, the Bull—April 21st to May 22nd.
GEMINI, the Twins—May 22nd to June 21st.
CANCER, the Crab—June 22nd to July 23rd.
LEO, the Lion—July 23rd to August 23rd.
VIRGO, the Virgin—August 24th to September 22nd.
LIBRA, the Balance—September 23rd to October 23rd.

SCORPIO, the Scorpion—October 24th to November 23rd.
SAGITTARIUS, the Archer—November 23rd to December 21st.
CAPRICORNUS, the Goat—December 22nd to January 19th.
AQUARIUS, the Water Carrier—January 20th to February 19th.
PISCES, the Fishes—February 19th to March 20th.

Further, the twelve Zodiacal signs are divided into four groups, the elements Fire, Earth, Air and Water, and these also effect your character. The four groups are as follows :
FIRE—Leo, Sagittarius, Aries.
EARTH—Taurus, Capricornus, Virgo.
AIR—Libra, Aquarius, Gemini.
WATER—Cancer, Scorpio, Pisces.
Of course, there are natural differences between two people born in the same period, depending on heredity, the exact hour of birth, whether they were born nearer the beginning or end of a planetary period, and so on, but in the main those born under the same sign share similar characteristics—and to some extent character shapes destiny.

YOUR HOROSCOPE—

FORTUNE is on your side if your birthday falls between December 22nd and January 19th. Your zodiacal sign is *Capricornus*, the Goat, and though you may not achieve success in life at first, the careful, painstaking way in which you will set about carving a path for yourself should enable you to sit back in peace and comfort in later life, and enjoy the result of your efforts.

Your friendship will be sought by almost all those who come into contact with you, for you make a most faithful and loyal friend, and they will see your sterling worth shining out of your eyes.

You will derive great pleasure from the affection of those around you, and if there are times, such as come to many of us in life, when you are feeling a little depressed or downcast, because you have not as many nice things as you would like, you should find comfort in remembering that the true riches of life are not bought with gold.

A little failing you should guard against is not always being able to make up your mind quickly enough, for you may lose valuable opportunities otherwise. To overcome this, you will need to cultivate some special ambition as an incentive to put your very best into your work and to force you to make decisions.

You are often rather reserved over the thoughts nearest to your heart and so are apt to brood over slights or injuries, imagined or otherwise, instead of speaking out to the one concerned and clearing matters up. However, once the air is cleared you are your charming self again, and do your best to make up for the little shadow that for a time had you in its grip.

As *Capricornus* is your sign, one of the "earth" groups, you are a child of the earth, and have your feet firmly planted on the ground. You are staunch and trustworthy and will stand steadily and loyally for all who rely on you.

Your Career

Your trustworthiness will stand you in good stead when choosing a career, for you will thus inspire the confidence of your employers. You will probably find that business life will suit you best, though, as you are also fond of the out-of-doors, you might also make a success of any work connected with the garden or with farming.

As Saturday is your lucky day, you should try to choose it for any special plans or undertakings.

Mr. " Right "

You will need to make a careful choice of the man you marry, but you could not do better than choose one who is born between June 22nd and July 23rd which period is ruled by the zodiacal sign of *Cancer*, the Crab.

Your *Cancer* sweetheart will be careful and persevering like yourself, and will usually attain his success in life by steady hard work. You will admire him for this, and together you should climb quietly up the ladder of success, for when two hardworking natures work in double harness there is little that can stand in their way.

He will share your love of neatness and order, while his faithfulness and loyalty will be as fine and deep as yours, so you should get

—If you were born between December 22nd and January 19th.

on well with each other in every way.

Your Second Choice

If your sweetheart's birthday falls between April 21st and May 22nd, under the sign of *Taurus*, the Bull, you have also quite a good chance of happiness with him.

He will be solid and dependable, just as you are, and as he is better able to make up his mind than you, he should be able to assist you just when you need a guiding hand most.

Being of a little more cheerful disposition than you, also, he will know just how to shake you out of those fits of the " blues " which may sometimes grip you. You should, therefore, be quite well suited.

Other Sweethearts

The men of other birthdates are not really quite so suitable for you, and if you decide to marry one of them you may find you need patience and tact with which to overcome the little differences in your characters.

But love can work wonders, and if you are quite sure that yours is strong enough not to let these little things get the better of you, then you may find happiness.

Your Engagement Ring

When the great day comes on which you are going to choose the ring which will set the seal on your love, you will perhaps like good luck to help you in your choice.

Your lucky stone, then, is the

CAPRICORNUS (Goat)

ruby, and if you choose a ring set with this stone, you may be all the more sure of good fortune attending you and your sweetheart.

Good Luck for Your Wedding

The most fortunate months for you to choose for your wedding would be October or November of any year.

If you have decided to have a pretty white wedding, you should strive to include some autumn leaves in your bouquet, or to see that they form a part of the church decorations, as their colour holds luck for you.

Perhaps, however, you are having a quiet wedding ? Then you might well choose a warm brown colour for your dress or suit, or else make sure that you are wearing something brown underneath.

If you do this you may be sure that you have done all in your power to encourage fortune to smile on you.

HAPPY you, if you were born under the zodiacal sign of *Aquarius*, the Water-carrier, between January 20th and February 19th ! Well-liked wherever you go for your bright, jolly ways in company, you will gather many friends about you, and this will please you immensely, for you like nothing better than to have people round you.

Those who know you really well, however, will have discovered that beneath your social gaiety lies also a more serious side to your nature, and that for sound, practical advice, as well as sympathy, you are the person to go to.

You like variety and change, and you will find that your life will hold both ups and downs, but whatever comes, you have the courage and patience with which to win through.

Faithful and reliable, you are nevertheless rather inclined, sometimes, to let your sense of responsibility weigh you down, and this is something you should try to fight against. Your thoughtfulness for others will win you a warm place in the hearts of the older folk with whom you come into contact, and, while there are few people so generous as you are, you should see that this does not lead you into being imposed upon.

You do not find it easy to forget an injury, but you are honourable and just, and you will always give people a fair hearing before you condemn them in any way. Perhaps you are a little too inclined to want your own way in life, but this is a failing you can overcome.

Being a child of " air " gives your character the breeziness and gaiety that makes others enjoy your company, though you must guard against going " up in the air " over trifling irritations !

You are home-loving and, while you do not show affection easily, yet once your love is given it is deep and true. You will make a good housewife, for you are thrifty and methodical, and will probably show excellent taste in the furnishing of your home.

Your Career

Because you are quick to learn and have a very good memory, you should be most successful as a teacher of almost any subject you care to take up. Domestic service, also, would suit you if you find such work appeals to you, while still another career you might do well at is nursing, because you are naturally patient and gentle with invalids.

You share your lucky day with the Capricorn folk, so you, too, should try to carry out any special plans or make big decisions on a Saturday.

Mr. " Right "

The man whom you should choose as your life partner is one whose birthday falls between September 23rd and October 23rd, under the sign of *Libra*, the Balance, for you will find he has most in common with you.

Your *Libra* sweetheart will be sweet-tempered and level-headed, and this, coupled with your own wise head, should take you a long way towards success together.

Both of you will be popular with your friends, for you share the charm of manner that makes you so, and you will both be happy when you are working to help others less fortunate than yourselves.

—If you were born between January 20th and February 19th.

A love of spending your leisure hours tramping the countryside is another characteristic you will have in common.

He has the same patience and courage with which to overcome the setbacks which may cross your path and, though wealth may one day come to you, you will be quite content with simple, homely things.

Your Second Choice

Perhaps your sweetheart's birthday falls between May 22nd and June 21st, under the sign of *Gemini*, the Twins? Then you should also find happiness together, for though you may disagree on minor points, you have quite a number of things in common.

He will share your love of home and bright surroundings, and he will be a real pal and companion to you. You will find that he is a little lacking in ambition and rather inclined to drift, but your understanding nature should enable you to give him just the help and counsel he needs to send him along the road to success.

Other Sweethearts

If you choose a partner who is not truly in harmony with you, you will find you need to make many allowances where his characteristics may clash with yours.

He may put down your gay ways as " flightiness," and so be irritated by them, not realising how sincere you are underneath.

If you do your best to show him a little more of your serious side, however, and feel that you care for him sufficiently to try to look at things from his point of view sometimes, you should find happiness.

AQUARIUS (Watercarrier)

Your Engagement Ring

Your lucky stone is the deep red garnet, and when you go on that happy expedition with " him " to choose the precious ring, you should encourage good fortune to be still further on your side by selecting one set with this stone.

You have a second choice in the amethyst, however, if you prefer this stone, and it should help you and your sweetheart to know only happiness during your engagement.

Good Luck for Your Wedding

May or September are the luckiest months for your wedding.

Your lucky colour being red, you should see that your bouquet is made up of deep red carnations or roses if you are going to be married in white.

Should you be having a quiet wedding, however, you might choose a frock in which red could be prettily introduced, or else see that you have at least a touch of red somewhere about you. Good fortune should then smile on you throughout your married life.

GOOD luck will never entirely desert you if you were born under the zodiacal sign of *Pisces*, the Fishes—February 19th to March 20th. Even when clouds are heaviest, something will turn up at the last moment to lead you into better times again.

Your character is curiously like two fishes swimming different ways, which is the symbol of your sign, for you have rather a dual nature. Because of this, other people are often led into thinking that you lack decision, but this is not really one of your failings. It is simply that you have such a strong sense of duty towards others that one side of your character prompts you to act, sometimes, in a way which calls forth the disapproval of the other side.

It is most important that you should live, as far as possible, in peaceful, happy, surroundings, for you are greatly impressed and influenced by the things about you, and are subject to sudden " moodiness " and sometimes, even, fits of depression. Fortunately, however, those do not last long and you are quick to gain fresh heart from any kind thought or action shown to you.

Deeply fond of children and animals, you do not like to pass either in the street without stopping to talk to them, and in consequence they are usually exceptionally good when in your care. You would make a good life partner for a man whose work was difficult or tiring, for you have that soothing influence that makes people feel they can relax and be at peace in your company.

You will be keen to learn all you can about the wonders of the world you live in, and you will naturally be fond of books and also of music.

You are very loyal to your friends, though you will only choose a few to whom you will reveal your inmost thoughts and dreams. Whenever anyone is in trouble or difficulty, they will come to you, for you are intensely sympathetic and also have a deep understanding of human nature.

Being a " water " child will account for your having a deep love of the sea and a longing to travel on it. Then, too, though you are naturally peace-loving and slow to anger, when once your temper is roused, the " storm " is heavy. It does not take you long to get over it, however.

You will love nothing better than to have a home of your own and a little family to look after, and you should make a success of marriage because you are tactful, adaptable and grateful for the affection shown you.

Your Career

You could not do better than choose nursing as a career, for you have the patience and the soothing presence required for this.

Being clever with your fingers as well, however, you might also do well at dressmaking or hairdressing, if these appeal to you.

For you, Thursday is the luckiest day, and you should see that you carry out all the most important schemes on that day.

Mr. " Right "

To choose the right life partner is most important for you, but if your choice falls on one born in *Scorpio*—October 24th to November 23rd—you could not do better.

Mr. " *Scorpio* " will be kind and tolerant, and will understand and

—If you were born between February 19th and March 20th.

help to shake you out of your sudden little moods of depression. In fact he will act like a tonic on you. He, too, will share your ideal of being pals as well as husband and wife, and will appreciate all the little things you do for him.

Both of you will take a deep interest in those who are sick, and you may be able to work together over this, for quite often *Scorpio* men become doctors. At any rate you should find he will make a devoted husband and a good parent.

Your Second Choice

It may happen that your sweetheart's birthday falls between June 22nd and July 23rd, under the sign of *Cancer*, the Crab. If so, you will find that you have a great deal in common, though you may not get on quite so well as you would with the *Scorpio* man.

You will find that there is much in your *Cancer* sweetheart that you can admire, and this will please you, as you like to look up to, and be proud of, the man you marry.

He will share a love of books and music with you, and he also possesses the same love of the sea, so that if you were called upon to travel or to make your home by it, you would both be quite happy over this. Then, too, he will share your fondness for children and animals.

Other Sweethearts

You are not likely to get on quite so well with the men of other birthdates, for they would not so easily be able to understand your " moodiness," at times, or to make a companion of you as much as you would wish.

PISCES (Fishes)

However, your understanding might well help you to overcome these little differences, so long as you were sure of your love.

Your Engagement Ring

You will be anxious for good fortune to smile on you, from the day when he takes you to choose the ring, onwards all through your engagement, and you can certainly help good luck to stay with you by choosing a ring set with your lucky stone, the amethyst.

Good Luck for Your Wedding

The most fortunate months to choose for your wedding are either June or November of any year.

Perhaps you are planning to be a pretty white bride ? Then you should certainly carry out the old rhyme and wear " something blue," for that is your lucky colour. If you have decided on a quiet wedding, however, then you could not do better than choose a dainty frock or outfit in blue, so that you may encourage happiness to walk with you through the future.

YOU are ready to grasp good luck with both hands if you were born between March 21st and April 20th, under the zodiacal sign of *Aries*, the Ram. You are born to lead, and you will not like it if your friends do not let you do so. However, as soon as they know you well, they will probably give way to you in this, for they will realise that you are perhaps better fitted than most people to do so.

A humdrum, quiet life does not generally suit you, for you are extremely active and like to be up and doing, interested in many things, and anxious to fight for what you want from life.

You might well try to curb those impetuous ways a little, however, for they may lead you to rush thoughtlessly into risks and dangers without first going thoroughly into whether you are doing the best thing or not. If you guard against this, you should go far towards success.

You have, perhaps, more courage than those of any other sign, but because of this there is no need to take needless risks and perhaps cause others to suffer on your account. Because you like to go straight to the point over most things, you get very impatient with those who like to work round a subject before they reach it, but if you see anyone in need of help you will do all in your power to ease their burden for them, for you are generous to an extreme.

You are quick and clever, but your impulsive nature will often lead you to say more than you mean, and then you will be sorry afterwards. You will make a good and capable wife, however, for your capacity for deep affection should lead to faithfulness in love and friendship, but you should

YOUR HOROSCOPE—

guard against an inclination to jealousy.

Another result of your forceful nature is a tendency to be obstinate, and to dislike admitting yourself in the wrong, but you have the strength of will to overcome these little failings and make something really fine of your character.

A child of " fire," some of the fieriness of your sign has entered into your nature so that you are apt to flare up quickly when your anger is roused. But you will calm down just as quickly.

Tuesday is the most fortunate day for you to carry out any special undertakings.

Mr. " Right "

The most suitable life partner for you to choose, is a *Sagittarius* man, his birthday falling between November 23rd and December 21st.

You will find him quick to acquire knowledge, and with the same desire as yourself for an active, interesting life. Being of a rather steadier, quieter nature than yours, he will be a good influence over you, and you will feel the happier for having someone so dependable at your side.

You will get on well together, also, because he is very sociable, and has great determination, and the latter, coupled with your own forceful, decided nature, should make for great success in life.

Both of you will be hospitable, and like to entertain your friends often, so that you should have a splendid chance of happiness together.

Your Second Choice

You have also quite a good chance of happiness if your sweetheart's birthday falls under the

—If you were born between March 21st and April 20th.

sign of *Leo*, the Lion, between July 23rd and August 23rd.

He, like yourself, will be full of courage, and will possess the power of exercising great influence over others. This asset should, therefore, stand you in good stead, for your tendency towards impulsiveness, which may sometimes cause you to make mistakes, needs the curbing influence that he would have over you.

You should also find your capacity for loving deeply, amply repaid by your *Leo* partner's faithfulness in affection. You may well make a success of marriage with him, therefore.

ARIES (Ram)

Other Sweethearts

If you choose a man who is not truly harmonious with you, you will probably find you are expected to give way over your opinions and plans quite often, while you might definitely clash over the fact that both of you would want to take the reins in the home.

Then, too, you would need to guard against sudden flares of temper, for, while they are all over in a few minutes as far as you are concerned, he might take them more seriously, brood over them, and be really hurt.

However, with strength of will, and true love on your side, you might well overcome these difficulties and know happiness.

Your Engagement Ring

In all the wonderful excitement of a visit together to the jeweller's to choose " the dearest little ring in the world," if you would still further wish to encourage fortune's favour, you should choose one set with your lucky stone, which is the popular diamond.

Then you should be able to look forward to engagement days that are full of happiness.

Good Luck and Your Wedding

For you, the months of July or December are the most fortunate for your wedding, and if you possibly can, you should resolve to be a white bride, for this is a particularly lucky colour for you, and you can still further add to your luck by carrying a bouquet of lovely white lilies or roses.

If you must choose a quiet wedding, however, you may still court good fortune by choosing a pretty dress or outfit of white or cream, and then you should know few clouds in the sky of your married happiness.

"ONE of the best!" That is how people will describe you if you were born under the zodiacal sign of *Taurus*, the Bull, your birthday falling between April 21st and May 22nd.

You are so good-natured and generous, kindly and easy-going, that other folk cannot help liking you. But though they think of you as a good sort, and one who, by your cheery ways, will hearten them when they are feeling depressed, only a few of your nearest friends realise that underneath you have a strong and serious side, capable of deep feeling.

You also have a strong sense of duty, and you would never let anyone down who relied on you. On the other hand, you will not let yourself be imposed upon and, straightforward and kindly yourself, you will not easily forget any injury that is done you.

Besides being deeply affectionate and loving, you will greatly appreciate any kind of beauty, and you will love to have nice things around you. Music, particularly, will appeal to you, and it seems to have a good and soothing influence over *Taurus* people.

Perhaps you are a little too stubborn where sticking to your own views about anything is concerned, and this is something you might strive to overcome, for none of us are entirely incapable of making mistakes.

You find your enjoyment in the practical, homely things of life, and you are well able to look after the welfare and comforts of others. You are ready to give up everything for those you love, but you should guard against a tendency towards jealousy which, if you do not strive to conquer it, may cause you unnecessary unhappiness. You have a very good memory, and you are clever with money, being able to make every penny do its work and a little bit more.

You are an "earth" child, dependable and reliable, a person to lean on in time of trouble. You will also know just what you want from life, and determine to see that your feet are set firmly on the way you mean to go.

Your Career

Because of your love of beautiful things, you should be most successful at dress-designing or florist work, where you can be among the colour and beauty of the flowers.

On the other hand, your love of music might help you to do well as a music teacher, if this career appeals to you.

Friday is your lucky day, so if you have anything of vital importance to do, see that you carry it out on that day.

Mr. "Right"

You need to be rather careful in choosing your life partner, in order to find one whose characteristics most harmonise with your own, but if you choose one whose birthday falls between December 22nd and January 19th, under the sign of *Capricornus*, the Goat, you should have a splendid chance of happiness.

Your *Capricornus* sweetheart has great powers of endurance, and he will also be very persevering and steady, qualities you will admire in him, while his love will be the kind that will last all through life.

He may be subject to fits of "the blues," but your warm affection will help him through them to cheerfulness again.

You will be pleased **because** he

—If you were born between April 21st and May 22nd.

shares your own strong sense of duty, and also, like you, is straight-forward and reliable, so you should find that your characteristics blend in very well together.

Your Second Choice

If your sweetheart's birthday falls under *Cancer*, the Crab, between June 22nd and July 23rd, you should also get on quite well together.

Both of you will be persevering, and share the capacity of achieving success if you set your minds to it and work with a will. You will probably find him just as fond of music as you are, too, and you should spend many happy hours in the enjoyment of this.

He may be inclined to be "moody," but here your understanding and common sense should help you to shake him out of his moods, and altogether you should be quite well matched.

Other Sweethearts

If you choose a partner who is not definitely harmonious to you, you would need to overcome your inclination towards jealousy, or there might be friction between you, while both of you might want too much of your own way.

Again, he might not share your love of home, being more anxious to go out on social pleasures, so that you would need a great deal of tact and patience to overcome these differences of character.

If your love is strong enough, however, you may quite well find you are able to do so, and so achieve happiness.

TAURUS (*Bull*)

Your Engagement Ring

Perhaps you know that blue is the special colour associated with love, and what stone could be prettier to choose for your treasured engagement ring than the sapphire? This is your lucky stone, and there should be no shadow over your engagement days if you choose a ring set with it.

Good Luck at Your Wedding

If you would have fortune smile on your wedding—and what bride wouldn't?—you should choose the month of July or December for the ceremony, and if you are having a white wedding you should carry blue delphiniums in your bouquet in July, or see that it is tied with blue ribbon in December, for this is your lucky colour.

Should you have a quiet wedding, then you would look charming and also court good luck in a pretty blue dress or costume. Then fortune should indeed smile on your married life.

YOU seem to bear a charmed life if your birthday falls between May 22nd and June 21st, under the zodiacal sign of *Gemini*, the Twins.

You are a puzzle to all who come in contact with you, including yourself, because you are generally trying to do two things at once, yet are never quite sure if you mean to carry either of them through. You are such a contradiction, and so changeable, that people become exasperated with you, but you have only to smile your own particular smile at them and they find themselves forgiving you at once !

Your brilliance and charm bring you many admirers, and you are always having love affairs which usually leave you with the firm belief that your heart is broken— until the next time !

This does not mean that you are a flirt, for you are really sincere each time, so long as it lasts. Your feelings are deep for the time being, but, like the butterfly, you are soon attracted elsewhere. In fact, " butterfly " is an excellent description of your gay, happy, elusive ways.

If your latest sweetheart is upset over parting, you will feel sorry about it so long as you think about it, but it will not remain long in your mind, for your spirits rise again in no time, and you are your usual light-hearted self.

But there is a sterling side to your nature, as your friends will vouch for. You are loyal to them, and you have plenty of intelligence and imagination. In fact, you love nothing better than to be able to find out all about the things that go on around you, and to study books for this purpose.

Gemini, like *Pisces*, is a double sign, and this explains why your nature seems to be a dual one. You will probably find that all through your life things happen to you twice over. You may marry twice, and wives born under this sign often have twins.

You should try to overcome a desire to rule the lives of others around you, for we cannot all live to the same pattern, while you should never let your witty sayings be at someone else's expense.

A child of " air," you are light-hearted and breezy, " up in the air " one minute, and down the next, but never down for long.

Your Career

Because, owing to a certain indecision in your nature, you prefer to have regular, settled work at which you do not have to make decisions for yourself, you should find your best success in secretarial work.

On the other hand, because you are generally quick at learning languages, you might also do well in any work connected with them.

Wednesday being your lucky day, you should carry out all important plans on that day.

Mr. " Right "

The most suitable life partner for you is one born under the zodiacal sign of *Aquarius*, the Water Carrier, his birthday falling between January 20th and February 19th.

Although you are fickle and changeable, when once you have met the right man for you, instinct will convince you of the fact as you have not been fully convinced before, and you will settle down steadily.

If your sweetheart is an Aquarian, then, he will be one whose high

—If you were born between May 22nd and June 21st.

ideals you can look up to, while he will give in to you in many ways—though not too much for your own good.

Just because he will not try to curb and rule you, you will probably be all the more firmly attached to him. Both of you will make friends of people with artistic interests and your home will be the sort of place where people drift in and out informally.

Your Second Choice

Your sweetheart's birthday may, on the other hand, come under the sign of *Libra*, the Balance, his birthday falling between September 23rd and October 23rd. In this case you should get on quite well together, for where you are perhaps too light-hearted and impulsive, his level-headedness, should balance up well.

He will be understanding and sympathetic over all your aims and interests, while his steadying influence will prevent you from acting too rashly at times.

With such a good wife as you will make when you once settle down, you should go far together.

Other Sweethearts

You are not likely to get on so well with men who are not truly in harmony with you, for they may look on your gay, breezy ways as "flightiness" and will be irritated by them unless you make every effort to show them your more serious side.

Perhaps, too, you would need to appreciate that there are times when silence is golden.

If you are quite sure that your love is the real thing, however, then

GEMINI (Twins)

you may well overcome these clashes in temperament and find happiness.

Your Engagement Ring

On the happy day when you go to choose the ring with "him," it would be well to consider that you may ensure even better fortune for yourself and your sweetheart by choosing a ring set with your lucky stone, the sapphire.

Then you need have no doubt that your engagement days will be happy ones.

Good Luck at Your Wedding

September, or your own birth month, will be very fortunate for you to choose for your wedding.

If you can manage it, you should be a lovely silver and white bride, for these are your lucky colours.

Should you have a quiet wedding, however, then you might choose a frock or costume of a delicate green colour. Because it is fortunate for you, you can laugh at the "unlucky green" superstition, and you will be courting good luck in your marriage.

IF you go the right way about it, you should certainly find fortune smiling on you if you were born under the zodiacal sign of *Cancer*, the Crab, which rules between June 22nd and July 23rd, though it may not always be in quite the way you expect.

You are rather a contradiction, because, being subject to fits of " moodiness," you are inclined to act according to the mood you are in at the moment and then, a little later, want to change your mind and do something entirely different ! This makes it a little difficult for those around you to understand you, though the few friends you make—you prefer a picked few to many—will know you to be loyal and able to keep a confidence.

You will need cheerful surroundings, fresh air and sunshine to bring out the best in you, for you are very quickly affected by the things around you. Extremely sensitive, you should strive hard not to take offence over little things, or to imagine hurts where none are intended.

Your feelings go deep, but because you hide them under such a deep reserve, people often take you to be hard and cold. You are greatly in demand at social gatherings, however, for then you really let yourself go in an effort to make a success of things, and people see the really charming side of your nature.

Perhaps you might guard against a little closeness over money matters, and a tendency to worry over trifles. In any big emergency, however, you are a great standby, and people will know they can rely on you.

You are very fond of your home and family, and in consequence should make a splendid housewife.

Your devotion to children, also, should make you a good mother.

You are generous-hearted, but rather inclined to be jealous, which is something you should fight against, while you are intelligent, industrious and painstaking, but unfortunately you resent criticism, even when it is only given from the kindly motive of helping you.

You are a " water " child and, as " still waters run deep," so are you apparently cool and undemonstrative, but deeply loving and loyal underneath.

Your Career

Having a deep love of the sea born in you, and because you long to travel on it, you should be very successful as a stewardess, though nursing—as you are very capable with invalids—should also be a career you might well follow.

Your lucky day is Monday, so you should carry out all the things of importance to you on that day.

Mr. " Right "

The life partner with whom you are most likely to find happiness is one born under *Pisces*, the Fishes, between February 19th and March 20th.

He will be trustworthy and reliable, like yourself, in any big emergency, though he may also share your inability to come to a decision quickly. However, because he has the same failing himself, he will be all the more ready to understand you.

His generosity will balance up your own rather too-careful ways, while both of you are home-loving and, though you will like a little variety and change now and then, his adaptable nature will enable

—If you were born between June 22nd and July 23rd.

him to fall in with whatever plans you make in this way.

Both of you are rather subject to "moodiness," but as each of you will strive to overcome this for the other's sake, it will be turning a disadvantage into an advantage.

Your Second Choice

Perhaps your sweetheart's birthday falls between October 24th and November 23rd, under the zodiacal sign of *Scorpio*, the Scorpion? Then with him as your partner you also have quite a good chance of happiness in marriage.

He has the strength of purpose to succeed in life where perhaps you are a little inclined to let things take their own course, while his decisiveness, also, will uphold you when you are inclined to be undecided.

He, too, will share your love of home, so altogether you should find you have made a good choice.

Other Sweethearts

If your sweetheart is one who is not truly harmonious to you, you would have to try to conquer your tendency to "moodiness," for he would probably take these attacks very much to heart, and then discord in the home might follow.

He might not be so fond of home life as you are, and you would have to be prepared to go out with him rather frequently, while you would also need to curb your tendency to exaggerate small worries, or he might be rather irritated with you.

You should be quite sure that your love is the real thing, therefore, before you take the final step.

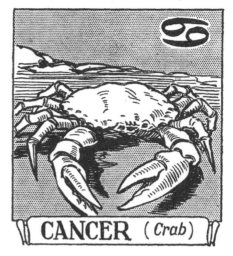

CANCER (*Crab*)

Your Engagement Ring

Your lucky stone being the emerald, when the happy day comes to go and choose your ring, try to have one that is set with that lovely stone.

This is the best way in which to encourage fortune to smile on you and your fiancé.

Good Luck and Your Wedding

For you, February of any year would be a very good month for your wedding, but you should not marry between the ages of twenty-one and twenty-eight unless you are very sure of your feelings.

There are few girls who do not look well in white, and if yours is to be a white wedding, try to place a tiny spray of ivy in your bouquet. If this is not possible, then you should wear some touch of green beneath your dress, for this colour is very lucky for you.

Should you decide on a quiet wedding, then you would look charming in an outfit of any pretty shade of green, and also you can feel you are encouraging fortune to make your married life a sunny one.

WHEREVER you are there will be laughter and gaiety, if you were born under the zodiacal sign of *Leo*, the Lion, between July 23rd and August 23rd, for you are a lovable person whose merry ways will gather hosts of friends around you.

Although you love bright and colourful surroundings and join whole-heartedly into any laughter and fun that is going on, you are not frivolous and empty-headed. Really, you are serious and a deep thinker when you like, and, through your fire and enthusiasm over any interest you take up, you have great power to inspire others to follow you.

Perhaps you might try to cultivate your powers of concentration rather more, for while you may begin something with tremendous enthusiasm, you are inclined to grow tired of it quickly and leave others to finish it for you. This is a pity, for you may lose wonderful opportunities through it.

You will stand by your friends through thick and thin, but if you take a dislike to anyone—and you have rather strong likes and dislikes —you will not trouble to hide the fact. Perhaps it would be kinder if you showed a little more tact at times, instead of being quite so downright when voicing your opinions.

You have an intense dislike of anything mean or underhand, and this high sense of honour in you, and your keen ambition and organising powers, should take you far in life if you do not try to have too many irons in the fire.

The idea of marriage means a great deal to you, but you would want a partner who would treat you as a real companion, one with whom you could discuss your thoughts

YOUR HOROSCOPE—

and feelings, confident that he will appreciate them.

Being very fond of children, you would make a good mother, and you would want the man you marry to share your interest in your little family.

A child of " fire," this explains your burning enthusiasm over anything you take up, and also your love of brightness and colour.

Your Career

Your love of colour and your strong artistic sense should enable you to make a great success in any work connected with furnishing, decorating or dress-designing, while you might also be a success as a dancing or music teacher, for you possess the necessary patience and influence over others that this work would entail. In any event, whatever you take up, your splendid enthusiasm should stand you in good stead.

Sunday is your lucky day, and you should make this the day for anything special you wish to undertake.

Mr. " Right "

For you the life partner who would be most in harmony would be one born between November 23rd and December 21st, under the zodiacal sign of *Sagittarius*, the Archer.

He will share your love of bright surroundings, laughter and fun, and you will both stand loyally by your friends.

Where you are rather outspoken, he will probably be rather more tactful, and will smooth down any awkward situation your downrightness may cause.

His more cautious, steadying influence, too, will balance up your

—If you were born between July 23rd and August 23rd.

rather too generous ways. You are both deep thinkers, and the enthusiasm you share will take you a long way together.

Your Second Choice

If your sweetheart's birthday falls under the Sign of *Aries*, the Ram, between March 21st and April 20th, you might also find quite a good chance of happiness.

The *Aries* man will make a very good husband, for he is usually of the type that adapts himself easily to domestic surroundings.

A characteristic you both share is a desire to express your own personality in everything you do. Neither of you care for routine work, or anything that does not bring your keen intellects into play, and this instinct should have a still greater influence over your joint success in life by being shared.

Both of you are capable of deep, lasting affection, so your love for each other should be based on a solid foundation.

Other Sweethearts

With a partner born at any other time you would probably find you will be expected to give up many of the interests you have hitherto followed so keenly, while he will most likely want you to be quieter and more restful than your natural high spirits would prompt you to be.

With the strength of will you possess, however, and with true love in your heart, you should be able to adapt yourself more to his tastes, and find happiness.

LEO (*Lion*)

Your Engagement Ring

What girl is not anxious that good fortune shall attend her engagement days ? On the wonderful occasion when you go with " him " to choose the ring, then, you should try to select one set with your lucky stone, the topaz. Then there should be little chance of any clouds gathering over you and your fiancé.

Good Luck at Your Wedding

Lucky months for you to marry in are April or December of any year.

Unless you want a white wedding, you would look lovely as a golden bride, for this is your most fortunate colour.

If your wedding is to be a quiet one, however, then you might choose a pretty frock or costume of golden yellow, or carry a bouquet composed of flowers of this colour. Then you may rest content in the knowledge that you have done all in your power to make fortune smile on your marriage.

GOOD luck will never be far away if you were born between August 24th and September 22nd, under the zodiacal sign of *Virgo*, the Virgin.

You are far-seeing and very practical, and you will weigh up both sides of a question very carefully before you make a decision. Hard-working and clever, too, you will love to have order and neatness about you, but you should be careful not to carry this to the point of " faddiness " in your home.

Your kindness and consideration for those who are not so fortunate as yourself, and your willingness to give them a helping hand, will win you the affection of many. You also have a deep love of flowers and animals, and are never so happy as when you are walking in the country with a dog.

Perhaps you are a little too sensitive, and you should try to harden yourself a little in this direction, for it may interfere with your progress in life, keeping you back where otherwise you might forge ahead.

You should be particularly careful to avoid worry and anxiety as far as possible, as this will have a bad effect on your health. You are also inclined to be a little too fault-finding, and you should strive to combat this before it loses you friends. Remember that if you look for the good points in others you will not have so much time to notice the bad ones.

It means a great deal to you to have the confidence and appreciation of those around you, and you will do your best to make yourself worthy of these. Your friends, therefore, should find that they can rely on you absolutely.

A child of " earth," you are firm and reliable, someone to turn to in difficulties, and who will never forsake her friends in adversity.

Your Career

With your liking for method and order, and your sound trustworthiness, you should find your best success in secretarial work, or in factory work if this should appeal to you.

On the other hand, you might do quite well in the teaching profession, but whatever work you follow you will need quiet, peaceful surroundings to bring out the best in you.

Tuesday being your lucky day, you should carry out all big undertakings then.

Mr. " Right "

The most suitable life partner for you is one whose birthday falls between April 21st and May 22nd, under the Sign of *Taurus*, the Bull.

He will not be as sensitive as you are, but he will be able to understand you very well, and this will enable him to shield you in many ways when, otherwise, your feelings might be hurt.

You both share the same hardworking, practical nature, while his shrewd common sense should go well with yours and be a great aid in finding success.

Perhaps you may find him a little difficult at times, but because he is easily influenced by those he loves, your own deep affection for him will help the waters of true love to flow smoothly, and you should find much happiness together.

Your Second Choice

Your sweetheart's birthday may come under *Capricornus*, the Goat, between December 22nd and January 19th, in which case you have

—If you were born between August 24th and September 22nd.

also a good chance of happiness with him.

He is persevering, and will work hard and painstakingly to carve a way for you in life. Like yourself he is trustworthy and reliable, but he may be inclined to lack decision and to need an inspiration before he will put forth his best work. You will be this inspiration, however, and should help him to go far.

You may find that he does not possess a very strong sense of humour, taking life, at times, a little too seriously, but you yourself are somewhat inclined to be over-serious, so you should be able to understand this trait in him.

Other Sweethearts

To keep harmony between yourself and your partner born at any other time, you would probably have to curb your desire to lead in most things, and give in to him quite often.

Your tendency to make mountains out of mole-hills, at times, might irritate him, too, unless you resolved to curb this. However, there is no task too heavy for true love to undertake, and if you really care for him enough, you should be able to rise above any little differences of opinion or character and find happiness.

Your Engagement Ring

Good luck is something every girl wishes to attend her engagement, and so you will be wise to encourage it to come your way right from the

VIRGO (Virgin)

breathless moment when you choose the ring. You may do this by choosing one set with jade, the beauty and unusualness of which would be much admired by your friends.

It is a stone which, from olden times, has been closely associated with love, so besides being your lucky gem it should bring double powers of good fortune to bear on your engagement.

Good Luck for Your Wedding

January or May of any year would be most fortunate months for your wedding, and if you are to be a white bride, you should see that there are touches of silver about your dress, for this is a very fortunate colour for you.

For a quiet wedding, however, you might choose a lovely frock of silvery grey in order to still further persuade fortune to smile on you and your husband.

YOUR HOROSCOPE—

" HOW I envy her ! " is what people will say of you if you were born under the zodiacal sign of *Libra*, the Balance, between September 23rd and October 23rd, for your sweetness of disposition and placid ways make it easy for you to enjoy life.

As your sign suggests, you have a well-balanced mind with a strong sense of justice, and you will consider no effort too great to set right a wrong you believe has been done to anyone. A help to you in this is your quickness in sensing things, and you will seldom find your intuitions are wrong. In fact, you could not do better than let your intuition help to guide you in all your undertakings.

You are clever, but inclined to feel that the effort of using your brains is too great and, because you will not exert yourself, you may find your best opportunities slip by you, unless you do your utmost to overcome this failing.

You will probably find that you will like or dislike a person almost at first sight, and here, also, you should find your judgment is generally correct. To those you like, you will be generous and a good friend, but you will have no patience with anyone who does not appeal to you.

Unselfish and affectionate, because of your sweet disposition, you will be popular at all social events, but you should beware of those who are jealous of your popularity.

Perhaps you are a little too sensitive where those you love are concerned, and you should strive not to let any little hurts go too deep.

You will find your friends like to confide their troubles in you, for you are very sympathetic, and will do your best to give them fresh hope if things look dark for them. You are a queer mixture of sunshine and showers, filled with the joy of life one moment, and sunk in the depths of despair the next. This is because you are an " air " child and, like a leaf in the breeze, are tossed sometimes up to the skies and sometimes down to earth, according to how life is treating you at the moment. Fortunately, however, those whom you love have great power to influence you, and can generally shake you out of your despondency very quickly.

Your Career

The work you are most likely to make a success of is hairdressing, or any kind of shop work, for you like change and variety about you, while you are honest and trustworthy in whatever you undertake.

Also, owing to an artistic streak in your nature, you might do well in the millinery line, for your fingers would be clever at putting novel touches to your work.

Your lucky day is Friday, and you should try to make all important decisions, or carry out big plans, on this day.

Mr. " Right "

Because marriage is almost essential to your happiness, you should choose a life partner who will give you the companionship and understanding you long for. The one most in harmony with you, therefore, is one born under *Gemini*, the Twins, between May 22nd and June 21st.

He will give you plenty of understanding and encouragement, while he is bright and sociable, which would fit in with your own popularity on social occasions.

—If you were born between September 23rd and October 23rd.

You will both be interested in all that goes on in the world, and will also share a love of the out-of-doors. He will be capable of the same deep affection, once he has given it, as you, and though you may find him subject to fits of depression at times, just like yourself, the effort you will each make to overcome this for the other's sake will be good for you both.

Your Second Choice

If your sweetheart's birthday falls between January 20th and February 19th, under the Sign of *Aquarius*, the Water Carrier, you might also find happiness.

He has a charming personality, and his cheery ways will do much to shake you out of your fits of the " blues." You will find, too, that your love of artistic things is shared by him.

Your *Aquarius* sweetheart will probably be rather more careful over money than you are, and this will be an advantage, for you are inclined to be a little extravagant.

Other Sweethearts

You might not get on so well with other men, for they might feel neglected through your popularity, while also they would probably take your sudden changes from joy to depression too much to heart. Your irritability, at times, might also cause friction between you.

If you make the effort to overcome these little difficulties for love's sake, however, you may well be happy with one who is not, in the ordinary way, truly harmonious to you.

LIBRA (Scales)

Your Engagement Ring

It is such a thrilling moment when at the jeweller's shop with " him " you see the rings spread out before you, and know that you are really about to select the one that will bind you together, and you will be so eager for fortune to smile on you.

Then see that you court good luck by choosing a ring set with your lucky stone, which is the beautiful opal. Often considered unlucky, for you it is most fortunate, for it is your birthday stone.

Good Luck for Your Wedding

Either January or June would be most fortunate months to choose for your wedding.

Perhaps you are dreaming of a white wedding ? Then you should be sure you have " something blue " about you, for this colour is very lucky for you.

At a quiet wedding, you might wear a pretty frock or suit of any shade of blue in order to court happiness in your marriage.

IT is up to you to make a success of your life if you were born between October 24th and November 23rd, under the zodiacal sign of *Scorpio*, the Scorpion, for you have it in your power to do big things if you set about it in the right way.

You have great strength of will and influence over others, and if you use these powers in the right way you should possess a very strong, forceful character, able to help those less strong than yourself along life's road, and to inspire and encourage any who are downcast.

The thing you should most guard against is lack of self-restraint for, while you can be one of the finest characters if you exercise self-control, once you let your forceful nature free to go its own way it may lead you to disaster. This is the keynote to your success, and is a point you cannot emphasise to yourself too highly.

You are very determined, and will refuse to allow anything to stand in your way when you have some aim in view, but you would be wise to make quite sure first that it is a really worth-while object you are striving after.

There is no " happy medium " with you. You know your own mind, and you do not trouble to hide the fact that you either like a person or you do not. Because of this, you are almost bound to make one or two enemies as you go through life, but when you make friendships they will be as firm as a rock, and will last a lifetime.

Owing to the influence of the Scorpion you may often find yourself having to wage war with yourself against the fire of jealousy, but those you love will always be able to bring out the best in your nature.

You will be keenly interested in anything you take up, and you have a deep love of beauty.

Being a " water " child, you are calm and unruffled on the surface, but may suddenly be stirred up by the depths of feeling hidden underneath.

Your Career

Because you are likely to possess a strong gift of healing, you would be most successful as a nurse. In fact, there are many callings you may follow with advantage. You should be good at anything requiring public speaking, or at salesmanship, because of your power to move those who listen to you, while you should make a clever organiser, and might also succeed as a teacher.

Your lucky day is Tuesday, and so you will be wise to choose that day for any special venture for which you desire success.

Mr. " Right "

You could not do better than chose a life partner whose birthday falls under *Virgo*, the Virgin, between August 24th and September 22nd, for you would get on very well together.

He will share your appreciation of beauty, while love of romance and all that is connected with it will be features of both your characters, helping you to find mutual happiness in many things.

Your *Virgo* sweetheart will work hard for you and the little home you will share, and while your forceful nature may cause you to want to lead the way at times, his deep understanding of human nature will help him to give in to you, unless he feels you are not quite in the right. This understanding will also enable him to guide you in many ways where

—If you were born between October 24th and November 23rd.

otherwise you might be rather too headstrong. Altogether, your characters should blend in very well.

Your Second Choice

You may also find happiness if your sweetheart was born between April 21st and May 22nd, under the sign of *Taurus*, the Bull.

You are both inclined to hastiness, and you may have occasional heated words, but as you share this trait you will understand one another the better, and your tiffs will be over the sooner. The similarity between you will probably help each of you to strive to control this fault, for you will see how foolish it is to give way to your feelings.

He should never give you cause for jealousy, because of his strong sense of honour, and so you will really be very well suited.

Other Sweethearts

Men born at other times are not so suitable for you, for they would not easily be able to understand your downright ways and your strong likes and dislikes. Also, they might be impatient of your tendency to jealousy, and friction might arise over this.

Perhaps the chief bone of contention would be your desire to lead in most things, when he might have exactly the same wish ! You should search your heart to make quite sure you could overcome these differences in character before you step into marriage, therefore.

Your Engagement Ring

There are such rosy dreams of the future in your heart when the great

SCORPIO (*Scorpion*)

day comes on which to choose the ring which spells " I love you," and you will be so anxious for fate to be kind and make them all come true.

Then, to persuade fate to smile on you, choose a ring set with your lucky stone, the aquamarine, which has caught the beautiful blue of the sea in its colour. Your engagement days should then be all happy ones.

Good Luck at Your Wedding

For you, March or July are both fortunate months when you are choosing your wedding day, and if you are to be married in white try to carry red flowers in your bouquet, for this is a very lucky colour for you.

Should you decide on a quiet wedding, you might choose a dress of wine red, if that colour suits you, or, if not, see that you have a touch of red about you somewhere in order to court fortune's favour in your marriage.

YOUR HOROSCOPE—

YOU will often find fortune smiling on you if you were born under the zodiacal sign of *Sagittarius*, the Archer, between November 23rd and December 21st, for you are naturally happy and sunny-natured, and will be popular wherever you go—though perhaps more with the opposite sex than your own !

People cannot help liking you for your frank, open manner and the spirited way you are ready to tackle life, wanting to get out of it the most you can, yet not, of course, by hurting other people.

Full of hope, quick-witted and clear-sighted, you are generally able to find your own way out of the difficulties that beset you. You are energetic and determined, too, and rather inclined to resent interference in your plans, or in your life generally.

You should be careful of accidents brought about through animals, though you are generally very fond of your dumb friends. Travel is not usually very fortunate for you, though you are quite likely to take long journeys and may even settle abroad.

Perhaps you are inclined to be a little too fault-finding and exacting, and to take offence where none was meant, so you should strive to overcome these little failings. You will probably have many love affairs, and are quite likely to marry twice. Companionship and love mean a great deal to you, but you do not care to be ruled by others, preferring to be the one to take the reins.

Being very generous, when married you will do anything for your husband and children, but you will like to have plenty of change and variety in your life.

A child of " fire," you have the flame of determination to make the best of yourself burning in your heart, but you should try not to have too many irons in the fire instead of striving to make a success of one thing at a time.

Your Career

Your quickness to learn and your ability to explain things patiently and clearly should lead you to find your best success in teaching, while your quick-wittedness and streak of originality should also help you to be successful at dressmaking or millinery.

Thursday being your lucky day, you should reserve all big decisions, or the carrying out of important plans, for that day.

Mr. " Right "

The most suitable life partner for you is one born between July 23rd and August 23rd, under the sign of *Leo*, the Lion, for he has a great deal in common with you.

He will have the same deeply affectionate nature as you have, and so you will never lack the devotion you would long for from your husband. Both of you will share, too, the same courage and determination to win through all obstacles, and so you should go far in " double harness."

Another characteristic you have in common is your influence over others, while he will share your generosity and love of home and family, so that you have every chance of happiness together.

Your Second Choice

Perhaps your sweetheart was born under *Aries*, the Ram, between March 21st and April 20th ? Then he, too, should be quite suitable for you.

—If you were born between November 23rd and December 21st.

Both of you are inclined to be hasty and to say more than you mean at times, but this similarity in disposition should make for closer understanding and sympathy between you.

You will find your *Aries* sweetheart sociable, like yourself, and determined to get on well, too, though you might find yourselves clashing because you both want to rule in the home. However, mutual love and understanding should smooth over any real difficulty on that score.

SAGITTARIUS (Archer)

Other Sweethearts

With a sweetheart who is not really harmonious to you, you would probably need to be content with a quieter, less varied life than you might really wish for, and also be satisfied with a husband who would be rather more inclined to drift than to show himself as ambitious as you would like.

Friction might also arise through your tendency to be fault-finding and rather exacting, but if you care deeply enough for him, you can mould yourself to suit his character better, and so find a very good chance of happiness.

Your Engagement Ring

In the joy you will experience when your engagement ring is actually on your finger, you will feel even happier if you know that you have done all you could to court fortune's favour by choosing one set with your lucky stone, the diamond, besides the fact that your friends will greatly admire this lovely stone.

Select a diamond ring, then, and you should know no shadow over your engagement days !

Good Luck and Your Wedding

The month of August is a most fortunate month for you to pick for your wedding.

Perhaps you have decided on a white wedding, and if so, you should see to it that you carry a bouquet tied with blue ribbon, for this colour is very fortunate for you.

If you are to have a quiet ceremony, however, then you could not do better than choose a dainty frock in the shade of blue that suits your colouring best. Then you should meet with only sunshine along the marriage highway.

"ASTRA"

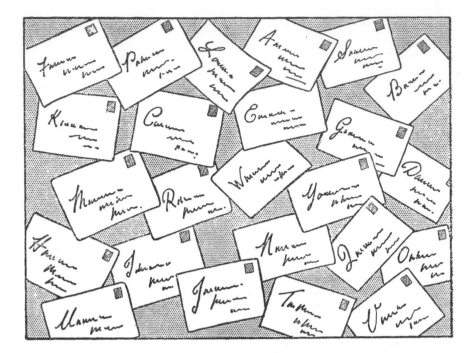

POSTMAN'S KNOCK

HERE is an enjoyable game to play. Take a pencil, close your eyes, and put the pencil-point down on the picture above. Then see which letter you are touching, look below and see what message Fate has for you. (If the pencil rests on an empty space, try again.) Or if you like, choose your own initials.

(A) " You have an unknown admirer."   (B) " Do not be deceived by appearances."   (C) " He is not to be trusted."   (D) " Look before you leap." (E) " Beware lest your heart rule your head."   (F) " Be patient ; all will come right in the end."   (G) " Persevere and you will win."   (H) " Mind your own business."   (I) " Faint heart never won anything."   (J) " Do not believe all you hear."   (K) " You will soon meet Mr. Right."   (L) " Kindness is never thrown away."   (M) " Do not judge him too harshly."   (N) " Some-one is trying to steal him from you."   (O) " He does not mean all he says." (P) " Try to see his point of view."   (Q) " His heart is the thing that matters." (R) " You must choose between them some time, but don't be in a hurry." (S) " Good fortune is waiting for you round the corner." (T) " Never mind, he's not the only pebble on the beach."   (U) " It's a difficult choice ; let your heart guide you."   (V) " Do not let pride ruin your life."   (W) " He's too shy to speak ; give him a little encouragement."   (Y) " The wedding bells will ring sooner than you expect."

CHAPTER III

Find Fortune in the Cards

*The meaning of the cards—Three simple methods of fortune-
telling—How to read them—Special lucky cards—Additional
meanings—Wishes—Easy-to-follow examples, etc.*

ALMOST ever since playing
cards were invented they
have been used for taking
peeps into the future, and it is
remarkable what correct forecasts
are sometimes made with them.

The telling of fortunes by cards
is a fascinating hobby, and one that
will make you popular wherever you
go, for we all love to be told about
our future, don't we ? At a party
that has become dull, for instance,
or on a rainy day at a boarding
house, the girl who can wile away
an hour by telling others their
" fate " will be in great demand.
The most hardened scoffer will be
unable to resist the temptation to
hear " what is coming to her " in
the future.

There are many different methods
of fortune-telling by cards. Some
are very elaborate, some so very
simple that they are unsatisfac-
tory ; some use the entire pack ;
others only thirty-six or thirty-two,
or even fewer, cards ; some give a
general survey of the future, others
are limited to finding an answer to a
single question, such as " Shall I
marry ? " or " Will my wish come
true ? " In this chapter you will
find good examples of both.

Here, to begin with, is the
" Threes " method, which is little

PLATE 2

6. The film rôles he plays are full of courage, charm, resource, strength with tenderness and a sense of humour. His eyes show that he possesses all these qualities.
Goldwyn.

7. The parts she portrays demand a reserved character that shrinks from betraying her inmost feelings, and there is much that the world does not know in the mind behind these eyes.
Metro-Goldwyn-Mayer.

8. A capacity for enjoying life, an easy-going good nature and a hearty sense of humour are clearly shown in the eyes of this popular star.
Paramount.

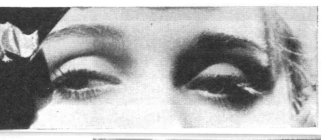

9. Unusually heavy are the upper lids of these eyes, a sign of a mind that thinks profoundly and considers a question carefully before coming to a decision.

10. Only someone with the sense of humour, the good-nature, and the knowledge of life that these eyes show could successfully portray the characters this favourite star does.

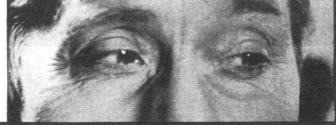

PLATE 3

11. Remarkable eyes, revealing ambition, and the great power of concentration and fixity of purpose which have already won her rapid success and will lead to greater triumphs.
Gaumont-British.

12. He enjoys life, and at first glance you might think him capable of nothing more than light-hearted frivolity, but these eyes also disclose strength and a capacity for deep feeling.
Paramount.

13. Wisdom, a profound knowledge of life, an almost uncanny understanding of human nature and an abundant sympathy, as well as intense conscientiousness.
Metro-Goldwyn-Mayer.

14. These eyes indicate a firm character, not easily ruffled or discouraged, and a great capacity for work coupled with keen enjoyment in doing it thoroughly and well.
Fox.

15. Unusual eyes these, and revealing an unusual character; unconventional, courageous, self-reliant, determinedly choosing its own path in life and refusing either to be driven or tempted from it.

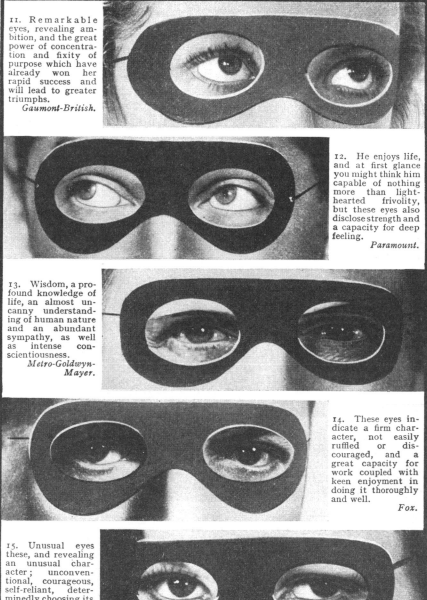

PLATE 4

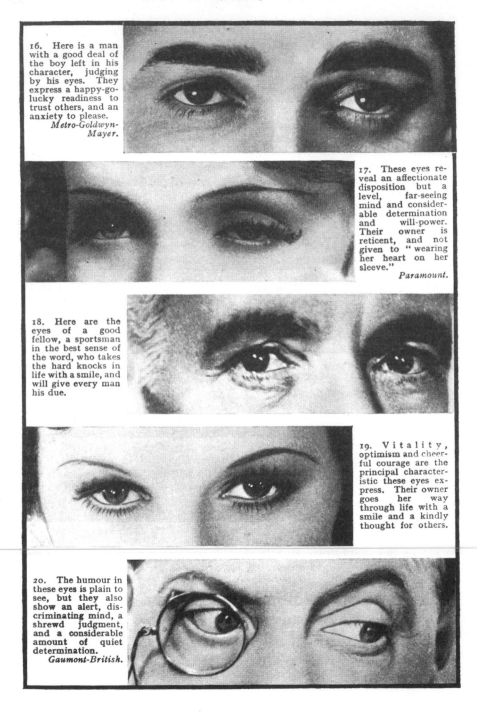

16. Here is a man with a good deal of the boy left in his character, judging by his eyes. They express a happy-go-lucky readiness to trust others, and an anxiety to please.
Metro-Goldwyn-Mayer.

17. These eyes reveal an affectionate disposition but a level, far-seeing mind and considerable determination and will-power. Their owner is reticent, and not given to " wearing her heart on her sleeve."
Paramount.

18. Here are the eyes of a good fellow, a sportsman in the best sense of the word, who takes the hard knocks in life with a smile, and will give every man his due.

19. Vitality, optimism and cheerful courage are the principal characteristic these eyes express. Their owner goes her way through life with a smile and a kindly thought for others.

20. The humour in these eyes is plain to see, but they also show an alert, discriminating mind, a shrewd judgment, and a considerable amount of quiet determination.
Gaumont-British.

Queen—A dark woman, unfriendly to you ; possibly a rival—unless a " personal " card.

Jack—A dark young man, not very honourable ; an enemy.

Ten—An unkind letter.

Nine—Danger or risk.

Eight—Illness.

Seven—Injustice.

Six—Interference.

Five—Worry (over matters other than money).

Four—Ingratitude.

Three—Indifference.

Two—An unexpected drawback.

Of course, the meanings of some of the cards will vary a little according to whether the sitter is a lady or a gentleman, and whether married or single, engaged or not, but there should be no difficulty in reading them correctly. For instance, the " proposal " card in the fortune of a married woman obviously cannot mean that she herself will receive a proposal of marriage ; it means that she will hear of a proposal to someone else—a daughter, perhaps.

The "Threes" Method

TO tell a fortune by the "Threes" method, as in many others, you first of all choose a " personal " card for your " sitter "—the person whose fortune is being told. You pick a Queen for a lady and a King for a gentleman, the suit according to his or her colouring—Hearts if very fair, Diamonds if moderately fair, Clubs if rather dark, Spades if very dark. The corresponding King or Queen, when it turns up, will represent the " sitter's " fiancé or fiancée—husband or wife in the case of married people—or the person with whom he or she is, or is destined to be, in love.

You lay the " personal " card face upwards nearest you on the table. Then shuffle the cards and ask your " sitter " to cut them three times. Then take the pack and lay the cards in threes, face downwards, arranging them as shown on page 35. Then turn up and read each set of three in turn, commencing with those nearest the personal card and proceeding from left to right and upwards, as numbered in the specimen lay-out on page 35. The sets nearest the " personal " card apply to events likely to happen sooner than those further away. Until you have learnt the meanings of the cards, refer to the book for each one.

Each set deals with a separate incident, event or situation, though you will sometimes find that two or more sets will link up into a chapter of the story of the future. The three cards in a set need not be taken in the order in which they lie. You will see, as you read their meanings, which naturally comes first, second and third.

If a reading does not seem clear, it can usually be understood and explained by using a very little imagination.

If you know something of your sitter's character, life and circumstances, it, of course, helps you to interpret readings that may otherwise be a little difficult to understand.

HOW TO READ THE CARDS

HERE, as an example, is a reading of the cards laid out as a specimen on page 35. You will see by this exactly how it is done.

The person who is having her fortune told is moderately fair, so the Queen of Diamonds is her " personal " card, and is placed at the bottom of the lay-out.

Set 1. You have **high ambitions** (Ace of Spades) which may lead you into **danger** (Nine of Spades), but if you persevere with courage you will reach **prosperity** (Ten of Clubs) in the end.

Set 2. You will **quarrel** (Five of Clubs) with a **dark man, not very well-intentioned** towards **you** (King of Spades), but the **friend-ship** card (Six of Clubs) shows that —if you do not let the cause of the quarrel rankle—he will be-come your friend.

Set 3. You will hear **news** (Nine of Diamonds) of the **engagement** (Nine of Hearts) of a **nice young man who is fond of you** (Jack of Hearts). The Hearts on either side of the Diamond show that the news is welcome.

Set 4. The **illness** (Eight of Spades) of a **nice woman who is very attached to you** (Queen of Hearts) will bring about a **short journey** (Eight of Diamonds). The fact that the third card is a Diamond indicates that the illness will not be serious, and a speedy recovery may be hoped for. If it had been a Club, it would not be quite so lucky, and a Spade would indicate news that was not so good.

Set 5. **Someone is thinking of mak-ing you a gift of money** (Ace of Diamonds) and **promotion in your work is in view** (Nine of Clubs)— tho two cards with somewhat similar meanings falling together make this very definite—but there is a delay owing to **money disappointment** (Three of Dia-monds). The presence of the Nine of Clubs, which is a lucky card, suggests that the difficulty will soon be overcome.

Set 6. The **ingratitude** (Four of Spades) of a **dark, unfriendly woman** (Queen of Spades) will lead to a **worry over money** (Five of Diamonds). The Diamond being the third card of the set indicates that the worry will pass.

Set 7. An **unexpected meeting** (Two of Hearts) with a **friendly dark woman** (Queen of Clubs) will lead to an **invitation** (Six of Diamonds). The lucky suits show that the in-vitation will be a welcome and pleasant one.

Set 8. There will be an **unexpected drawback** (Two of Spades) about a **change of residence** (Four of Diamonds), and a **sudden change in your work** (Two of Clubs) will follow.

Set 9. I see a **lovers' tiff** (Five of Hearts), but a **friendly young man** (Jack of Clubs) will **help to smooth things out** (Six of Hearts). You will make it up—provided you do not let false pride stand in your way.

Set 10. You will be **worried** (Five of Spades) over being **treated unjustly** (Seven of Spades), but a man who is a **true friend** (King of Clubs) will stand by you. This is not a very lucky set, but the presence of the King of Clubs promises that all will come right.

Set 11. **An untrustworthy young man** (Jack of Diamonds) will **interfere** in your affairs (Six of Spades), but **all will turn out right in the end** (Seven of Clubs), so do not worry.

Set 12. Your **loyalty** (Four of Clubs) will lead to a **better in-come** (Seven of Diamonds), which will bring you **great contentment** (Seven of Hearts).

Set 13. I see a **new job** (Ace of Clubs), which after some **delay** (Three of Clubs) will turn out to be a **change for the better** (Eight of Clubs).

PERSONAL CARD

THE
"THREES" METHOD
(see page 33).

Set 14. You will receive a **love letter** (Eight of Hearts) from a **not very honourable young man** (Jack of Spades), to whom you are **indifferent** (Three of Spades). If you are wise you will ignore it.

Set 15. A **meeting** (Ace of Hearts) with a **kind man who is fond of you** (King of Hearts) will bring you **an unexpected gift or money** (Two of Diamonds).

Set 16. **Doubt** (Three of Hearts) and the receipt of **an unkind letter** (Ten of Spades) will lead to a **long journey or sea voyage** (Ten of Diamonds). (This is not a very lucky set, but those on either side are so good that the incident is not liable to have any serious results.)

Set 17. A **proposal of marriage** (Four of Hearts) from the **man of your heart** (King of Diamonds) will lead to **married happiness** (Ten of Hearts). This is a splendidly lucky set.

The " Six Sevens "

HERE is another system, a little more elaborate than the " Threes," but in some ways more definite.

For this you do not need a " personal " card, and though you take the complete pack in your hand you only deal forty-two cards, just as they come. (The remainder have no part in the fortune you are telling, and are laid aside.)

After you have shuffled the cards, and your " sitter " has cut the pack three times, you lay them out face upwards in sets of seven as shown on page 37. The first set reveals the future as it directly affects Yourself, the second one as it effects your Lover (or Lover-to-be), the third your Home, the fourth your Friends or Relations, the fifth your Work and the sixth Money.

You then read each set according to the list of meanings on pages 32–33. In this method they must always be read in a certain order—the centre one first, the top next then the bottom, then the upper and lower ones on the left, and, finally, the upper and lower ones on the right, as shown in the numbered diagram on page 37.

The positions of the cards in the set have a meaning of their own. The centre card is the most important, and often determines the character of the whole set. The top position shows power over the others—except the centre one—the bottom is less powerful. Those on the left show the progress of the fortune, and those on the right how it will turn out in the end.

Of course, the six sets link up to make a complete fortune, since they are bound to affect each other. And the positions of the outside cards in relation to the nearest cards of the next set may tell something. (For instance, if the Jack of Hearts—the " lover " card—fell in position 3 of the " yourself " set, and the Queen of Clubs—a kind woman friend—in position 2 of the " friends and relations " set, it would indicate that your lover and a friend of yours were on excellent terms; but if the Queen of Spades—an unfriendly woman—were in the same position, it would show that among your friends and relations you have a rival, or some woman who dislikes your lover or will try to do him harm.)

To show you clearly how to use the " Sevens " method, here is an example of reading the cards laid out as a specimen on page 37.

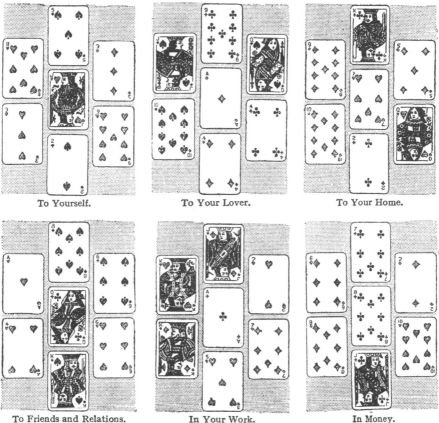

| To Yourself. | To Your Lover. | To Your Home. |

| To Friends and Relations. | In Your Work. | In Money. |

HOW TO LAY OUT CARDS FOR A READING BY THE
"SIX SEVENS" METHOD.

Example of Reading by the "Six Sevens" Method

What is Coming to Yourself:

Set 1

1. Your lover (Jack of Hearts). For this card to fall in the centre of your set is a splendid sign, and indicates that he will be your true lover for life.
2. Worry (Five of Spades).
3. Sudden or unexpected drawback, or obstacle (Two of Spades).
4. Love letters (Eight of Hearts)
5. Shyness or doubts (Three of Hearts).
6. Disappointment over money, (Three of Diamonds).
7. An engagement (Nine of Hearts).

Explanation

There is someone who is truly in love with you. You are worried about some unexpected drawback or obstacle, but his love letters will overcome your doubts. There will also be a little money worry, but in the end a ring will twinkle on your third finger. The general position shows true love surmounting doubts and difficulties and triumphantly conquering in the end.

Set 2

To Your Lover :

1. Somebody is thinking of giving him money (Ace of Diamonds). (This card falling in the centre of the set suggests that the intention is really serious and the amount substantial.)
2. Promotion in work (Nine of Clubs).
3. A change of residence (Four of Diamonds).
4. An unfriendly man (Jack of Spades).
5. An unkind letter (Ten of Spades).
6. An unfriendly dark woman (Queen of Spades).
7. Loyalty (Four of Clubs).

Explanation

Someone is certainly thinking of giving him a substantial sum of money, and he will get promotion in his work, which will involve a change of residence. An enemy will cause trouble with an unkind or malicious letter, and an unfriendly dark woman will play a part, but his loyalty to you will remain unshaken. The general position indicates money success for him, but attempts to cause trouble between him and you. (The fact that the " loyalty " card comes in suggests that the trouble caused has to do with you and not his work.) He is, however, staunchly true to you—but you need to be on your guard, and will be wise to warn him against false friends. To have the " loyalty " card in the " lover " set is a splendid sign, and when it comes in position 7 it shows that his love endures and in the end triumphs over all that has gone before.

Set 3

To Your Home :

1. Contentment (Seven of Hearts).
2. A kind man (King of Clubs).
3. A sudden change (Two of Clubs).
4. News (Nine of Diamonds).
5. A long journey or sea voyage (Ten of Diamonds).
6. Worry over money (Five of Diamonds).
7. A kind and loving woman (Queen of Hearts).

Explanation

Contentment reigns in your home, but a kind dark man, the head of the house (because the card comes at the top) will experience a sudden change in his work. He will receive news (not bad news, because it is not next to a spade card, and probably about money, because it comes above a diamond) which will entail a long journey or sea voyage. There will be money worries, but they will be softened by the help and sympathy of a kind and loving woman. Although there are troubles, this outlook is far from unlucky, for there are no spades in the set, and so the troubles should not be serious, and the presence of the Queen of Hearts in position 7 shows loving hearts and friendship keeping the home happy through everything that may befall.

Set 4

To Your Friends and Relations :

1. A dark woman attached to you (Queen of Clubs).

2. Illness (Eight of Spades).
3. A dark man (King of Spades).
4. A meeting (Ace of Hearts).
5. A proposal of marriage (Four of Hearts).
6. Interference (Six of Spades).
7. Help in a love affair (Six of Hearts).

Explanation

A dark woman friendly towards you will suffer illness (severe, because the illness card is at the top of the set, but probably not alarming, as no worry card is present). A dark man is attached to her, and a meeting is followed by a proposal of marriage. There is, however, interference on someone's part, and your help is asked. As to this, of course, you must use your own judgment and act for the best.

Set 5

In Your Work :

1. A new job (Ace of Clubs).
2. An untrustworthy young man (Jack of Diamonds).
3. A lovers' tiff (Five of Hearts).
4. A kind-hearted man (King of Hearts).
5. A wealthy man (King of Diamonds).
6. An unexpected meeting (Two of Hearts).
7. A rise in wages (Seven of Diamonds).

Explanation

This set is not a very easy one to read as there is a curious absence of Clubs—or " work " cards.

You will get a new job, but it does not appear to be a very well paid one, as there are few Diamonds in the set except court cards, but it may possibly be with a wealthy firm. An untrustworthy young man in a position of authority will take advantage of a lovers' tiff. (This is a little difficult to understand, but possibly you may be sufficiently upset for it to affect your work.) But a kindhearted man who is very well disposed towards you and a wealthy man will together take an interest in you, and after an unexpected meeting you will get a rise in wages.

The general fall of the cards indicates that in spite of the untrustworthy man you will be successful in your work. The King of Hearts turning up in connection with you promises happiness, and the King of Diamonds is a very lucky card in money matters.

Set 6

In Money :

1. A change for the better (Eight of Clubs).
2. All goes well (Seven of Clubs).
3. A true friend (Jack of Clubs).
4. An invitation (Six of Diamonds).
5. A short journey (Eight of Diamonds).
6. Unexpected money (Two of Diamonds).
7. Marriage (Ten of Hearts).

Explanation

The mixture of Clubs and Diamonds indicates that you will make your money by work (had the set been largely composed of Diamonds, this would suggest that money would come to you unearned—through a legacy or in some similar way), but there are enough Diamonds to indicate a good deal of money. Soon your financial position will improve, (the card being in position 1 suggests that it will improve considerably). All will go well, partly due to a man who is a true loyal friend (probably, since Clubs are above

A method of finding out if, and how, a wish
will be fulfilled.

him, somebody where you work). You will receive an **invitation** and take a **short journey** as a result of which you will be able to be **married** and live happily ever after. (There are no cards after the marriage card to suggest anything spoiling your happiness.)

Additional Meanings

REMEMBER that in addition to the special meanings of the cards and their positions, there are additional meanings caused by the influence of the cards that lie next to them. Hearts lying next to an unlucky card—especially if on both sides of it—almost wipe out the bad luck, and Diamonds or Clubs certainly reduce it. They at least indicate that the consequences will not be so serious as you may at first have feared.

The King of Hearts is a very lucky card indeed, and brings affection and happiness even if he falls among unlucky cards. In the same way the Jack brings love that conquers trouble and sorrow and makes up for everything. For either of these, or your own card —according to your colouring—to fall in the "yourself" set is very lucky, and it is nearly as good if either of them falls in the "lover" set.

Two or more Jacks in the "yourself" set suggests unimportant love-affairs; Kings, serious ones. Four Kings together means the fulfilment of your dreams. The same cards in the "lover" set indicates that your boy has many friends—good or bad according to the cards. In the "work" set they indicate that men will play an important part in your working life. Four Jacks together mean great success in your work.

Queens, in the "yourself" set indicate girl friends, in the "lover" set rivals or girl friends of "his" whom you may have to be on your guard against. Four Queens together mean that you will have a gay time.

Three Aces in any one set are lucky, and may mean a fresh start after a setback, but four, especially if the Ace of Spades is upside down, are a bad sign, and is a warning to avoid quarrels and go carefully in all that you do.

Three or four Tens together mean "good luck," Nines are also lucky and mean "good news," Eights, "a change," Sevens, "great happiness," Sixes, "help," Fives, "opposition," Fours, "success," Threes, "delay," and Twos "something sudden and unexpected." A Heart, Diamond and Club of the same value falling together are better than cards of all four suits, or three including the Spade.

Wishes

HERE is a simple way of telling your " sitter " whether he or she will or will not get a particular wish, and the circumstances that will affect it.

Shuffle the pack and tell your " sitter " to cut the cards three times as before, concentrating on one wish with all his or her thoughts. Then deal the cards one at a time, laying them face upwards on top of each other until either your sitter's " personal " card—according to his or her colouring—or the Nine of hearts—the " wish " card—turn up. (If the wish card turns up before the personal card it is luckier than the reverse way.) Then go on dealing the cards, laying them in a semi-circle until the other card—" wish " or " personal "—turns up. Discard the remainder of the pack.

If the Ace of Spades lies in the semi-circle, your sitter will not get his or her wish—in this case it is wise to try the fortune three times, shuffling well and cutting each time. If the Spade Ace turns up only once in the three times, the wish will probably come true eventually ; if twice, probably not ; if three times certainly not.

If the Ace of Spades is absent the wish will come true sooner or later. The nearer the " wish " and " personal " cards come together, the sooner or more certainly the wish will be realised ; for them to fall next to each other is a very lucky sign indeed.

The cards that lie between the two—you may, of course, have to make a circle of the whole pack !— foretell, according to the meanings given on page 32, the events and circumstances that help or delay the fulfilment of the wish.

On page 40 is an example, with the King of Diamonds as the " personal " card !

Explanation

Your wish will come true fairly soon, but it will be affected by an **unexpected meeting** (Two of Hearts) with an **untrustworthy man** (Jack of Diamonds) which will cause you **worry** (Five of Spades). **Indifference** (Three of Spades) will cause **a change** (Two of Clubs), but **sympathetic help** (Six of Hearts) will come from a **friendly dark woman** (Queen of Clubs). There will be a **short journey** (Eight of Diamonds) involving some **risk** (Nine of Spades), but **all will go well** (Seven of Clubs) and bring you your wish.

" CARTA DESTINA."

CHAPTER IV

Tell-tale Tea-leaves

How to read the future from tea-leaves in the form of numbers, stalks, dots, squares and other shapes—Fortune from the dominoes —Fate in the sand.

THE girl who can tell her friends' fortunes from the tea-cups is always popular, and to do this requires no special ability or study—just a knowledge of what the tea-leaf shapes represent, a little imagination, and common sense.

You see, you must use a little thought when telling fortunes— you must remember the type of person you are dealing with, her character and circumstances. For instance, a tea-leaf shape resembling a church, which for a single girl means that she will soon be married, must obviously have a different meaning when it appears in the tea-cup of a wife. In the latter case, it stands for a christening.

If you keep in your mind the disposition of the person whose tea-cup fortune you are telling, you can elaborate the meanings of the pictures to a great extent, and make quite a long and fascinating tale of it.

First of all, the one whose tea-

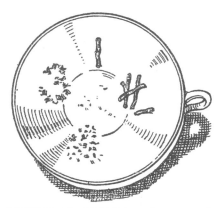

A FIGURE 3, a long STALK, crossed STALKS and a group of DOTS.

Here you see a SQUARE, an OBLONG and a CIRCLE or RING.

cup is to be read must leave a few drops of tea in the bottom of the cup, and then twirl the cup slowly in her *left* hand three times, finally turning it upside-down to drain in the saucer. All this she *must* do herself.

When the cup is drained, you take it up and carefully study the leaves until you find resemblances to well-known objects among them. They may be very crude and ill-shaped pictures, but often just the slight suggestion of an object is sufficient to act on as a guide. Sometimes a very vague shape will take a definite form if you look at it with your eyes half-closed.

Another thing to remember is to read round from left to right of the cup, otherwise you might spoil the luck of the person whose fortune you are reading.

A clear cup, with no leaves at all, is a sign of a complete absence of trouble for that person. A lucky sign indeed !

Numbers

Where the tea-leaves form numbers, these are their meanings :

1. Happy, care-free days are coming.

2. Some pleasant happening will occur twice in the near future.

3. A great wish will be fulfilled before long.

4. Success in work.

5. A pleasant surprise.

6. You are going to make many friends.

7. A time of contentment is in store.

8. A slight disappointment.

9. Much better and happier days are coming.

Stalks

Stalks indicate people. Long, hard stalks mean men ; thin, shorter stalks, women, and these people will be fair or dark according to the lightness or darkness of the stalks.

When stalks stand out clearly, it shows that these people will bring happiness ; if they are cloudy and jumbled with other leaves, they may be the cause of slight disappointments.

Stalks standing straight up denote friends ; any which are crossed indicate enemies. Stalks slanting at all angles are a warning to be on guard against mischief-making by these people.

You can recognise in this cup an ANCHOR, BIRD, CAT and CASTLE.

This tea-cup shows a typical EGG, HAND, KEY and JUG.

Groups of Dots are a sign of money coming. Small, single dots denote letters on the way. A big dot standing alone means a present.

Squares stand for joy and peace, **Oblongs** for quarrels. Large complete **Circles** mean continuous happiness, but any break in the circle, or a stalk crossing it, means disappointments.

Where a symbol is found standing out alone, quite clearly, whatever the sign denotes is almost bound to come true; when it is muddled and cloudy, there is likely to be some doubt about its fulfilment; possibly difficulties in the way which will first have to be overcome.

Here are the meanings of other shapes you are likely to find:

Acorn.—Great success is likely to start from humble beginnings.

Anchor.—A trip across the water is likely, with something pleasant on the other side.

Arch.—Something very unexpected is going to happen.

Arrow.—Someone is falling in love with you.

Basket.—A present—something very useful.

Bird.—Very good luck is coming in some form or other.

Boot.—A journey to some new abode.

Bridge.—A big problem will soon be solved.

Butterfly.—Happy days are in store.

Castle.—A very dear wish will soon be fulfilled.

Cat.—Beware of false friends.

Crab.—Be on your guard against those who are trying to come between your sweetheart and yourself.

Cross.—Trouble is coming, but if you keep a stout heart it will very soon pass.

Dagger.—Some danger is threatening, but it will not harm you.

Dog.—You will have a very faithful friend.

Duck.—A journey with someone very dear to you.

Ear.—Pleasant news is on its way.

Earring.—Your life will not lack for luxury.

Egg.—A change is coming.

Eye.—A big opportunity will occur—look out for it, or you may miss it.

Feather.—Very good luck indeed. The larger the feather, the better the luck.

Fish.—Something good is coming to you over water.

Flowers.—A happy married life.

Gate.—Somebody stands in the way of your desire.

Grass.—Ease and luxury in life.

Hand.—If pointing upward, some big wish will be granted—downward, disappointment.

Hat.—A surprise visitor, bringing good news.

Heart.—An engagement is foreshadowed. It will be a very happy one.

Hive.—Future prosperity.

Inkwell.—A letter will contain pleasant tidings.

Ivy.—True love is on its way.

Jewel.—You will be remembered in somebody's will.

Jug.—You will lose something you are rather attached to.

Key.—You will learn something very useful, which will help you in gaining your desires.

Kite.—Your ambitions are lofty ; you will need much patience and perseverance.

Ladder.—Married life will bring both joy and prosperity.

Leaf.—One, a letter—if more, it means you will have to choose carefully between many admirers.

Letters.—Letters of the alphabet indicate the initials of people destined to have a great influence on your life.

Loaf.—Domestic bliss.

Moon.—Romance lies in wait. A crescent moon is very lucky.

Mountain.—People of wealth and power will help you on in life when you are most in need of it.

Mouse.—You are worrying yourself needlessly over something.

Nail.—A false friend will try to harm you, in vain.

Needle.—Some little troubles are in store, but they will be followed by much joy.

Nose.—You will make a great discovery soon.

Owl.—Luck in love.

Pail.—Married life for you will mean much hard work, but love will sweeten the days.

Pen.—Somebody is expecting a letter from you. Why don't you write ?

Pin.—A fascinating stranger will cross your path.

Pipe.—Domestic happiness and long life.

Recognisable above are a KITE, MOUSE and SCISSORS.

You can see here a SHIP, STAR, WHEEL and TREE.

Rattle.—Loving children will bless your days.

Ring.—A wedding in the family. Any break in the ring indicates a disappointment in love.

Rose.—Good luck in life and in love.

Saucer.—A married life full of content.

Scissors.—A quarrel with your sweetheart, but it will have a happy ending.

Ship.—A letter is coming from over the sea.

Spider.—Money from an unexpected quarter.

Star.—Joy and prosperity in abundance. Very lucky indeed.

Thistle.—You will never be very rich, but always very happy.

Tree.—You may expect to be moving to a new neighbourhood.

Trunk.—Happiness lies at the end of a journey.

Umbrella.—If open, great good luck, especially in love. If closed, there will be a few disappointments.

Vase.—You will perform a good deed and reap a valuable reward.

Wall.—Something will come between you and your sweetheart, but love will soon put things right.

Watch.—Somebody you little suspect cares for you.

Wheel.—An opportunity is awaiting you now. You must hurry to take advantage of it.

Wings.—You will shortly hear surprising news.

Worm.—A critical problem will confront you ; think well before making a decision.

Yacht.—Your sweetheart has good news for you. He also needs your help.

You will find a specimen teacup fortune on page 47.

Let the Dominoes Decide !

ANOTHER way of peeping into the future is with Dominoes. You should lay a complete set face downwards on the table, shuffle them well together, then draw one. Here is what each foretells :

Double-Six.—Wealth will be yours some day.

Six-Five.—A wonderful love awaits you.

Six-Four.—You will never want.

Six-Three.—Luck in love.

Six-Two.—A very welcome present is coming.

Six-One.—You will do a kindly deed.

Six-Blank.—Beware of scandal harming you.

Double-Five.—Change of abode, bringing better times.

Five-Four.—A big stroke of luck is at hand.

Five-Three.—A surprise visitor.

Five-Two.—You have a rival in love.

Five-One.—Love will loom large in your life.

Five-Blank.—A choice lies before you.

Double-Four.—Much pleasure at a coming party.

Four-Three.—A happy surprise in store.

Four-Two.—Beware of mischief-makers.

Four-One.—An enemy will fail to harm you.

Four-Blank.—A very unexpected letter.

Double-Three.—A sudden wedding in the family.

Three-Two.—You are going on a long journey.

Three-One.—A delightful discovery.

Three-Blank.—An anxious time, followed by great joy.

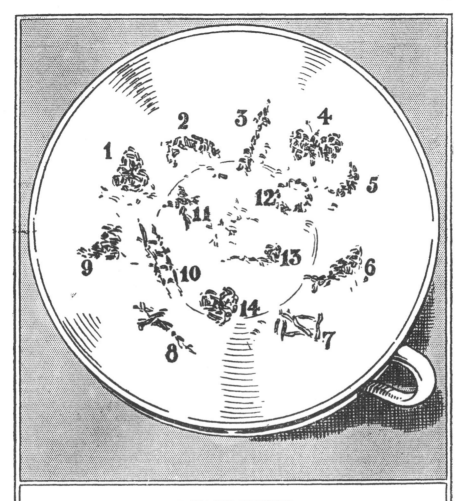

A TEACUP FORTUNE

THIS shows you just the right way to tell a friend's fortune, supposing, for example, the tea-leaves left in her cup are as shown above :

" The ACORN (1) in your cup tells that you will rise in life, while the ARCH (2) indicates a surprise. The ARROW (3) near it suggests that this surprise concerns love, which will come from an unexpected direction. Happy days are promised by the BUTTERFLY (4) and the CRESCENT MOON (5) near it tells that the happiness will come through romance. The FISH (6) foretells something good coming to you from over the water, but I see from the GATE (7) below it that some hindrance will delay this. Danger is threatened by the DAGGER (8) but the BOOT (9), which means a change of residence, will probably avert this. The LADDER (10) following, indicates that this change will go with marriage, and that joy and prosperity will accompany it. The CROSS (11) stands for trouble, but it will obviously pass, for the RING (12) again indicates marriage, with happiness and long life promised by the PIPE (13). That your courting days will be happy ones is assured by the HEART (14)."

Double-Two.—Folk are jealous of you.

Two-One.—A change in your affairs.

Two-Blank.—A long and happy life.

Double-One.—A very lucky find.

One-Blank.—Somebody is watching you carefully.

Double-Blank.—Disappointments may arise, but good will follow.

You are allowed to pick three Dominoes, but only one at a time. After picking the first, read its message and replace it, shuffling again, and so on.

To pick the same Domino twice is very lucky; three times is luckier still. You must not pick more than three Dominoes for yourself, or you will break the charm.

See Fate in the Sand !

A MOST fascinating way of telling fortunes at a party is by sand.

A tray with a rim round it, or a large plate, must be filled with fine sand and made perfectly smooth and level.

The tray is then placed on the table, and the girl who wishes to know her fate should take a pointed pencil—it must not be too short—and, holding it at an angle, let the point rest very lightly on the sand in the centre of the tray. The pencil should be held at the extreme end and with just the tips of the fingers.

She must then close her eyes and remain as still as possible while somebody else counts twenty-five. At the end of that time the pencil-point will in all probability have made various tracings in the sand. These will tell her fortune.

A faint, irregular line without shape, means many changes in her life. Tiny, broken lines show that the tracer is likely to have many sweethearts as well as many friends.

Long, well-defined lines mean good luck and great success; small, deep ones indicate the coming of money after hard work.

Large circles mean disappointments; small circles happy marriage. Squares mean pleasant surprises; deep, jagged lines show many ups and downs in life, while heart-shapes indicate a very happy love affair which will end in perfect wedded bliss.

" BOHEA."

CHAPTER V

Features and Fate

How to judge " his " character from his Head—Hair—
Eyebrows — Eyes—Nose—Mouth—Chin—Ears—Neck—
Hands—How he walks and sits, etc.

MOST of us consider that we can " size up " a man we meet for the first time, if not quite at a glance, at any rate after looking at him and talking to him for a little while—unless he is an exceptionally " deep one."

To a certain extent this is true, for a man's face does betray his character to some extent, to any-one who is in the least observant. We all know the difference between a strong face and a weak face, a clever one and a silly one, an honest one and a shifty one.

But these are general impressions and can sometimes be misleading. There is more in it than that. There are many other details of a man's character that can be read by less obvious signs if you study the subject a little, and sometimes these additional traits modify, for better or worse, your first general impression, and they will enable you to form a judgment of a man whose general appearance is not easy to read.

It is well worth while to give the subject a little study, for it is plainly a great advantage to be able to sum up the character of any man you meet, and to tell whether he is to be trusted or not ; and when it is a question of a possible Mr. " Right," nothing could be more important than to read him rightly from the very beginning.

So here are some hints that you will find of the very greatest help in judging character from the appearance.

The Head

FIRST of all, take the head. It is not always true to say that a big head is a brainy one and that a small one has " nothing in it," but as a general rule the man with a large, massive head is clever, or at any rate capable, and determined. He will get on in the world. If the other signs agree—and it is impossible to judge a character by one feature alone—he also will be affectionate, loyal, generous and considerate. In the little things of life he may be easy-going, but he will insist on having his own way about the big ones, and once he has made up his mind, it will be difficult to change it.

This does not mean, of course, that a man with a small head does not possess some of these qualities, but *too* small a head, in proportion to the body, is often a sign of a small and shallow mind, and a vain, self-satisfied nature.

Now take the shape of the head. Generally speaking, a man with a square or round head is practical and sensible, especially about money matters. He is steady, reliable and confident ; you can depend upon him in an emergency : but he is not as a rule romantic or very " understanding."

The very long, narrow head belongs to the man who is more likely to be an ardent lover. He is more sensitive, imaginative and sympathetic, more likely to understand your thoughts and emotions and to enter into and share them. But he may not make so solidly satisfactory a husband ; he has not, as a rule, the determination that gets a man on in the world, and you are not likely to find him quite the same tower of strength to lean on in time of trouble as the more round-headed man.

A head that is high above the

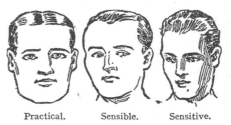

Practical.   Sensible.   Sensitive.

ears, combined with a broad, upright forehead, usually belongs to a brainy man—but often an unworldly one who is not competent to tackle the everyday practical problems of life. The forehead that slopes backward—unless the slope is *too* pronounced—does not by any means denote lack of brains, but rather that they are applied in a more practical way.

A man whose forehead bulges at and just above the eyebrows is usually good at outdoor games ; bulges at the side, level with the eyes, indicate a mastery over figures; similar bulges at the top corners of the forehead mean a love of music.

The shape of the back of the head reveals a great deal, too. If, seen in profile, it curves well out behind the ears, and then into the neck, the owner is probably of an affectionate disposition, fond of home and children, and will make a loyal and devoted husband. The head that is almost a straight, upright line often belongs to the

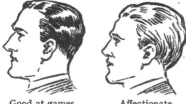

Good at games.   Affectionate.

hard, ruthless, dominating man who tramples roughshod over the feelings of others. The head that seems positively to slant outwards at the very bottom is generally the sign of a self-indulgent man, too fond of physical comforts, easy-going if he is kept comfortable, but "difficult" if he has to exercise self-denial.

These are general rules that may be modified by other features. You will find how to read the "bumps" of the head in detail in Chapter XI.

The Hair

THERE is a general idea that coarse hair is a sign of a coarse nature, and fine hair of a refined one, but there is no scientific reason to believe that the texture of the hair is to any extent a reliable guide to character. But it is true that stiff, wiry hair is seldom found in men of a weak and yielding disposition. The man with curly hair is often supposed to be very loving. It is more true to say that he is fond of being loved, and sometimes even flirtatious.

Neither does the colour of the hair indicate a great deal, but here again there are one or two exceptions. The popular belief that people with fiery red hair often have tempers to match, and a rather jealous and moody disposition, is a true one ; and as a general rule black-haired folk have a more passionate disposition than those with brown or fair hair.

The Eyebrows

QUITE an amount of character, too, is revealed in the eyebrows.

Thick, bushy brows, that overhang the eyes like eaves, usually go with a rather rugged character, straightforward and with little use for trivialities or the "trimmings" of life. Often they stand for a stubborn determination, or even obstinacy, and very "set" ideas. These eyebrows are often found in men with a great love for a country life. Thin, weak eyebrows, on the contrary, frequently betray a lack of decision ; they are sometimes a sign of poor health.

High, arched eyebrows are generally a sign of a sensitive, refined nature, and a sympathetic and understanding disposition. The man with eyebrows like these will consider your wishes before everything—but you will probably have to be careful not to wound his feelings, for he is easily hurt, and inclined to take things to heart.

Very straight, level eyebrows go, as a rule, with an honest, straightforward nature. The owner may not be very clever or possess great personal charm, but you can rely on him, sure that he will never " let you down."

Eyebrows that draw down over the eyes indicate a thoughtful, and often reserved, nature. If *very* depressed they may be a sign of a not altogether straightforward character.

Ruthless.   Self-indulgent.

If the eyebrows tilt a little upwards at the ends they show that valuable trait—a sense of humour. The man with such eyebrows will be a jolly companion, always able to see the funny side of things and to laugh his way through the troubles of life.

Eyebrows that meet over the nose are sometimes, though not always, a sign of bad temper.

The Eyes

EYES reveal character more by their expression than anything else, and this is a thing impossible to lay down rules about. The alert, twinkling eye; the dull, lifeless

an alert mind, quick to observe and to profit by all they see.

Half-closed, lazy-looking eyes go with a thoughtful, often an imaginative temperament, but their owner is frequently not very energetic or industrious.

Eyelids that droop at the corners usually stand for a love of ease and the comforts of life.

A full, rather prominent eye is a sign of a good memory and an accurate, conscientious turn of mind.

The deep-set eye is that of the thinker, and the man who is better at directing the work of others than in doing it himself.

Eyes set rather wide apart—the

CHARACTER IN EYEBROWS

Strength.   Weakness.   Sympathy.   Straightforwardness.   Humour.

eye; the hard, cold eye; the lazy eye; the soft, affectionate eye— each tell its own tale plainly.

But here are a few details that may help you to form a judgment from the eyes of anyone you meet— bearing in mind, of course, that his other features must also be taken into consideration.

The colour counts for very little, really, except that black or very dark eyes stand for a warmer, more passionate character than grey ones —though grey-eyed men are often capable of a very deep, sincere, loyal and lasting love.

Very round, childlike eyes with an expression of constant surprise, naturally belong to people who believe all they are told and are easily taken in.

Wide-open eyes generally mean

average distance between them is the width of an eye—usually belong to a thoughtful, rather dreamy man. Those rather close together, if they are steady, stand for determination, especially a determination to get on. But this type of eye, if it is shifty and restless, may mean that their owner is not altogether to be trusted. Do not, however, distrust every man whose gaze does not meet yours long and steadily; he may merely be nervous or shy.

A fleshiness above the eye is, often a sign of a self-indulgent nature, fond of the comforts of life. A fullness below generally belongs to the man who is a good talker, and perhaps something of a writer. He has a gift of words in one way or another. (See Plates 1 to 8.)

This nose shows strong character. | This one a sensitive nature. | This one reveals humour.

Noses

THERE is a great deal of character in a nose.

A big, prominent nose generally stands for character and capability. If it is accompanied by a strong chin, it belongs to the man who gets things done and pushes his way on in the world. A wide, flattish nose, on the other hand, is often a sign of laziness.

A straight, very thin nose usually stands for a sensitive, refined nature —even a fastidious one ; its owner may be a little difficult to get on with, because nothing but the best satisfies him.

A very sharp nose, especially if the owner also has thin lips, is often a sign of meanness.

The man with a turned-up nose is usually a good sort, cheery and easy to get on with, and is very often lucky. Without being particularly clever, or possessing many of the qualities that make for success in life, he has a way of " falling on his feet." (See Plates 11 and 12.)

Mouths

MOUTHS give their owners away perhaps more than any other feature.

A big mouth is usually a sign of a generous, broad-minded, easy-going nature. Too small a mouth is a sign of over-cautiousness ; if it is small, thin-lipped and very well formed it often stands for selfishness.

Very thin lips may stand for meanness, but very thick ones are also a bad sign. The man who has them is apt to be too fond of his own pleasures.

The nicest men have moderately full lips, the lower one thicker than the upper—a sign of an affectionate nature and at the same time a strong, well-controlled one.

A long upper lip often goes with a well-developed sense of humour. (See Plates 9 and 10.)

A determined mouth. | A self-indulgent one. | An affectionate one.

Chins

CHINS usually tell their own story.

The square, massive chin belongs to the man of determined will, who goes his own way and brushes aside those who try to oppose him. Much nicer is the firm but rounded chin. This stands for an affectionate disposition, strong yet tender—it belongs to a man who is both a splendid lover and a really satisfactory husband.

The very receding chin that slopes away backwards into the neck is a sign of both weakness of intellect and of character.

Grim resolution. | Firmness of will. | Weakness of character. | Well meaning but weak. | Whimsical humour.

Mischievous.   Generous.   A busybody.

The long chin is not a really strong one, but is sometimes a sign of obstinacy—which is quite a different thing from determination—and narrowness of mind. Men with such chins are often subject to fits of depression, and have difficulty in making up their minds. They are very anxious always to do the right thing, but are worried by doubts as to what the right thing is !

The small chin is a weak sign if it recedes, but it may be as firm as the heavier type, though less ruthless.

The narrow chin belongs to the sensitive, imaginative type of man, often with high ideals and high principles, but not too well suited to the struggles of life.

The pointed chin usually indicates a humorous, whimsical kind of mind, apt to be unconventional, but sometimes with an uncertain temper. (See Plates 13 and 14.)

Ears

EVEN a man's ears have a message for those who can read their meaning.

The small ear that lies flat against the head is usually a sign of refinement and good taste. The man with ears like these may, however, be finicky and difficult to please— not altogether an easy man to get on with. Small ears that stand out from the head indicate self-confidence and an ability to organise, direct and control the work of others.

Large ears that stand out are not handsome, but they usually belong to a generous and kindly man, anxious to please, and usually straightforward and dependable. Large ears that lie against the head usually stand for shrewdness and a good business instinct. The man with ears of this type is usually a hard worker and makes money.

Ears with a little point at the top generally indicate a keen sense of humour and even a mischievous nature ; they belong to the type of man who loves to play practical jokes. Ears inclined to point at the bottom are found in men strictly honourable in their dealings and fair in their judgments, but very often intolerant of the weaknesses of others.

The ear with a large lobe—the lower part—indicates generosity, and often a love of music. The ear with *very* little lobe is a sign of an interfering busybody who wants to mind everybody's business but his own. (See Plate 15.)

The Neck

EVEN the neck can reveal character to a certain extent. The long, thin neck usually be-

A fighter.   Fond of money.

Affectionate.   Intolerant.

longs to the sensitive, imaginative type of man, and sometimes accompanies ill health.

The man with a short, thick "bull" neck is stubborn and difficult to manage. He will go his own way, and will not be convinced by argument, though very often he can be influenced by an appeal to his emotions.

He's stolid.　　He's a good sort.

The Hands

THE shape of the hands is discussed in Chapter VII, but apart from this, there is something to be learnt from the way men hold their hands.

The tightly clenched hand often belongs to the man who is a born fighter, who sees life as a struggle and himself as battling his way through it ; this, however, must be read in conjunction with other signs. It may merely be due to nervousness.

The man whose fingers hook noticeably in towards the palm is fond of money and possessions and power. He is often selfish and not always entirely honest. This type of hand is not often met with, and do not confuse it with the loosely half-closed hand, which is a sign of a strong yet tender nature.

The hand that is normally held wide open, with the fingers apart, generally stands for a weak, undecided character and a lack of brain power. It belongs to the man who is easily "taken in" and easily led. But the hand that, when it is deliberately held open, spreads well out is a sign of a good-hearted nature.

The man who waves his hands about a great deal is enthusiastic, even excitable, and often not entirely to be depended upon.

The man who has a knack of pointing one finger to emphasise what he is saying is given to "laying down the law" and is usually intolerant of the opinions of others. (See Plate 16.)

How Does He Walk ?

A MAN'S walk will often betray his character.

It is easy to recognise the short, quick, uneven steps of the nervous man who is always in a hurry but

He's lazy.　　He's nervous.

seldom gets anywhere ; the slow, rather wandering walk of the dreamer ; the vigorous stride, with head and shoulders thrust forward, of the man who hammers his way through life regardless of others ; the soft, cautious tread of the man who tries to turn everything to his own advantage, and the firm, steady straightforward walk of the trustworthy, manly man.

—and Sit

EVEN in the way he sits a man may give himself away.

The man who always sprawls in a chair will expect to be waited on right and left, rather than to be helpful to others. He who perches on the edge of his chair as if he intends to rise again at any moment is unsure of himself and apt to be erratic. The one who cannot be still, but is constantly shifting his position is obviously restless and dissatisfied ; he is not the type who makes his way doggedly on to success, nor is he reliable.

The man who habitually sits with his knees apart and his feet firmly planted on the floor may be a little slow in thought, but he is very sure. He may not be a romantic lover or quick to understand and humour a woman's ways—he is, in fact, rather fond of getting his own way—but he is solid, reliable and trustworthy.

Best of all is the man who can sit quietly, easily and comfortably. There is nothing extreme about him ; he is the all-round good sort who will make a splendid life-partner.

"IOGO."

CHAPTER VI

Luck in Marriage

Fortune on your wedding-day—The month and day to choose—
Wedding superstitions—Luck for the bridegroom—The wedding-
ring—Luck in the house—Omens of the months, etc.

THE wedding-day is so important an event in a girl's life that it is not surprising there are so many charms and

superstitions connected with it. Indeed, there are so many things which foretell good or ill-luck that the bride-to-be must keep her eyes and ears wide open if she wishes to look into the future.

Choosing the Day

IT is well to choose your wedding-day with care, for once it has been fixed, it is considered unlucky to put it off, except in unavoidable circumstances. Choose, if possible, a time when the moon is full, and then remember the old rhyme :

" *Monday for health,*
Tuesday for wealth,
Wednesday the best day of all.
Thursday for crosses,
Friday for losses,
Saturday no luck at all."

While Lent weddings are said to be unlucky, the forty days following

Easter are lucky with the exception of any that fall in May, which used to be considered a downright unlucky month for marriages.

June, the month of roses, is held to be the luckiest month of all, but if you cannot be married in summer, November and December are the next luckiest months.

Scots lassies often choose the last day of the year in order that they and their new-made husbands may see the New Year in together as man and wife. It is in Scotland, too, that it is held to be unlucky to have your banns called in one year and be married in another.

The following verse gives the old superstitions concerning the luck of wedding months :

" Married in January's hoar and
    rime,
  Widowed you'll be before your
    prime ;
  Married in February's sleepy
    weather,
  Life you'll tread in tune together ;
  Married when March winds shrill
    and roar,
  Your home will lie on a distant
    shore ;
  Married 'neath April's changeful
    skies,
  A chequered path before you lies ;
  Married when bees o'er May
    blossoms flit,
  Strangers around your board will
    sit ;
  Married in month of roses—June,
  Life will be one long honeymoon ;
  Married in July, with flowers
    ablaze,
  Bitter-sweet mem'ries in after-
    days ;
  Married in August's heat and
    drowse,
  Lover and friend in your chosen
    spouse ;
  Married in September's golden glow,
  Smooth and serene your life will go ;

Married when leaves in October
    thin,
  Toil and hardships for you begin ;
  Married in veils of November mist,
  Fortune your wedding ring has
    kissed ;
  Married in days of December cheer,
  Love's star shines brighter from
    year to year."

Here is another rhyme which tells a slightly different story :

" Marry when the year is new,
  Always loving, kind and true.
  When February birds do mate,
  You may wed nor dread your fate.
  If you wed when March winds blow
  Joy and sorrow both you'll know.
  Marry in April when you can—
  Joy for maiden and for man.
  Marry in the month of May,
  You will surely rue the day.
  Marry when June roses blow
  Over land and sea you'll go.
  They who in July do wed
  Must labour always for their bread.
  Whoever wed in August be
  Many a change are sure to see.
  Marry in September's shine
  Your living will be rich and fine.
  If in October you do marry,
  Love will come, but riches tarry.
  If you wed in bleak November
  Only joy will come, remember.
  When December snows fall fast
  Marry and true love will last."

If the initials of the bride and bridegroom are the same it is lucky, in spite of the old rhyme which tells us that :

" To change the name and not the
    letter,
  Is to change for worse, but not for
    better."

But if, when placed together, the initial letters of their names and surnames spell any word, it is not considered a good omen, unless they should spell " love," and then a happy married life is certain.

The Wedding Dress

UNLESS they are going away in their wedding dress, most brides prefer to be married in the customary white, for, the old rhyme tells us :

" *Married in white,*
You have chosen aright.
Married in green,
Ashamed to be seen.
Married in grey,
You will go far away.
Married in red,
You will wish yourself dead.
Married in blue,
Love ever true,
Married in yellow,
Ashamed of your fellow.
Married in black,
You will wish yourself back.
Married in pink,
Your spirits will sink.
Married in brown,
You'll live out of town.
Married in pearl,
You'll live in a whirl."

If it is going to be a very quiet wedding, and the bride's name is Mary, then she should be married in blue, and in any case every bride should wear :

" *Something borrowed and something blue,*
Something old and something new."

The " something old " ensures that her friends shall be faithful when they are needed, the " something new," for success in her new life, the " something borrowed," that she may take with her the love of her family, and " something blue " as the emblem of constancy.

If a girl marries before her elder sisters, they must wear green garters at her wedding.

The bridegroom must not see his bride in her wedding dress before she stands with him at the altar, and she should not look at herself in the mirror after her toilet is completed, but in case she should be tempted to break this rule—and the temptation is very natural !—she must avoid putting her gloves on until she has actually turned from the mirror, for without these she is not fully dressed, and no ill-luck would follow that last peep in the glass. If she should look at herself even after the gloves are on, then the ill-luck may be averted by putting another pin in her veil.

The Wedding Wreath

NOWADAYS, in this country, the wedding wreath is always of orange blossom, but at one time it was twined of ears of corn as a symbol of prosperity. Orange blossom was said to have been brought first to this country by pilgrims from the Holy Land, and not only are the fragrant white flowers regarded as an emblem of purity, but the plant itself is an omen of prosperity, for in the East the orange tree bears fruit and blossom at one and the same time.

The Wedding Veil

AT one time the wedding veil took the form of a square of linen held over the heads of both bride and bridegroom. Later it was thought that it was only the bride who needed a veil, and thus the present-day custom began, the bride going into church with the veil down and coming out with it thrown back as a sign that she is now a wedded wife with no need for maiden blushes.

The Wedding Day

" HAPPY is the bride that the sun shines on ! " Many a bride recalling this old saying has been worried because a shower of rain fell on her wedding day, yet in

Germany the girl who sees a shower of rain on her wedding morn is delighted, for she believes it is a sign that all her tears will have been shed before and not after her marriage, so any girl who goes to church in a shower may remember this belief and be comforted.

If, on her wedding morning, the bride is awakened by the singing, or even the chirping of a bird, it is a very good omen. So it is to see swallows fly past her window, while if a robin should come to sing on her window-sill she may count herself as fortunate indeed.

She must be careful not to break anything on her wedding morn, or she will quarrel with her husband before the year is out. Should she by chance have such an accident, she may avert the misfortune by breaking two other things on purpose—even old flower-pots will serve; but she should be very careful not to break the heel of her shoe, or she will quarrel with her husband's family.

If there is a cat in the house she must feed it or the cat, to spite her, may bring on a shower of rain ! (This is an old superstition which is, no doubt, founded on the belief that cats were the friends and companions of witches.)

It is lucky if the cat sneezes.

Though every bride will, of course, read the marriage service through before her wedding day, she should not do so within twenty-four hours of the service itself. She must not try on her wedding ring, and the ring itself must not be enlarged, or she will be left a widow ; a correct fit can always be assured if a ring is chosen of the same size as that of the engagement ring.

If, when she comes to put on her wedding dress, a small spider is found in its folds, this foretells that she will never lack money ; the spider must never be killed, but placed carefully out of doors.

Sometimes, out of sheer nervousness, a bride will cry on her wedding morning. These tears need not alarm her, for they are a sign that she will shed very few after her wedding.

In some parts of Austria the bride's mother gives her a handkerchief of the finest linen. This is called the " Tearkerchief," and is for use in drying the tears the bride may shed on leaving her old home. After the wedding the handkerchief is folded away and never used again.

On no account must a bride go to church with a borrowed handkerchief, so let the " something borrowed " be some other trifle.

On the way to church it is unlucky to meet a pig, a hare or a serpent, but to see a lamb or a dove is a very good omen.

When she enters the church, if she sees her bridegroom before he sees her, she will rule him ; if, however, it is he who has the first glance, he will be master.

A thunderstorm during the ceremony means quarrels, but if the sun breaks out on the way home the quarrels will not be very serious ones.

On entering the church, and also on entering her house after the ceremony, the bride should step with the right foot first. She must also be careful not to make any mistakes when signing the marriage register.

The first man to kiss the bride when she is a wedded wife is said to ensure himself a year's good luck. At one time it was the clergyman who did this, but nowadays it is often the best man who claims the privilege.

When the bridesmaids help to undress the bride they must take great care not to leave a single pin in any of her garments, and the pins taken from the wedding veil must all be thrown away.

For a bridesmaid to keep a pin is generally said to prevent her own marriage—although in Brittany these pins are eagerly sought, for they promise marriage within the year.

A bride must not keep her wedding bouquet; it is usually distributed among her friends. One old custom is for the bride to toss it over the heads of the guests, and if a single girl catches it, she will be wed before the year is out.

A curious old Scottish custom, which is still followed in some parts of the country, is for the bridegroom's mother to meet the newly-wedded pair at the door of their home, and to break a currant bun over the head of the bride, thus ensuring them prosperity in the future !

If the couple are going to set up housekeeping in a new house, a piece of silver should be set in the door-sill, and if a friend can induce a hen to cackle in the house before they enter it, so much the better for them.

One quaint old custom took the form of a plate of cake crumbs, plate and all, being thrown from an upper window as the bride alighted from her carriage. If the plate remained unbroken it was a bad sign, but if it were smashed the more pieces there were the more years of good fortune it promised the happy pair.

In some country villages it was the custom, if there were still unmarried daughters left at home, to pour a kettle of hot water down the steps directly the bridal couple left for their honeymoon, in the belief that before the water dried up another match would be made, the wedding " flow on," and another couple soon pass over the same ground.

Nowadays, a bride is usually driven to church in a car, but when horses were used they had to be grey, as these were supposed to protect the bridal couple from witch-craft.

EVERY WOMAN'S LUCK BOOK

The casting of old shoes after the honeymoon carriage dates back from olden days when, on the occasion of her marriage, the bride's father gave one of her shoes to her bridegroom as a sign that he was now her master.

In some parts of the country the shoe-throwing ceremony did not take place until after the newly-married pair had set off on their honeymoon. Then the girls ranged themselves in one line, and the bachelors in another. An old shoe of the bride's was thrown as far as possible, and the girl who got to it first was promised marriage within a year. When she had picked up the shoe she threw it at the men, and the man whom it hit could reckon that his bachelor days were numbered.

If a bride wishes to rule in her new home, she must put her right foot before that of her bridegroom when they stand at the altar together. If, when they return home, she and her newly-made husband stand together before a mirror while she is still in her wedding dress, good luck will follow them.

For the Bridegroom

THOUGH, as may be expected, most of the charms and superstitions are for the bride, there are certain things which it is considered lucky or unlucky for a bridegroom to do.

He must not drop his hat on the wedding day, and he must be still more careful not to drop the wedding ring as he is about to place it on the finger of his bride.

A tiny horseshoe carried in his pocket will bring him luck in love, and any money that he pays out on his wedding day should be in odd sums. No one should hand him a telegram on his way to church.

In Scotland a Highland bridegroom left his left shoe undone so that no witch might cast a spell over him.

As orange blossom was for the bride, so rosemary, " for remembrance," was for the bridegroom, and sometimes the wedding guests wore sprigs of this plant, too. Here is what one clergyman preaching a wedding sermon some three hundred years ago said about it :

" The rosemary is for married men. It helpeth the brain, strengtheneth the memory, and is very medicinal for the head. It also affects the heart. Let this rosmarinus, the flower of men, ensign of your wisdom, love and loyalty, be carried not only in your hands, but in your hearts."

According to the month in which he was married, so the bridegroom might know what to expect of his bride. Here is the character of the bride for each month :

January. A good housekeeper, careful with money and far-sighted.

February. A loving wife, a good mother, and a loyal friend.

March. Somewhat extravagant, and given to gossip.

April. Good-looking, but inclined to flirt.

May. Handsome, good-tempered, and cheerful in disposition.

June. Generous, impulsive, and apt to be quick-tempered.

July. Good-looking, fond of dress, and rather impatient.

August. Practical, and a good housewife.

September. Amiable, liked by her neighbours, and helpful to her husband in business.

October. Pretty, inclined to flirt, and given to jealousy.

November. Very impulsive, generous, and quick-tempered.

December. Extravagant, fond of change ; a good hostess.

The Wedding Ring

FROM the earliest times rings have been used in the marriage ceremony, though they have not always been of gold, some of the first ones being of lead or iron.

The wedding ring is said by some to be placed upon the third finger of the left hand because, according to an old belief, there is an artery leading there straight from the heart—a pretty idea which will appeal to all lovers, who will echo the words of an old poet :

" *And as this round*
  Is nowhere found
    To flaw, or else to sever,
  So let our love
  As endless prove,
    And pure as gold forever."

In ancient days the bridegroom first placed the ring on the top of his bride's thumb with the words, " In the name of the Father," then on the forefinger as he said, " and of the Son," then on the middle finger, adding, " and of the Holy Ghost." He then placed it on the third finger as he said, " Amen."

It was once the custom—a pretty one that some couples still like to follow—to have a motto engraved inside a wedding ring. Here are some of the most favoured :

" *My love is fixed, I shall not change ;*
  I like my choice too well to range."
" *My love is true to none but you.*"
" *Be true in heart though far apart.*" (A very suitable motto for a sailor's ring.)
" *Many are the stars I see, but in my eyes no star like thee.*"

" *My promise past shall always last.*"
" *United hearts death only parts.*"

Luck in the House

SINCE the majority of people pass most of their time in the house, it is only natural that many old charms and beliefs should be associated with household things, and here are some of the signs and omens in which people have believed for centuries past.

Candle. A spark on the wick of a candle means a letter from a friend. If there is a big glow, a present will come with the letter.

Clothes. If by accident you should put on a garment inside out, it means a pleasant surprise during the day, but you must continue to wear it the wrong way or you will lose the luck. To put shoes on the table is a sign you will hear bad news. If a child's petticoat is longer than her frock it indicates that she is more beloved by her father than her mother.

Cricket. To hear a cricket means there is money coming to you. If you have been lucky in your old home, and are moving to a new one, take a cricket with you and you will take your luck, too.

Dog. If a strange dog howls three times outside the house you will hear of an illness.

Fire. Should a bright spark fly out upon you there is a pleasant surprise coming your way, while if a piece of coal flies out, it means money. Should the fire burn only at one side, a parting is foretold, while a piece of coal hanging from a bar indicates that you may expect a visit from a friend.

Foot. For the sole of your foot to burn is a sign that you will shortly tread on strange ground, while if, during the night, you slit a sheet with your toe, it is a sign that you will soon be moving to a new house.

Letters. Never dry a letter before the fire if it contains a request for something. If you do, your request will not be granted.

Matches. To light three cigarettes with the same match will bring misfortune upon one of the three smokers

Mirror. As everyone knows, it is unlucky to break a mirror, as this signifies breaking your own image. But if you can gather up all the pieces your ill-luck will last only seven days, instead of the traditional seven years.

Moon. The new moon should never be seen through glass. To see it on a Monday means a gift during the week. If you can contrive to see the new moon for the first time while looking over your right shoulder and wish when you see it, your wish will come true.

Peas. If you find a pea-pod containing ten peas, you will have a pleasant surprise before the day is out.

Picture. Should a picture fall without reason, you will hear of a death. (Of course, should the cord have been frayed this superstition does not hold good.)

Salt. While it is unlucky to spill salt, for, " As many grains of salt you waste, as many tears you'll shed," yet the misfortune may be averted by throwing a pinch over your left shoulder.

Stairs. To stumble up the stairs is a sign of a wedding, while it is unlucky to pass anyone on the stairs of a private house.

Umbrella. To open an umbrella in the house is to bring bad news. To drop your umbrella means a disappointment unless someone else picks it up for you. If you pick it up yourself, take it by the ferrule end.

Water. To spill water is a sign that you will take a journey.

ROUND THE CALENDAR

Luck-Lore of the Months

January

THE omens of this month centre mostly about the New Year, and the old custom of first-footing must be given pride of place.

Just before midnight on New Year's Eve, the house should be tidied, the fire banked up, and as the clock strikes, then the door should be set wide that the old year may go out and take any ill-luck with it. The house is then ready for the first-footer.

To bring the best kind of luck the first-footer should be a dark man, and unless he brings some gift with him it will be a sign that the year will be a lean one. If he brings a cake, then you will have plenty, if a fish, then good luck will be yours ; a lump of coal is also a good omen, while if he should offer a coin, even a farthing, all your undertakings during the year will be attended with success.

Housewives should make sure that their clocks have been wound, for illness is foretold if a clock stops as the New Year is coming in.

In this old rhyme you may find a forecast of the weather by the way the wind blows on New Year's night :

" *If on New Year's night wind blow south,*
It betokeneth warmth and growth ;
If west, much milk, and fish in the sea ;
If north, much cold and snow there will be ;
If east, the trees will bear much fruit ;
If north-east, flee it, man and brute."

PLATE 5

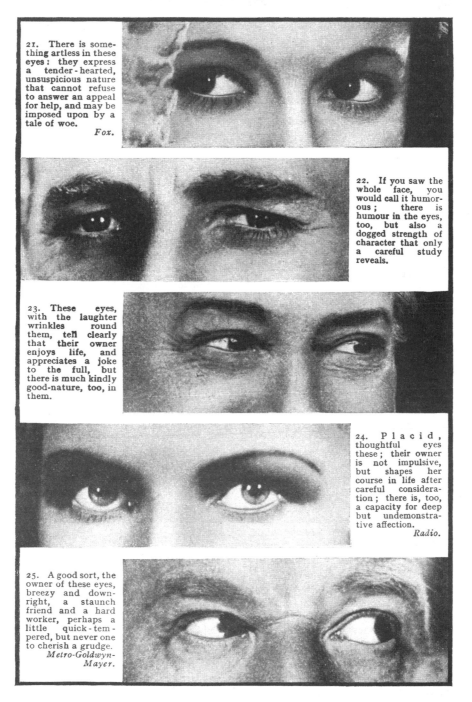

21. There is something artless in these eyes: they express a tender-hearted, unsuspicious nature that cannot refuse to answer an appeal for help, and may be imposed upon by a tale of woe.
Fox.

22. If you saw the whole face, you would call it humorous; there is humour in the eyes, too, but also a dogged strength of character that only a careful study reveals.

23. These eyes, with the laughter wrinkles round them, tell clearly that their owner enjoys life, and appreciates a joke to the full, but there is much kindly good-nature, too, in them.

24. Placid, thoughtful eyes these; their owner is not impulsive, but shapes her course in life after careful consideration; there is, too, a capacity for deep but undemonstrative affection.
Radio.

25. A good sort, the owner of these eyes, breezy and downright, a staunch friend and a hard worker, perhaps a little quick-tempered, but never one to cherish a grudge.
Metro-Goldwyn-Mayer.

PLATE 6

26. These eyes reveal a sensitive, affectionate nature and a goodhearted, tolerant attitude of mind; their owner would never judge his fellows harshly, but would be lenient to their faults.
Paramount British.

27. A very level mind lies behind these eyes, and a shrewd and critical judgment. Their owner has an " infinite capacity for taking pains " and demands the same standard of thoroughness from others.
Paramount.

28. It is not only the twinkling eye with laughter-lines round it that expresses a sense of humour. More than one very successful comedian has heavy-lidded eyes such as these.
Metro-Goldwyn-Mayer.

29. These are the wide-open eyes of a receptive mind, always ready to take in fresh facts and impressions, and to learn from them and turn them to profitable account.
Warner.

30. Penetrating eyes these, that take in far more than they may appear to. They belong to a mind that can go straight to the heart of a matter, discarding the things that do not count.

PLATE 7

31. These eyes show a mind alert and yet thoughtful, quick to see the possibilities of a new idea, but considering it carefully before adopting it and carrying it out. *Paramount.*

32. These are kindly eyes ; their owner is a friendly soul and wishes the whole world well ; the thought of suffering or injustice rouses him to indignation.

33. The owner of these eyes has a very decided temperament. Outwardly she appears placid, for she conceals her emotions, but actually her feelings are deep and strong. *Paramount.*

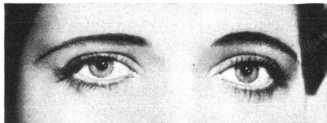

34. Here is a man who has experienced the ups and downs of life, and learnt much. He is a good friend to the deserving but will not tolerate being imposed upon. *Gaumont-British.*

35. Exuberant vitality dances in these eyes, unquenchable enthusiasm, untiring energy, and a desire to be constantly "up and doing." There is determination here, too.

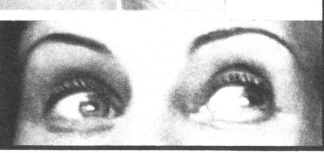

PLATE 8

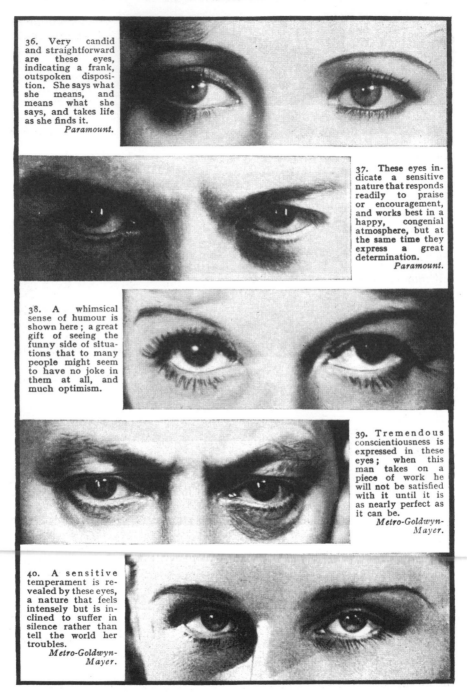

36. Very candid and straightforward are these eyes, indicating a frank, outspoken disposition. She says what she means, and means what she says, and takes life as she finds it.
Paramount.

37. These eyes indicate a sensitive nature that responds readily to praise or encouragement, and works best in a happy, congenial atmosphere, but at the same time they express a great determination.
Paramount.

38. A whimsical sense of humour is shown here; a great gift of seeing the funny side of situations that to many people might seem to have no joke in them at all, and much optimism.

39. Tremendous conscientiousness is expressed in these eyes; when this man takes on a piece of work he will not be satisfied with it until it is as nearly perfect as it can be.
Metro-Goldwyn-Mayer.

40. A sensitive temperament is revealed by these eyes, a nature that feels intensely but is inclined to suffer in silence rather than tell the world her troubles.
Metro-Goldwyn-Mayer.

February

ST. VALENTINE'S DAY holds the luck of this month, and as the charms and omens of this day are described in Chapter XII, it is only necessary to mention the weather-lore.

Candlemas Day (February 2nd) was held to show the kind of weather which might be expected throughout the year, and shepherds with their lambs judged it a very bad sign if the sun peeped in their huts, for :

" *If Candlemas Day be fair and bright,*
Winter will have another flight ;
But if Candlemas Day brings clouds and rain,
Winter is gone and won't come again."

March

THERE are no specially lucky days in this month, which to ensure a good summer should be windy and dry, while dust blowing is the sign of a good year for the farmer.

" *A peck of March dust and a shower in May,*
Makes the corn green and the fields gay."
" *A peck of March dust is worth a king's ransom.*"

April

EASTER usually falls in this month, and there are several old beliefs connected with the festival.

Potatoes planted on Good Friday do better than those planted on any other day of the year, but no other undertaking must be begun on this day.

Hot cross buns should be eaten, for they protect the house from fire, and if one is eaten before seven in the morning, a wish will be granted.

On Mothering Sunday children should be sure to take a Simnel cake home to their parents.

Holidaymakers naturally look for a fine Easter, but a wet one is a better indication of a good summer.

" *A wet Good Friday and a wet Easter Day foreshows a fruitful year.*"

May

AT one time Whitsun was marked by many quaint customs, such as letting a dove from the roof, and by dancing on the village green, but these have all died out, and only the old superstition concerning May weddings remains, and that is fast vanishing, except in a few districts.

For a good harvest this month should be dry, " *A May wet was never kind yet,*" while most of us know the old saying bidding us, " *Ne'er cast a clout till May be out* " —though some people hold that this applies not to the month but to the hawthorn blossom.

June

THIS is the lovers' month, and girls who meet their sweethearts, become engaged, or get married in June, should find fortune favour them.

June is named after Juno, who was supposed to have all women under her special protection, and to look favourably upon any plans undertaken by women in this month.

Since this is the first of the holiday months, fine weather is hoped for, yet farmers like a wet June for :

" *A dripping June,*
Brings all things in tune."

July

A MONTH specially favourable for making friends, but those who are taking their holidays in this month should hope for fine weather on the first, since :

" *If the first of July it be rainy weather,*
It will rain more or less for four weeks together."

August

THE month for holiday friendships, but do not put too much faith in them, for an old superstition tells us August friends are fickle friends.

September

A FINE first day of this month is said to foretell a fine month altogether. As this is the seventh month, it is a lucky one for planning any new business undertaking.

October

THE " magic " of October lies about Hallowe'en, and its charms and superstitions are described in Chapter XII.

From October weather you are said to be able to foretell the weather for early spring :

" *If October brings much frost and wind,*
Then are January and February kind."

November

A LUCKY month for planting fruit trees if you make sure you dig the hole on the first day.

November 11th is Martinmas, and if there are heavy frosts before that date the rest of the winter will be mild.

December

" A GREEN Christmas makes a fat kirkyard," the old saying tells us, while snow on Christmas Day is lucky for those who walk in it.

" *A child that's born on Christmas Day is fair and wise and good and gay.*"

Each mince-pie eaten in a different house means a wish to come true during the year.

December 28th (Holy Innocents' Day) is an unlucky day to start a new undertaking or to make a new friend.

Christmas decorations should be burnt before Twelfth Night, or they will bring bad luck on the house where they are left up.

"LUNA DI MIELE."

CHAPTER VII

Hands of Destiny

Palmistry reveals character and foretells the future—Types of hands—Fingers and thumbs—The mounts—The Lines of Life, Fate, Heart, Marriage, etc.—Other signs and their meanings.

EVERYBODY knows that our hands reveal a great deal about our characters. By the shape of a hand, its texture, and other points, anyone who has studied the matter at all can form a very good idea of the character and disposition of its owner.

But if you learn something about the science of Palmistry you can go further than that. Those curious lines and markings that are upon every palm will be like a map to you. Examining the hands of your friends you will be able to tell a great deal about their characteristics, their gifts, their virtues and failings ; you will be able to foretell, too, important events likely to happen in their lives, and may even give a timely warning of an impending trouble of some kind that may be averted if the right action is taken.

It is not possible to give in this book a complete course of instruction in the art of Palmistry, but the information contained in this chapter will equip you to read many interesting things in the hands of your friends.

No two hands are alike. The markings upon your hand are different from those on anyone else's, and almost every mark has a meaning. That is why palmistry is such a fascinating study, and you can spend endless hours of interest and entertainment in finding out the secrets hidden in your own hand and in those of your friends.

First of all, we will deal with the different *types* of hands, of which there are seven.

The " Elementary " Hand

THIS is the least desirable type to possess, indicating as it usually does that the person possessing it is rather dull and slow-witted, though likely to be determined and obstinate when she wants her own way, even if that way is not the right one.

This hand is thick, heavy and rather clumsy, the fingers inclined to be short, and bearing square, coarse nails. Fortunately this hand is found the least often of any, for its possessor would probably not be very happy, prone as she would be to jealousy, and lacking the courage to help her through the difficult times that come into all our lives now and then.

A person with this hand would

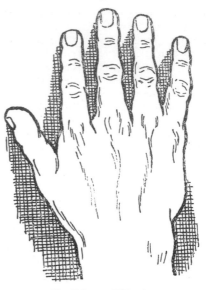

The " Square " Hand.

not possess a great deal of ambition or initiative, and would prefer to work under someone else, and only have to obey orders.

It is not very likely that either you or your friends will own a hand of this type, however, since with the changing times, and the better opportunities we are all receiving in life to make something better of ourselves, the characteristics it stands for are becoming rare.

The " Square " Hand

IF you have a hand that looks rather square in shape, of medium size, with the fingers square and the nails rather short but well shaped, it is one to be quite satisfied with, for it shows that you are very practical, with a love of neatness and order, while you are usually very keen to do " the right thing " according to the accepted rules.

You are likely to be very determined—almost stubborn—but as

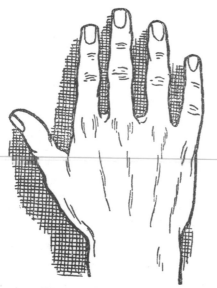

The " Elementary " Hand.

you are more often than not in the right, this is not really such a bad failing. One of your good points is that you will meet the rough patches of life with plenty of courage, resolved to fight through them as quickly as possible.

You are slow to make up your mind, but once you have reached a decision it will be almost unshakable, while, because your head

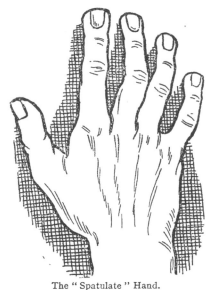

The "Spatulate" Hand.

will always rule your heart, you will feel a little impatient with people of the dreamy, romantic type.

Perhaps you hide your feelings rather too much, leading others to think you cold, but you have a deep love of home and family in your nature. Having a strong sense of justice, you are conscientious and trustworthy, and generally win your success in life through sheer hard work.

The "Spatulate" Hand

IN this type of hand the fingers are spread out and flattened rather at the tips, the palm starting

rather broadly at the wrist, and narrowing in slightly as it meets the fingers.

Perhaps you have a friend with this type of hand, and if so, you will be able to tell that she is one of the restless, outspoken type of people, who want to be left to go their own way in life, even if it happens to be the wrong way.

She will feel that she must have change and variety, and will probably get tired of one job and want to change to another quite often. She will be interested, too, in all sorts of unusual schemes or ideas, though she will not be foolish about them ; she will only choose those which her practical common sense tells her have a firm foundation.

Of course, in every type there are those who go to extremes, but these are only exceptional cases, and we are not likely to come up against many of them.

Your friend with the spatulate hand will be calmly confident of her own ability to make a success of whatever she has on hand, while she will be courageous and rather lucky in her undertakings.

The "Conic" Hand

IF you have a hand of medium size, with the tips of the fingers rather pointed and bearing long-shaped nails, you are very artistic, with a deep love of pretty things.

Perhaps you are rather too fond of the good things of life, and disposed to sit back and enjoy yourself rather than make the most of the gifts which are yours. You are inclined to be a little too impatient, while you might do better if you could concentrate a little more.

You are generous and warm-

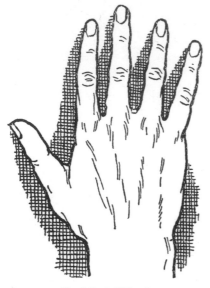

The " Conic " Hand.

deep thinker, full of dreams and ideals, and quite content with her own company most of the time. Because of this she will be rather aloof, and you may think her unsociable. However, she has a deep understanding of human nature.

She should do splendidly in the teaching profession, for she will go to any amount of pains to explain things, and her patience is remarkable. Unfortunately she has not a great deal of sympathy with others, and unless she is asked for help she will most likely be too busy with her own life to give it.

This friend of yours will care little for money or any other kind of material gain, preferring to live in her dreams and ideals, and you might advise her to try to come down to earth a little more, as it will be to her advantage.

hearted, but you are rather inclined to moodiness. Until you settle down with the right partner you will go from one love affair to another, for your feelings will not go very deep in any of them, and a new face will soon attract you away from an accustomed one.

You are sociable, and therefore popular among your friends, while you will never refuse your ready sympathy to anyone in need. If your little finger is long, this will endow you with great tact, and you will be able to handle difficult situations successfully.

The " Philosophic " Hand

YOU will know this type by its long, rather thin shape, and somewhat knotty-looking joints. This type is not met with so often as the previous three, but you may find that one of your friends possesses it.

If so, you can be sure she is a

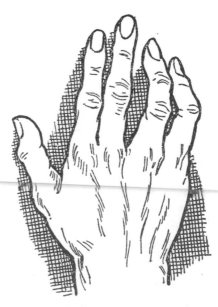

The " Philosophic " Hand.

The " Psychic " Hand

THIS is a type which is less generally found, but when you do meet with it you will know it immediately, for it is long and beautiful, its fingers rather pointed, and bearing lovely almond-shaped nails.

If you should happen to have it, I am afraid you will be rather too apt to have your head in the clouds and to let opportunities pass you by because you are too wrapped up in your thoughts to grasp them. You will find it very difficult to look at things in a practical way, and you are perhaps a little too easily influenced by others.

Your health may need care, as you are inclined to be delicate, but you can overcome this by taking the necessary precautions. Rather sensitive, you are inclined to fits of depression at times, but those you care for should be able to shake you out of them.

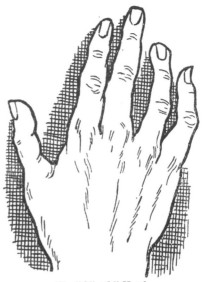

The " Mixed " Hand.

The "Mixed " Hand

STRANGELY enough, this type of hand, containing some of the characteristic features of other types, is quite often found, and if you possess it you will notice that its mixedness is mostly in the fingers. For instance, one may be " spatulate " and the others " conic," or two " square " and two " psychic."

You will be able to take up many different interests if you have this hand, and you probably possess a clever and active mind, but because of this you may try to have too many irons in the fire, and so succeed at none. This is something to guard against, therefore.

Perhaps you are a little too inclined to be restless and anxious for much change and variety in life, and consequently you may have many ups and downs of fortune. However, you will generally manage to remain cheery and smiling, while you will certainly be popular, for

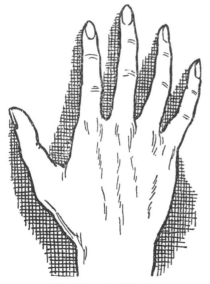

The " Psychic " Hand.

your different experiences will make you interesting and amusing in company.

THE fingers of our hands, too, give indications of character, and these must be taken into consideration when we are reading our own hands and those of our friends. The meaning in their shape should be read in conjunction with the meaning in the shape of the whole hand, as one may modify the other.

The Thumb

THIS is divided into three sections, or phalanges, the top one, where the nail is, denoting will-power, the second reason, and the third, at the base of the thumb, which is really the mount of Venus —this will be dealt with later— standing for love.

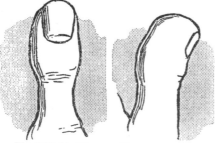

The "Waisted" Thumb.   The "Undecided" Thumb.

If the first phalange of the thumb is long and strong, this indicates self-confidence and an energetic will, while if it is of medium length, you will quietly accept what comes in life. If this phalange is too long, you are likely to be rather dictatorial and want to force people into your way of thinking, while if too short, you will be rather undecided. When the thumb is "waisted," you have a clever brain.

The second phalange should be rather longer than the first, and fairly thick. When it is the same length as the first, and the thumb is long and straight, you will have a sensible, firm character, but if the thumb is only moderately long, you will not be a leader among others, but you will have good judgment and wisdom.

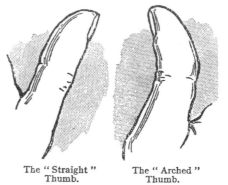

The "Straight" Thumb.   The "Arched" Thumb.

Perhaps you may find that your thumb has the first phalange short and the second long and thick. Then you will know that you are rather too cautious, and find it difficult to make up your mind. You make plans, but often fail to carry them out. With both phalanges strongly developed, you will be very fortunate and successful.

When the third phalange is thick and well developed, you are apt to let your feelings run away with you, and to be too headstrong, but if only moderately developed, then you will be kind and affectionate, well spoken of by all. If you have only a small, flat phalange then you will be of a colder, more practical nature.

You may have a friend whose thumb is widely separated from her first finger; then you can tell her that she is of the type who likes to go her own way, without help from others, anxious to succeed only on her own merit.

While if, on the other hand, the thumb is very close to the first finger, your friend will be cautious and afraid of acting on her own, while she may also be inclined to closeness over money matters. If the thumb arches backwards at the top, then she will be full of courage and ready to brave all obstacles.

The Fingers. The knotted type of finger that goes with the " Philosophic " hand indicates that you are careful and painstaking, fond of learning the innermost tricks of things, and ready to go to any amount of trouble to do so. In fact, you will be determined that nothing shall stand in your way, in this respect. You love nothing better than to solve problems which are puzzling others, and you will be most careful as to detail.

If the fingers are rather smooth, you will be full of bright ideas, but you may be too eager to rush into things without stopping to think whether it would really be wise or not.

Perhaps, too, you will be somewhat thoughtless in little things, and rather too wrapped up in your thoughts to consider the feelings of others. This will be even more so if your fingers taper off to a point.

When smooth fingers are long also, this indicates that you are methodical and particular—sometimes, even, giving more thought to details than to the bigger things in life. This is something you might try to correct a little, for it may hinder you on the road to success.

You may notice that a hand you are " reading " bears very short fingers, and then you will know that the owner is one of the sharp, quick people who must always be doing something, and are always in a hurry. She may be hasty-tempered, too, but her " flare-ups " will soon be over, because she will be in too much of a hurry to keep up a quarrel or nurse a grievance.

She will probably be clever and possess quite a good fund of humour, but you might suggest that she should think a little longer before she speaks, for quite often she will say something on the impulse of the moment, and be sorry afterwards.

Another may have less supple and rather more stiffly-jointed fingers which are set close together ; you may tell her that she is rather too cautious, afraid to take any step before she is quite certain where it will lead, and so in this way is likely to lose opportunities. She might

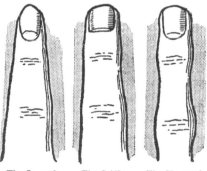

The Smooth, Pointed Finger.   The Stiffly-jointed Finger.   The Knotted Finger.

also trust her friends more, for she will find in most cases that confidence will call forth confidence in return.

Short fingers which are thick and rather clumsy have not a very happy meaning, so let us hope that none of your friends possess them, for they indicate a rather selfish, self-centred nature, more concerned with following her own pursuits than helping others.

If your fingers are very supple, arching backwards, you will be charming and witty, but you may find it rather difficult to keep a secret. You should do your best to overcome this fault, or you may lose friends through it.

Sometimes—though fortunately it is rare—a hand bears naturally crooked fingers, and unless there are redeeming points in the rest of the hand, this indicates a grasping, rather sly nature. Let us hope you do not find fingers like these in the possession of any of your friends.

You may discover that your fingers are set rather well apart, and this shows that you are generous, and perhaps a little inclined to fritter your money away instead of saving for a rainy day.

Probably, too, you will be rather determined, wanting to go your own way, and fretting against anything or anybody who might try to stop you. In fact, you would rather break away from all family ties than be forced to do something against your will.

If your fingers are fairly thick and fleshy at the top, or first, phalange, you are likely to be rather sensitive, and to imagine hurts where none are meant at times. Should your fingers be thick at the base, or third phalange, you are perhaps too much inclined to drift through life, feeling that it is too much bother to make the effort to fight for success, though you will be fond of the things money can buy, all the same.

In Palmistry, each finger of the hand has a name :

The Finger of Jupiter. This is the first finger, and if it is rather long you will like to take the lead among your friends, and to try to make them think along your own lines. It might be as well for you to remember that " pride goeth before a fall," and so strive not to think of yourself as always knowing better than others.

The Finger of Saturn. If this, the second finger, is unusually long, you will be of the patient, plodding kind, slow to make up your mind, yet usually deciding on the right course when at last you do so.

Keen on learning all about the interesting things in life, too, you will often be found poring over deep books, while though you have a splendid amount of patience, you may be lacking in humour.

The Finger of Apollo. If, when reading a friend's hand, you find the third finger is very long, you can tell her that she has a love of beautiful things and colourful surroundings, while success should come to her through any artistic work.

The Finger of Mercury. If one of your friends has a long little finger, she will be brilliant and clever, able to sway others by her power of speaking convincingly. Tactfulness, too, will be one of her strong points, and she will never hurt the feelings of others if she can help it. Whenever there is friction between her friends, she will be the one to smooth it over and bring back the smiles to their faces.

The Nails. Perhaps more than any other part of the hand do the nails show most plainly any signs of ill-health from which you are suffering, or are likely to suffer unless you exercise the right amount of care.

If your nails are a fairly good size, well-shaped and smooth, you are active and healthy, with a good circulation, while should they be short and squat, almost broader than they are long, you may have a little weakness of the heart. You should, therefore, guard against over-strain and being too energetic, see that you have plenty of sleep and not too much excitement. If you take these precautions, you have no need to worry about this tendency.

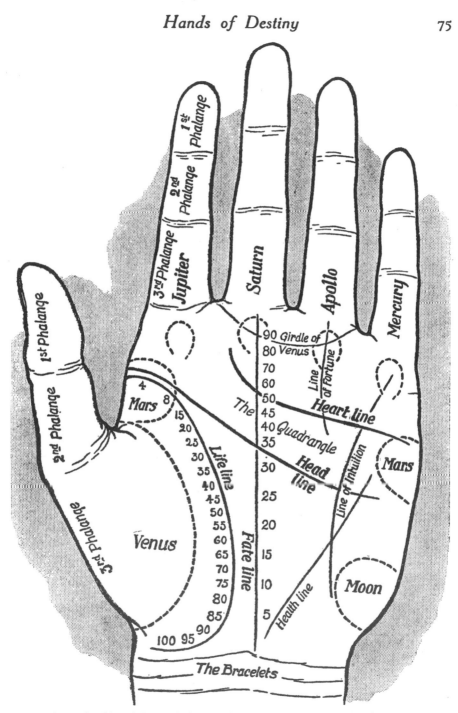

A complete Map of the Hand, showing the mounts, principal lines, bracelets, etc.

You may find one of your friends has ridged and rather rough nails, somewhat dull in colour ; you will know that she does not take all the care she might with her health, and that both her circulation and her liver are out of order. You may console her with the fact that it rests in her own hands to get her health back to normal, however, by being more careful over her choice of food and taking more exercise.

A nail of this shape shows a tendency to throat trouble.

A nail showing a liability to chest weakness.

Long, narrow nails that are rather curved tell you that their owner may be subject to chest trouble.

Perhaps you have a friend with rather small, triangular-shaped nails with little colour and polish. You will know that she may have a tendency to paralysis if she does not take care to lead a quiet, simple life, avoiding any kind of nervous strain.

Throat trouble is also indicated by the finger nails, and if you have nails something like those possessed by a person with a weak chest, but which are a little shorter and better coloured, you may know that you have a tendency to suffer from little ailments connected with the throat, and would be wise to take care of it by gargling frequently, keeping away from hot, overcrowded places as far as possible, and also avoiding chills.

Then you may overcome this weakness.

Finger-nails reveal character, too. Perhaps your nails are small and neat, and of a fairly deep colour ? Then you are brilliant and witty, but inclined to be hasty and to flare up into a temper if any little thing annoys you. Fortunately the storm will blow over quickly, but nevertheless it is something you should try to check. Also, you may be irritated by those who are not so quick at seeing things as you are, and may sometimes voice cutting remarks about this.

The owner of short, moderately pink nails will be bright and gay, always ready to enter into any fun that is going on, and keen to be " up and doing " all the time. Her high spirits will make her popular, and

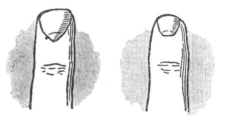

A nail like this indicates a tendency towards paralysis.

This nail shows a risk of heart trouble.

she will constantly cause those about her to laugh at the rather clever jokes she makes.

You may have a friend with short, brittle and thin nails, however ; you may then tell her that she is of the type that needs plenty of rest in order to keep up her strength and vitality.

Perhaps you have fairly short but broad nails ; if so, you will want to go out and battle for all you aim at in life, only feeling satisfied if you have won any success entirely through your own efforts.

You will be extremely fond of arguing, just for the fun of it, so to speak, but you do not like to be proved in the wrong.

The Palms

THE palms of the hands, too, indicate our characters according to their appearance and texture. If your palms are firm and springy, and your fingers also supple, you will be clever and never at a loss to know how to act in an emergency, while you will think no task too great when you are striving for success. You will like to strike out on new ideas for yourself, and often they will bring splendid results, so that people will come to know you are one whose advice is worth having, and will come to you for it. Probably your head will always rule your heart, but this does not mean you are hard—only practical.

A very thick, soft palm, if you find it among your friends, will tell you that its possessor is of the drifting type, content to let others battle through life while she sits back and looks on. She will like the good things of life, however, and will expect others to provide them for her. Perhaps she will be rather self-centred, too, and her friends will find her one of the " borrowing " kind.

A flat, dry hand means that its owner is rather cold and reserved, slow to form friendships and rather apt to consider herself a little above most of the people she meets. You might advise her to take a little more interest in others, and a little less in herself, if you are friendly enough to be able to talk so outspokenly, for she could be charming if she tried.

A palm of this sort, together with a long-shaped hand, shows a rather wilful, determined person, inclined to fits of the " blues " when she sees other people are better off than herself, and rather inclined to jealousy, too. This is something she should do her utmost to overcome, for it may well stand in the way of her life's happiness.

If you have a palm that is rather cupped, or hollowed out, you are one of those who must work perseveringly for all they attain, and you may meet with set-backs and hindrances that will try your patience. However, if the other indications in your hand are fortunate, all will come right in the end, and you will be rewarded for your efforts to surmount the obstacles placed before you.

IF you place your hands side by side, palms upward, you will see that the lines on them do not exactly match. In fact, in some instances—more especially in the case of older people—they differ a good deal, and before we go on to deal with the " mounts," this may need a little explaining.

The reason lies in the fact that your left hand is the one which tells you what you have the power to do in life, and your right hand indicates how you use these powers as you go along life's roadway.

Because of this, you may find new lines appearing on your hands with the passing years—lines which stand for opportunities you have made for yourself through your own efforts ; new work you have taken up for which you may not have had a natural aptitude, but which you have, nevertheless, mastered through sheer perseverence, or new friendships you have formed. You will see by this how interesting a study palmistry really is.

The Mounts

BEFORE we deal with the lines on the hand, look closely at the " mounts "—the soft, fleshy bumps beneath each finger. Each is named after a planet, and whether they are strong or weak in your hand, has an important meaning.

Probably there will be one mount in particular which stands out more than the others, and this is something important to note if you would gain a really accurate reading of your characteristics.

Jupiter. This mount comes beneath the first finger, and if it is well shown you will be very ambitious to succeed in life, knowing just what you want, and being full of the determination to get it by your own efforts. You will be keen and trustworthy, and so should succeed, while you will also be popular at social gatherings, for you have a bright, gay side to your nature that cheers others up and prompts them to seek your society.

Anxious to be the leader among your friends, you will find that in most cases they will give way to you, realising that you are really more capable than they are.

Let us hope this mount is not *over*-developed, however, for then you may be proud, and too wrapped up in yourself and your own ambitions to care about how others are faring along the road of life.

You may be inclined to be overbearing and dictatorial, too, which will make you enemies unless you try hard to overcome these failings.

Should you find that the mount of Jupiter is very flat, then you are inclined to be selfish and to want other people to do things for you without having to raise a finger yourself.

Saturn. If this mount, which comes under your second finger, is the most prominent on your hand, it means that you are clever and studious, quick at learning things, and one who is most trustworthy and dependable. You will rarely be at a loss to know what to do, no matter how difficult a situation you find yourself in, and in consequence you should be most successful in a business career.

If the mount is *over*-developed, this is not so good, for the indication is that you may be subject to " moodiness " and depression, while you are likely to be rather aloof and reserved. Because of this, your friends may find it hard to understand you.

This mount may not be shown on your hand at all, but we will hope this is not the case, for it will mean that fortune will rarely favour you, and you will have to win your way in life entirely by your own hard work.

Apollo. If you find this mount, which comes under the third finger, well shown on a friend's hand, you can tell her it is a fortunate one to have, for it tells that she is very intelligent, and at the same time gentle and kind-hearted. She will always be able to look on the bright side of things, and when clouds gather round her she will never give up hope.

She will probably be rather a bookworm, while she also loves colourful and artistic things, and will take a great pride in her home. You might perhaps warn her against being too impetuous.

Should your friend have this mount *over*-developed, however, then she will be extravagant and money-loving, always wanting to know the whys and wherefores of things, and inclined to have too good an opinion of her capabilities.

If this mount is absent altogether, then your friend will be slow-thinking, and not over brainy. She will probably be content to drift along in a rut all her life.

Mercury. When well-developed on your hand, this mount, beneath the fourth finger, will endow you with very gay and cheerful qualities. You will be quick to think and act, and always ready for any fun that is going. You will probably be brilliant and dashing, too, and your ideas may carry you a long way towards success.

An *over*-developed mount of Mercury would mean that you are inclined to boastfulness, and you might never get very far in life unless you forced yourself to work.

If this mount is not shown at all, then you are rather slow and plodding, and may only be helped to success by the efforts of others on your behalf.

Mars. There are two mounts of Mars, one between the thumb and first finger, and one in the middle of the outside edge of the hand. The one near the thumb, if well developed, shows that you are one of those people who will rise bravely above any trouble which may come your way, through sheer courage and will-power. Full of " vim," also, you will want to be " on the go " from morning till night, and you may be inclined to rush headlong into things without first counting the cost.

The mount on the outside edge of the hand, if well shown, means that you will work till you drop, if need be, to carry out any aim you have in mind, while you will be looked up to and admired by many of your friends for your strength of character.

Should either of these mounts be shown to excess, in this case it is fortunate. If the first, you will have wonderful courage, and will think

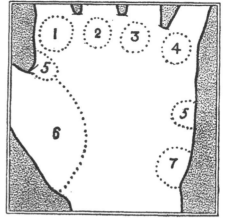

The Mounts. (1) Jupiter. (2) Saturn. (3) Apollo. (4) Mercury. (5) The two mounts of Mars. (6) Venus. (7) The Moon.

nothing of sacrificing yourself for the happiness of someone you love. Danger, too, would have no fears for you ; you may need warning against taking unnecessary risks.

An excess of the second mount of Mars shows that you have great powers of endurance, though you may be inclined to be a little dictatorial. You will be very forgiving towards those who have wronged you.

We will hope that these mounts are not entirely absent from your hand, for this indicates a person afraid to make decisions, and nervous even to the point of being timid ; the type likely to lose her head in a moment of crisis.

Venus. If this mount, coming beneath the thumb, is well developed, it shows a generous, affectionate nature, kind-hearted and sympathetic. You will possess a deep love of beautiful things, and will very likely be musical.

Anxious to please, you have the tactfulness that will keep you on the right side of almost everyone with whom you come into contact.

In one of your friends you may

find this mount *too* well developed ; you will know that she is inclined to fickleness in love, while she will let vanity play too big a part in her life. She will prefer, too, an dle life rather than an active one.

Let us hope you are not entirely lacking a mount of Venus, for then you will be cold and rather self-centred, not unselfish enough to put your love of others before yourself.

Moon. Should this mount—it comes just above the wrist on the outside of the hand—be the one that stands out most on the hand, it indicates that the owner has a deep love of beauty, while she will also be rather musical. She is the kind of girl who is easy to get on with, and her manner will never jar on you. Her imagination, if she does not carry it too far, should help her to success.

Perhaps she will have this mount *too* well marked ; in this case she will be subject to fits of depression and " moodiness," while she will often feel discontented with her lot in life when she sees others better off than herself.

You might advise her to try to cure herself of becoming quickly irritated with those who do not agree with her views, or wish to fall in with her plans.

If the mount of the Moon is entirely absent, then your friend will be rather slow and plodding, lacking in sympathy and imagination, and inclined to be hard on anyone who makes mistakes, though she is not above making them herself, sometimes.

AFTER the mounts, comes the interesting network of lines, some faint, some much more clearly shown, which you will find on your palms. When reading the hands, the left is the more important,

because it shows what we are given to make of our lives, and you should remember that, to give a correct reading, you must take all the points and consider them together— the shape of the hand, the fingers, the nails, the mounts, the texture and then the lines, for each will have its influence on the other, modifying or heightening the qualities they stand for.

The Life Line is the most important line on your hand, so we will deal with this first. It begins, or " rises," as we call it, just beneath the mount of Jupiter under the first finger, and gives you a good idea of the probable length of your life, as well as indicating what kind of health you may expect.

The Life Line curves round the mount of Venus, beneath the thumb, and ends somewhere near the wrist ; the farther it reaches, the longer your life will be.

If, on your hand, the line is long, deep and well coloured, you are likely to enjoy a long and happy life, with good health and few reverses of fortune. Should the line be broad and pale, and rather resembling a chain, however, then you would be wise to take care of your health, for you are not naturally very strong. You can quite well guard against illness, however, if you will take the necessary precautions.

The chain may only be shown for a short way along the line, which grows stronger and clearer afterwards ; in this case you may know that there will be a great improvement in your health at that point in your life.

Again, if on one hand you see the Life Line broken at a point about the middle of the palm, but you also see that, in the other hand, the Life Line continues unbroken all the way, then this is a sign that

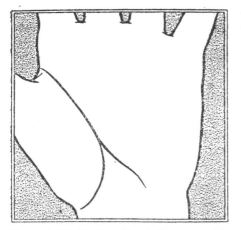

Fig. 1. A Life Line branching to the mount of the Moon.

you may suffer a bad illness where the break is shown, but that you will recover well and live to a good age.

You can count the length of your life from the line's beginning beneath the mount of Jupiter, downwards. About the middle of the line would be the fortieth year; with that as a guide you should be able to reckon the years quite easily (see page 75).

When there is a division in your Life Line, and one branch runs across to the mount of the Moon (see Fig. 1), you are likely to leave the place where you are living and go somewhere new, while if the line is broken and one half commences before the other stops, you will probably go abroad to settle.

When you see a number of tiny lines running downwards from the Life Line, you will know that you are inclined to be lacking in vitality, and should take plenty of rest, while you are also subject to fits of depression, now and then, looking rather more on the gloomy side of whatever comes to you than the bright side.

If you see similar lines running *upwards* from the Life Line, however (see Fig. 2), then you are fortunate in being naturally strong and healthy, always expecting the best from life, even when shadows cross your path, while you will very likely be full of the joy of life, ready to enter into any fun that is going.

Long lines, which lead from the Life Line to any other important lines, or to the mounts, have also something to tell us. Perhaps you can see one on your hand running up to the mount of Jupiter? Then this is very fortunate, for it means that you will accomplish whatever you set out to do in life through having fortune on your side, as well as owing to your own steady efforts. In fact, if you do what your instinct prompts you, there is every indication that you should become exceptionally successful, and perhaps even gain considerable wealth. See that you make the most of this tendency, therefore, by not letting opportunities pass you by.

When you are studying a friend's hand, you may see a line from her Life Line running on to the mount of Saturn; you can tell her that

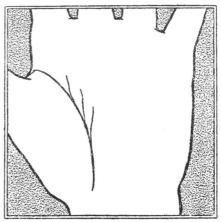

Fig. 2. Tiny lines running upwards from the Life Line.

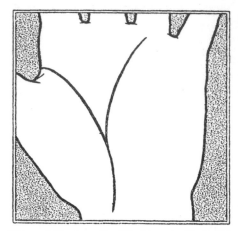

Fig. 3. A line from the Life Line running to the mount of Apollo.

she has a quick and clever brain, which she can use to great advantage in business life, while she will be honest and trustworthy, inspiring the confidence of all who know her. Good fortune might also come to her through elderly people, either relatives or her employers, if she is tactful enough to keep on the right side of them. If her sweetheart is connected in any way with gardening or mining, she should be very lucky.

A line running from the Life Line to the mount of Apollo (see Fig. 3), if you see it on your sweetheart's hand, indicates that he has a lucky streak in him, being probably one of those people who seem to be able to turn their hand successfully to anything. There is a decided opportunity coming for him to win money and fame, so long as he keeps steadily at whatever work he has chosen.

If, on your own hand, a line from the Life Line reaches the mount of Mercury, you will be tactful and diplomatic in your work, inspiring your employers to put you in a position of trust, while you will also have considerable influence over

people through your ability to talk them round to your way of thinking. You are likely to make a success of any form of teaching, while any work connected with money or with writing would also be fortunate for you.

Should you see, on a friend's hand, a line crossing her Life Line to the mount of the Moon, you will know that she will experience a great change in her life, perhaps travelling to, and maybe settling in, a distant land.

An Island (see Fig. 4) on your Life Line means that at about the time indicated you are liable to illness, and extra care should be taken of your health in order to avoid it. A long island near the end of the Life Line shows a tendency to become an invalid for the last years of life.

Perhaps, at one place, your Life Line passes through a Square ? (see Fig. 5). Then this will tell you that though you may be liable to danger through ill-health or accident, some lucky influence will be working for you, and you will come through none the worse for it.

On a friend's hand you may notice a number of fine lines crossing the

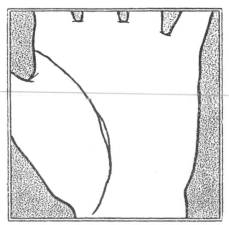

Fig. 4. An island on the Life Line.

Life Line near the beginning, and this will show that her childhood days may have been shadowed by unhappiness in the home, or relations may have stood in the light of her career until she branched out for herself.

Another friend may have lines crossing the Life Line at intervals from the mount of Venus, though we will hope there are not many of these, indicating, as they do, that she will meet with set-backs and worries, probably caused, in most cases, by the mistakes of others.

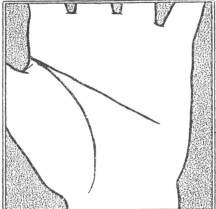

Fig. 6. The Life and Head Lines joined at their beginning.

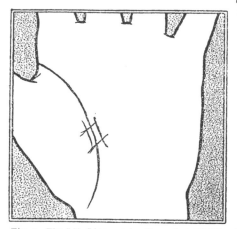

Fig. 5. The Life Line passing through a square.

Sometimes these lines may mean disappointment over a love affair, but in most cases this will turn out for her good in the end.

When the Life Line and the line immediately above it, which is the Head Line, are joined together at their beginning and continue so for a little way (see Fig. 6), you will be steady and sure, taking your time to make a decision, but generally judging soundly as a result, while, should your Life and Head Lines be divided by a wide space, you will probably possess much courage, with which to fight life's

battles. You will prefer to strike out on your own, winning your own way up the ladder of success— and you will generally get there, too.

Sometimes you may see a line running parallel with the Life Line down the mount of Venus (see Fig. 7), and this tells you that there is someone in your life who has a very great influence over you. It is probably someone you are very fond of, since they are able to sway

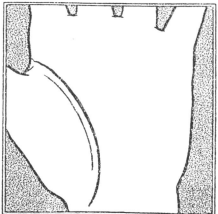

Fig. 7. An Influence Line running beside the Life Line.

your views and opinions. If there are more than one of these lines, then there is, or has been, more than one person influencing you. Usually the influence lasts only for the duration of the line, which you can judge by comparing it with the Life Line.

You should take care not to confuse this Line of Influence with the Line of Mars which also runs along beside the Life Line in some hands, but which is rather

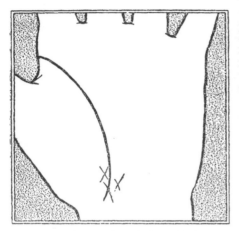

Fig. 8. Crosses at the end of the Life Line.

more strongly marked than the Influence Line. If you find this line on your hand, and it is well coloured and unbroken, it will be a strengthening influence on your Life Line, helping to counteract any illness or worry marked on the actual Life Line itself.

You may notice on a friend's hand that the Life Line ends in a lot of little lines, and this will tell you that whatever kind of good fortune she enjoys during her life, she will not end it very well off. However, unless this is shown in both hands it is only a possibility, which she can avoid by being rather more careful over putting by for a

" rainy day " than she might otherwise be.

If you see Stars or Crosses near the Life Line on a friend's hand, you will know these for worries and setbacks which will have to be met, particularly if any part of them actually crosses the Life Line. In this case, the trouble is mainly caused through the interference of friends or relations.

Several Crosses (see Fig. 8) shown at the end of your Life Line in one hand only, indicate that you are pleasant and clever, making amusing company all through your life, but should they also be shown in the other hand, this is not so fortunate, showing that you may try to have " too many irons in the fire " and so fail to make a marked success of anything.

The Head Line. Next in importance to the Life Line, the Head Line shows what kind of mind you have, and how it will influence you to act in life.

The most fortunate place for this to begin or " rise " is on the mount of Jupiter, like the Life Line. If this is so on your hand, and you see the line is clear, unbroken and long, you will know that you are the fortunate possessor of a bright, clever mind, full of ideas and capable of carrying them to a successful conclusion.

You will be rather determined, and like to have your own way in most things, but you will be popular, for all that. You will have, too, the ability to judge wisely in whatever situation you find yourself, and this will be a great advantage in business life.

Your strong sense of justice will cause you to champion those whom you think are being treated in any way unfairly, and you will be untiring in your efforts to help them and to put things right. Another gift is your good memory, which will help you in whatever career you follow, while you will also be able to concentrate on whatever you are doing, despite any distractions.

Perhaps, however, your Head Line is joined to the Life Line at its beginning? (see page 83). This shows that you are rather careful and cautious, preferring to weigh up matters carefully before you take any definite step, and therefore you can generally be relied upon to do the right thing.

You might, perhaps, try to cure yourself of being over-sensitive, and not having enough faith in your power to take responsibilities on your shoulders, for these things might stand in your way at times.

You may have a friend, whose Head Line is close to, but a little separated from the Life Line (see Fig. 9). This is a sign that her courage to face life's battles is intensified to the point of recklessness.

If the Head Line rises on the mount of Mars, you should advise the owner not to let little trials and

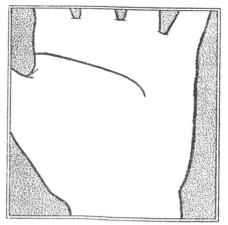

Fig. 10. The Head Line running downwards near the end.

setbacks worry and discourage her, as she is very inclined to do.

Then, too, she may be rather irritable with those who do not share her own views or see eye to eye with her on any particular subject, and she would be wise to check this if she does not want to lose friends through it. She may be rather fickle, too, both in her friendships and love affairs, though she will feel deeply about them so long as they interest her.

A Head Line which is very straight and clear indicates that its possessor is steady and practical, her head, in most cases, ruling her heart. She will be conscientious and persevering at her work, and through this and her natural common sense, should get on well.

If you are reading your sweetheart's hand, and you see that his Head Line starts running downwards near the end (see Fig. 10), you will know him to be straightforward and level-headed, dependable in his affections, and someone to lean on in time of trouble.

Perhaps, however, the line is sloping all the way? Then you

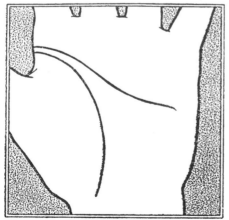

Fig. 9. The Head Line a little separated from the Life Line.

can tell him that he will be full of ideas that should carry him far if he goes the right way to work in carrying them out, while he will probably also be musical, and appreciate beauty, liking to be in bright, cheerful surroundings.

Your own Head Line may be of the kind that runs right across the hand, curving upwards at the end. In this case, you will be very fortunate, for you should earn money through your practical " braininess " in business, while you are very trustworthy and reliable when it is necessary for you to handle any big undertaking.

A short Head Line, should you find it on a friend's hand, will show that she is the kind who is content to drift along more or less in a rut, and cannot quite see why anyone else should want more interest or variety. She will be rather one-sided, too, only able to look at a matter from her own point of view, which is something you should advise her to try and overcome, as she will give people the impression that she is narrow-minded and obstinate. She should also try not to take offence too easily.

Happy you, if you should find that your sweetheart's Head Line curves rather decidedly upwards, for this will tell you that he has a brilliant and clever mind, capable of carrying out a responsible job, and forging ahead to what he has set himself as a goal. You can place your future happily in his hands, therefore, and know that he will never let you down.

Sometimes the Head Line is forked (see Fig. 11), and this is a fortunate sign, so long as it is a small fork, telling you that you have the gift of imagination, while your common sense will never allow you to act rashly or unwisely.

Should one branch of the fork

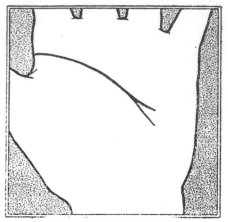

Fig. 11. A forked Head Line.

run down towards the mount of the Moon, then you will be tactful and diplomatic, charming as a hostess and in great demand socially. Perhaps you should see that this does not turn your head too much.

The Heart Line. This, as it suggests, is the line which is chiefly connected with our affections and love affairs, while also, of course, it has a bearing on our health.

When the Heart Line is well marked, unbroken and clear, with no chained appearance, you have a strong, reliable heart, and a happy, contented personality. Your love, when it is given, will be loyal and true, and should lead to happiness in marriage.

The line may rise in several different places, but it is most fortunate if it does so on the mount of Jupiter (see Fig 12), a little higher up than the lines of Life and Head. If it begins too high up, however, right at the base of the finger of Jupiter, then this is not so good, for you are apt to let your feelings run away with you, and to do and say things which you will be sorry for afterwards. This may bring you unhappiness, besides causing others who may be concerned, to suffer also.

If your Heart Line rises between the fingers of Jupiter and Saturn, this is better, for then you should be less impulsive and more stable in your affections, forming friendships wisely rather than impulsively.

You may find a friend's Heart Line beginning on the mount of Saturn, which will tell you that she may be intense in her feelings and affections, but that she will be undemonstrative about them, often leading people to form the mistaken opinion that she is cold and haughty. She may be lacking in sympathy and insight into human nature, too, while you should advise her to curb her strong tendency towards jealousy. Much bitterness and heartache may come to her if she does not crush this failing.

Perhaps you have a friend whose Heart Line commences high up on the mount of Saturn, almost on to the finger ? Then this will tell you she is rather exacting, wanting to monopolise all the time and affection of anyone who wins her regard, while she will be inclined to

suspicion and jealousy, too. To anyone who was prepared to devote themselves to her, however, she would be very staunch and loyal.

If the Heart Line runs very close to the Head Line on your hand, this will indicate that you are rather eager and impulsive, inclined to " count your chickens before they are hatched," while your heart will almost always rule your head, not always with good results.

You may see the Heart Line running straight across the palm on your sweetheart's hand, and then indeed you may congratulate yourself on having won his love, for he will be deeply loving and loyal, thinking of you first and foremost, ready to sacrifice his own wishes and desires to fall in with yours, and wanting only to devote himself to making you happy.

Don't let him " spoil " you, therefore ! Because he loves so deeply he will not be able to escape the demon of jealousy, but if you are wise and appreciate his otherwise sterling worth, you will never do anything to arouse this.

It may be that on a friend's hand the Heart Line, rising from the mount of Saturn, is unusually broad, yet not well-coloured, and this will show that she possesses a cold and calculating nature, and is one who will generally have her own interests in view before those of other people.

She will not make many friends, for she will prefer to keep a good deal to herself, while she will have little sympathy with anyone who comes to her for advice in their troubles.

Sometimes the Heart Line has a chain-like appearance (see Fig. 13), and this tells clearly of a fickle, careless nature, who treats love lightly and has many flirtations. " Off with the old love, on with the

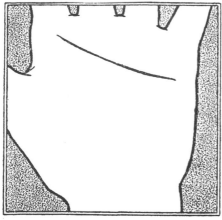

Fig. 12. The Heart Line commencing on the mount of Jupiter.

your friend will have a very happy marriage, which will bring out the very best in her and make her a charming person to come into contact with.

When your Fate Line ends on or near the mount of Saturn, there will be splendid opportunities offered to you in life, and it will be up to you to take full advantage of them. Probably you will meet with adventures in following your career, but they will only help you on to success.

If your Fate Line ends on or near the mount of Jupiter, you will achieve all you set out for in life, and you will be popular and admired for your steady, practical ability. You should guard against a tendency to think too highly of your own ability, however.

A friend whose Fate Line ends on or near the mount of Apollo is likely to be very artistic, fond of lovely things around her, and never so happy as when she is in the country amid nature's own beauty. If the line is particularly clear and strong, she may gain riches in later life either through her own success, or through a good marriage.

Your sweetheart's Fate Line may end on or near the mount of Mercury, in which case he is likely to do very well in business, inspiring the trust of his employers, and proving himself well worthy of a position of responsibility.

Sometimes the Fate Line ends at the Heart Line, and this is often the sign of disappointments in love, though when the Heart Line itself is a very good one, you will win through them to happiness in the end.

When the Line of Head stops the Fate Line, you may make mistakes or lose good opportunities through being too hasty in your

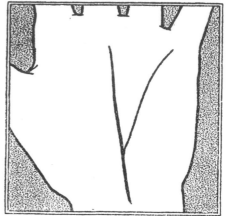

Fig. 17. A decided branch upward from the Fate Line.

judgment, but this tendency loses much of its force if it is not borne out by the other lines in the hand.

A broken Fate Line is not always a bad sign, and if the line is well marked after the break, without any other lines crossing it, the break will stand for some big happening which may change the course of your whole life. Should the lines run side by side for a little way, then the change may decidedly be for the better. A decided branch upward (Fig. 17) shows marked improvement in your position in life.

If you see little lines branching upward from your Fate Line, this is a fortunate sign, indicating that you will do well for yourself in your chosen career, and there is every opportunity for advancement both in position and money. Should there be branch lines running downwards from it, however, this is not so good, for it means that you will probably have to struggle hard to make your way, having to overcome many obstacles and setbacks in doing so.

When you see a chain-like Fate Line on a friend's hand, this will tell you that she is her own worst enemy, losing opportunities through her own foolishness, and bringing trouble upon herself by her rash actions. If the Fate Line runs double for part of the way, this indicates that someone will have a great influence over this friend's life, swaying her to follow in the way they point out, rather than the way she has chosen for herself.

Age, on the Fate Line, is counted upwards, instead of downwards as on the Life Line.

The Line of Fortune. If you have this line (see Fig. 18) shown on your hand, running high up on the mount of Apollo, you should certainly do well in life. This is the line that represents fame, wealth and prosperity, and according to where the line begins, so shall we know how and when these will come to us.

Should the line rise from the Life Line in your hand, you may take this as a good sign, showing success and good fortune, either won by your own efforts and hard work, or through inheriting from relations.

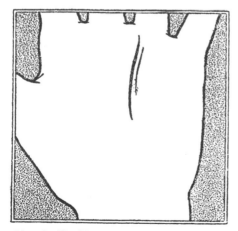

Fig. 18. The Line of Fortune doubled on the mount of Apollo.

The lower down on the Life Line its beginning, the more certain will you be to obtain fame. So if you are fortunate enough to possess this line you have much to look forward to.

You may find a friend who has the Line of Fortune rising from the mount of the Moon. Then you can tell her that her good fortune will be attained by some unexpected stroke of good luck, and partly through the influence of other people in her life. If she marries early, then this good fortune will come to her through her husband.

Your sweetheart may have the Line of Fortune beginning near the mount of Mars, which comes in the middle of the outside edge of the hand, and this will show that he may make mistakes at first in his career, so causing setbacks which will have to be overcome. He will therefore have to wait until later on in life before winning success, but when at length he does so, it will be because he has really made an effort and used his former mistakes as stepping-stones to better things.

Your Line of Fortune may commence from the Heart Line, and in this case you will know that you are one of those who love beautiful things and colourful surroundings, appreciating natural scenery deeply, and therefore with a longing to travel. You will not be practical enough, however, to obtain real wealth or fame through your following of art.

When the Line of Fortune rises from the mount of Venus, travelling up the hand side by side with the Life Line, any success or improvement of position will be made through the owner's marriage to a wealthy or famous man. She is not of the type who will carve out a way for herself, for she is inclined to drift along, more interested in the enjoyment she can get out of life than the work she can put into it.

If you see a friend's Line of Fortune forked where it runs on to the mount of Apollo, you will know that success will come to her through one channel only, and she may have to try several careers before she finally finds the one which will lead her to the right one.

If this line breaks up into many small ones, however, it indicates that the possessor will be one who is inclined to have " too many irons in the fire," and because she gives her undivided attention to none of them she will not find success.

When, instead of breaking up or branching, the Line of Fortune is doubled where it runs over the mount of Apollo (see Fig. 18) then you are likely to be much in the public eye, making a name for yourself, and winning a splendid position in life. The double lines should appear on both hands, however.

Lines that run cross-wise through the Line of Fortune indicate obstacles to be overcome, in some cases brought about through the jealousy or envy of others.

When the Line of Fortune is broken up into several lines and these appear to be tied together, you are too taken up with your anxiety to shine in the eyes of other people to find real success.

If the Line of Fate is better marked than the Line of Fortune, success will come to you without a great deal of money.

The Health Line. This line should rise from the base of the hand, near the wrist, and run up towards the mount of Mercury. If it is well-coloured, straight and clear, you will be the fortunate possessor of a strong, healthy constitution, while

should it run unevenly up the hand, then this should warn you that your health needs taking care of in order to overcome a tendency to weakness.

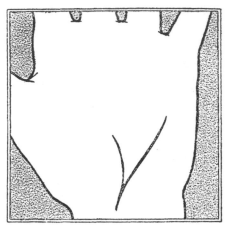

Fig. 19. A branch from the Health Line running towards the mount of Jupiter.

A branch line running from the Health Line to the Line of Fortune indicates a rise in position or a change in business, and may be brought about in connection with your health.

Perhaps, in a friend's hand, you see a branch from the Health Line running towards the mount of Jupiter? (see Fig. 19). You will know from this that her health will prompt her to travel a good deal, and that she will know considerable change in her life.

A double Health Line is a very good sign, showing wonderful health and great success, while if you do not find the Health Line marked at all in your hand, this shows that your constitution is very strong and that you will be one of those fortunate people who never know a day's illness in their lives.

The Line of Intuition. This is a line which is not found in every hand, but if you possess it, the indication is that you are intelligent and intellectual.

You should find the line rising somewhere near the mount of the Moon (see Fig. 20), running round towards the mount of Mercury. If the line is well marked, straight and clear, it tells that you have a good deal of intuition, and a keen understanding of human nature. That is, you will be able to understand how people are feeling or thinking even though they themselves do not give any indication of these things.

Probably you will be deeply interested in trying to look into the

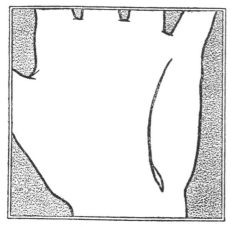

Fig. 20. An Island at the beginning of the Line of Intuition.

future, while should an Island mark the beginning of the line, you are likely to possess the gift of second sight.

If the Line of Intuition is uneven or branching, it shows that the possessor is one who will carry her imagination too far, indulging in flights of fancy which will lead her nowhere, instead of applying practical common sense.

When the Line of Intuition makes a clear and well-formed

triangle with the Lines of Fate and Head, it is said to indicate a clever palmist, while any lines running across the line towards the Life or Fate Lines indicate long journeys, probably across water.

The Girdle of Venus. This is a line running in a half-circle from between the first and second fingers to between the third and fourth fingers (see page 75), and its meaning varies according to the type of hand on which it is found.

In the thick, well-padded hand it is not a good sign, for it adds to the already strong tendency of its possessor to be lazy and luxury-loving, liking nothing better than to have all her spare time filled with parties and other gay pursuits.

When the girdle is shown on the artistic types of hands, such as the Conic or Psychic, however, it increases the possessor's deep love of beauty and pleasant surroundings, while it also adds to her powers of imagination and understanding.

The Marriage Lines. These lines run round the outside edge of the hand, beneath the Finger of Mercury towards the palm (see Fig. 21), but only the longest line or lines should be taken to represent marriage. If you see other and shorter lines running beside your chief Marriage Line these simply indicate love affairs which have had a considerable influence over you.

If, as well as a deep Marriage Line, you should see a cross on the mount of Jupiter, from its position you should be able to tell about what time in your life the marriage will take place.

Should the cross be high upon the mount then you will be married very young, while if it is more in the middle of the mount then you will be married round about twenty-five. When the cross is lower down, then your marriage will not be until you are middle-aged.

Little lines running from the Heart Line towards your Marriage Line indicate that your love goes very deep and will be the biggest thing in your life, but if the Marriage Line is forked, it means a broken engagement. Should the Marriage Line slant downwards towards the Heart Line, then there is a possibility that your husband will pass on before you.

When a number of little lines cross the Marriage Line there is a likelihood that your marriage will not be a very happy one, heated words and differences of opinion causing discord between you.

The number of children you will

Fig. 21. A Marriage Line.

Fig. 22. Lines indicating children, running up from the Marriage Line.

have is indicated by small lines running upwards from the Marriage Line (see Fig. 22). Clear, well-marked lines tell you that your children will be strong and healthy, will have long lives and win success, while the line among them which is the longest will show that one will outlive the others, and make the greatest name for itself.

The Bracelets. These are the lines on the wrist (see Fig. 23), and if they are clearly shown and un-

broken they indicate health, wealth and happiness.

If you should see these lines badly formed on a friend's wrist, you will know that she is inclined to be extravagant and fond of show

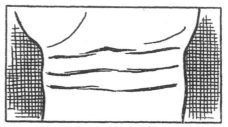

Fig. 23. The bracelets.

in the way of clothes and worldly possessions.

A cross shown in the middle of the bracelets tells you that you may have to work hard at the beginning of your life, but these early efforts will lead to good fortune.

The Travel Line. Perhaps you see a little line running straight down towards the mount of the Moon from your Life Line ? Then you are likely to make at least one big sea journey during your life.

A Travel Line which ends in a Cross indicates that you will achieve the aim you had in view when making the journey, while if a friend's Travel Line runs through a Square, she may narrowly escape some accident on a journey.

Squares. Whenever these are shown on your hand they tell you that some misfortune or accident will be turned away by a stroke of good luck.

Crosses. These, whether you see them on the mounts or the lines, generally mean that you will have obstacles to overcome in connection with the characteristics belonging to the mounts or lines on which they are found.

Stars. These are always of importance, showing success and fame, again according to the lines or mounts on which they are found. Should you see a Star on one of your fingers this is particularly fortunate, indicating a most outstanding stroke of good fortune.

The Grill. This is not a very good sign to have on your hand, for it usually indicates a disappointment, or some happening which will cause you considerable worry. It is made up of lots of little lines crossing one another.

The Quadrangle. This is the space between the Head and Heart Lines, and if there are many lines marked on it you will have a good deal of worry and trouble, but if it is fairly clear and broad you will have few worries, and a generally peaceful life (see page 75.)

Triangles. These are fortunate, for they show that you are quick-witted, clever and intelligent, and should do well for yourself in your chosen career.

Islands. Unfortunately, these are nearly always bad signs, so we will hope there are none shown on the lines of your hand, for in the Lines of Life, Head and Heart they indicate illness, and in the others misfortune of other kinds.

You should remember, when reading anyone's hand, that all the different points about it should be taken into consideration and considered together before you can give a really correct reading, but if you keep this in mind, together with all the information contained in this chapter, you should be quite a successful palmist.

" PALMYRA."

YOUR COLOUR—AND YOUR DESTINY

CHOOSE the ribbon of your favourite colour and trace it through until you find the symbol at the end. The MERRYTHOUGHT stands for " A wish attained," the RING for " Marriage," the HORSE-SHOE for " Good Luck," the THIMBLE for " Single bliss," the MONEY BAG for " Wealth," the BELL for " A wedding," the SWASTIKA for " Success," the BUTTON for " Married contentment," the BOOT for " Travel and change."

CHAPTER VIII

Lucky Stones

*Fortunate stones to choose—Why you should wear them—Ring
days—Lucky colours and their meanings, etc.*

FROM the earliest times gems
of all kinds have been favourite talismans, or charms,
said to exert a special influence on
their wearers. Though, as will be
seen in another chapter of this
book, there is a birthday stone for
every month, each stone has a special
meaning of its own, and is said to
possess a particular magic.

Agate. This is the " friendship "
stone, and is said to attract people
to its wearer. If you have a friend
you particularly wish to keep, give
her an agate, for it will help to bind
the friendship.

Amber. This is the stone for
health. Those who suffer from weak
throats are said to derive benefit
from wearing a string of amber
beads.

Amethyst. In earlier times this
pretty stone was worn as a charm
against intemperance of any kind.
It is the jewel associated with St.
Valentine, and is thus a favourite
with lovers, but to have its full
effect it should be worn on a
Thursday. It is most suited to a
blonde, or to a girl with a fair complexion, and is the only stone which
may be worn when in mourning.

Aquamarine. This stands for "faithfulness"; it is also a charm for those setting out for a long journey over the sea. It is thus a most suitable mascot for a girl to give her sailor sweetheart.

Beryl. This stone means "doubt," and is thus not a favourite with lovers, but if set in the form of a heart it means humility.

Bloodstone. As, perhaps, its name may imply, this stone stands for "courage," and is a most suitable mascot for a girl to give to her sweetheart if he is going to undertake any task which requires bravery.

Carbuncle. This was a stone much esteemed by the ancients, who believed that it inspired brightness and gaiety in its wearer.

Chrysolite. A stone for those who are inclined to a gloomy outlook, for it is said to drive away sad thoughts and also to be a charm against witchcraft.

Coral. This is really a child's stone, for it is supposed to preserve infants from dangers of all kinds. This is the reason so many rattles are made of, or ornamented with, coral, while a row of these beads is often worn as a charm against accidents.

Diamond. The favourite stone for engagement rings, no doubt because it stands for "virtue," but its first meaning was "courage," and its name is derived from the Greek word "adamas" which means "invincible." To gain the help of its full powers, you should wear it on the left side, this bringing it nearer to the heart.

Emerald. This stone was once a favourite gift between lovers, as it was believed to lose its colour should either the giver or the receiver prove unfaithful. It is also a charm for weak sight, and it was once believed that a serpent became blind if it looked on an emerald.

Garnet. A stone for sweethearts, since it means "constancy."

Jade. This is the stone for "luck," which is the reason so many mascots are made of it. The Chinese wore it to ensure long life and it is also said to be a help in digestive trouble.

Jasper. The symbol of "endurance." This is really a man's stone, as it is reputed to bestow the masculine virtues.

Lapis Lazuli. This is the stone for "truth" and "single-heartedness," possibly because of its clear blue colour. It is also believed to be a charm against diseases of the skin.

Lodestone. The girl who is longing for the love of a particular young man should certainly have this about her, for it is said to have magnetic qualities.

Moonstone. A "mascot" stone, supposed to bring good luck to all those who wear it. It is also said to be a charm against accidents for the traveller.

Onyx. This was believed to be a witch's stone, and brought bad dreams to its wearer, but if worn with a moonstone, it can have no ill effects.

Opal. Many people believe this stone to be unlucky, and brave would be the girl who would choose it for her engagement ring. Despite these beliefs, however, the ancients prized the opal very highly indeed. In old Mexico, it was regarded as a sacred stone, and in Turkey it was believed that it came direct from heaven in a flash of lightning. It is a "moon" stone, and should be worn on a Monday. It is said to lose its lustre when worn by one who is unfaithful to the giver. Opals are more lucky if set in silver, which is the moon metal.

Pearl. This is the symbol of purity, and is said to inspire the affection of the person to whom it is given, but it also stands for "tears," and is therefore seldom chosen as a lover's gift. If it is set together with a sparkling stone, such as a diamond, this belief ceases to hold good, however.

Porphyry. A delicate compliment may be conveyed by this stone, for it says : " I admire your beauty."

Ruby. This should be worn by the girl who is finding that the path of true love does not run smooth, for it is said to cause all obstacles in the path of happiness to melt away, to repair broken friendships, and, also, to improve the memory.

Sapphire. This lovely stone has long been held to be the symbol of " devotion," while in olden times it was often worn in the belief that it strengthened the sight.

Topaz. Topaz is the money stone. It will bring you luck in all business enterprises, and is a good stone for a girl to give to her sweetheart if he is setting up in business, or for her to wear herself when at work.

Turquoise. This pretty stone stands for success in love, and is said to keep its colour only when in sympathy with its wearer. Should she change her affection, the stone fades from blue to a greenish tint.

Ring Days

WHILE the stones in an engagement ring have their own meanings, the day on which the ring is put on has its special significance, too.

Sunday is a lucky day, and promises you a faithful, loving husband who will love and cherish you according to his marriage vows.

Monday. A day which should be chosen by the girl who is ambitious, since it foretells that her husband will be successful in all he undertakes, and will rise in the world.

Tuesday. This prophesies a short engagement and a wedding sooner than you anticipated.

Wednesday. A good day, for it signifies that you will have few cares in your married life, which will be free from serious illness.

Thursday. The girl whose ring was slipped on during this day may quarrel with her fiancé before the wedding, but there will be a reconciliation, and the disagreement will not affect her wedded happiness.

Friday. This day is the least lucky of all, for it means that you will be parted from your sweetheart ere the wedding bells ring out. But if your love is true, you will come together again.

Saturday. A lucky day, and one which promises you money with your marriage.

The engagement ring which is put on under the mistletoe has a luck of its own, and even if it is of pearls, the magic berries charm away the " tears," and change them into happy smiles.

Lucky Colours

ALL through the ages it has been believed that different colours exert different influences and have special meanings of their own. We all have our own colour, which will help to bring us good fortune, and here is a list of the different colours and the meaning attached to them.

Red. This colour will be lucky for the girl who is inclined to be depressed and to take a gloomy view of life. It has a tonic, stimulating effect, but it must not be used too freely or it may prove irritating.

Blue. This is a real lovers' colour, for "blue means true," and blue has always been the colour for faithfulness. It is also said to have a soothing effect on nervous people, therefore the girl who is too quick-tempered and over-easily excited should choose a blue colour scheme for her room.

Purple. This is the colour for royal mourning, and for everything regal. It also stands for success, luxury and social advancement, and should be chosen for her lucky colour by the girl who is keen to get on in the world.

Yellow. This is supposed to be the luckiest colour of all, and to have a happy effect on its wearer. It is the colour for money rather than for love, and should be worn when beginning in a new job. A "yellow" room is said to induce a cheerful frame of mind.

White. This colour signifies purity and innocence. It is more of a guard against evil influences than an actual luck-bringer.

Green. This is said to be the fairies' colour, and must be used by mortals with caution. It is the hue of spring, and is therefore the emblem of hope, but lovers had better beware how they use it. It is thought to be unlucky to be married in green, though several brides have in recent years defied this superstition. There is an old rhyme which says :

" *Married in May and kirked in green,*
Both bride and bridegroom won't long be seen ! "

Several rhymes show the old belief that lovers should always prefer blue to green.

" *Yellow's for jealousy,*
Green is foresworn,
Blue is the bonniest colour that's worn."

" *If you love me, love me true ;*
Send me ribbon and let it be blue ;
If you hate me, let it be seen,
Send me a ribbon, and let it be green."

" *Those dressed in blue have lovers true,*
In green and white, forsaken quite."

Brown. This is the colour of wisdom. A girl who is setting out upon her career will find it lucky, and even more so if mingled with orange.

Orange. This colour by itself stands for marriage, and the girl who is engaged, and who wishes the engagement to be short, should choose this colour.

If a girl thinks her lucky colour does not suit her, there is no need for her to wear much of it for it to bring her good fortune. She can wear a ribbon of that colour where it does not show, or even a handkerchief edged or embroidered with it will work the charm.

" PETREA."

CHAPTER IX

Reading " his " Writing

Character can be judged from anyone's handwriting—Size, slope and the shapes of letters have their meanings—Certain letters and what they reveal—Is he Mr. " Right " ?

ANYBODY can tell *something* from the handwriting of another person. We can all recognise the careful, well-formed characters of the painstaking man, the slapdash scrawl of the untidy one ; the very ornamental, " flowery " writing and the very neat, plain hand each reveals something of the character of the writer to anyone who gives the matter a moment's thought.

But those who have studied the reading of character from handwriting go much further than that. A brief study of a few lines written by someone quite unknown to them will reveal a surprising number of facts about the writer's disposition and temperament. Not only the general character of the writing, but a hundred little details, have a message for those who know how to read it ; in the crossing of a " t," the dotting of an " i," or the shape of an " s," a man may " give himself away " to anyone skilled in what is called " Graphology."

In this chapter you will find some hints that will help you, too, to judge character from handwriting. " His " letters may tell you things about him that you do not know, reveal fine qualities that you do not yet suspect him of possessing.

But remember that, as in all

First of all, the size. Most people write a medium-sized hand, but some writing is noticeably large, and some is minutely small.

Very large writing (1)—provided, of course, that the other signs agree —is an indication of a versatile character. The writer can do a number of different things, and do them well. The man who packs his life with a number of varied in_

1. *Does many things*

2. *Does one thing well*

terests usually has very large handwriting.

Extremely small writing (2) means exactly the reverse—the type of man who specialises in doing one thing and doing it really well. This usually includes, as a matter of course, considerable powers of concentration.

Now take the question of *pressure*. Is the writing heavy or light ? This is not quite the same thing as thick or thin, because some people use a thick pen lightly and others a fine pen heavily. If you examine a specimen of handwriting carefully, you will be able to tell if the writer has pressed heavily upon his pen or not. Remember, however, that people who write a great deal, and quickly, are apt to use a rather

methods of character-reading, you must not jump to conclusions too quickly. The signs must be considered as a whole, and not judged separately. Our natures are made up of various tendencies that seldom work together quite in harmony ; they counteract each other, modify each other, hold each other in check, and to bear this in mind is the secret of successful character-reading. A handwriting that carries a clear sign of weakness of character may also include an indication of strength ; you will judge by this that the writer is neither entirely strong or completely weak, but strong in some ways and weak in others—such as the man who is hard in business dealings, but easily influenced by the bright eyes and tender lips of the girl who knows how to appeal to his softer side.

General Indications

THE first thing in delineating a handwriting is to consider the main characteristics.

3. *Material*

4. *Too Sensitive*

lighter pressure than those who write little and slowly. You may have to make allowances for this.

A heavy pressure (3) is an indication of a forceful and determined character, who enjoys the material things of life—food, comfort, money and possessions—rather than the more spiritual things—literature, music, art and high ideals. The heavy writer may perhaps be good-natured, generous, and have other fine qualities, but he is not often the type who will willingly sacrifice himself for an ideal—or for anyone else.

An extremely light pressure (4) usually belongs to the idealistic person who cares little for material things ; often he is quite unworldly, and far too sensitive. You may find him attractive ; he will almost certainly arouse your sympathies, but he is not likely to be a rock to lean on in time of trouble or a strong arm to protect you in the hurly-burly of life.

The next thing to consider is—does the handwriting run *uphill*, on the *level*, or *downhill ?*

Writing that climbs upward (5) indicates, as you might expect, an optimistic and hopeful nature ; that which trails downward (6) is the writing of one who is subject to depression, and apt to look on the black side of things and expect the worst to happen ! The steeper the ascent or descent, the greater the writer's hopefulness or melancholy.

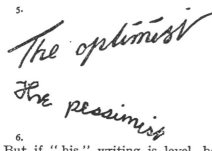

5.

6.

But if " his " writing is level, he has a well-balanced temperament in this respect, neither hoping unwisely for things he has no sound

reason to expect, nor worrying about imaginary catastrophes that will probably never happen ! Remember this, though—that your writing reflects your moods, and a letter written in a fit of depression by a normally hopeful person may show a tendency to droop downward, a thing that might lead you to judge his character wrongly if you had only this one specimen of his writing, and no other indications to go by.

Next, are the letters *upright*, *sloping forward*, or *sloping backward?*

9. Ardent.

8. Cold

7. Undemonstrative

10. Affectionate

11. Loving

12. Emotional

These are important signs, for, taken with other indications of character with which we shall deal later, they reveal the amount of affection, or capacity for affection, in the writer's nature.

Very upright writing (7), especially if well rounded, is a sign of a pleasant, kind, even-tempered and easygoing disposition, but not a demonstratively affectionate one. The husband who is devoted to his wife, and works hard to provide her with the comforts of life, but seldom kisses her or calls her anything more affectionate than " dear," and who has a positive horror of embraces and endearments in public, usually has this upright handwriting. If your own writing is similar, you will be happy married to a man of this kind, but if you write a sloping hand you are not likely to find him an ideal mate, for there is a risk that in time his outward coldness will chill your love.

Writing that slopes slightly backward (8) is often an indication of a cold nature ; the writer has actually little affection in his temperament. It is the writing of the man who has " no use for women," and though these men are often exasperatingly attractive, they are disappointing as lovers and husbands.

Very backhand writing, however (9)—especially if it has big, plain capitals, sprawling letters, and long, heavy cross-bars to the " t's "— can be a sign of a very passionate nature kept severely under control. This man may be capable of intense affection, but he is apt to be very jealous and possessive ; he can, though, be very fascinating. To be happily married to a man of this type, you need to be of a warmly affectionate nature, with either similar backhand writing, or the style that slopes well forward.

Writing that slopes forward a *little* (10) indicates a nature a little warmer, a trifle more demonstrative than the absolutely upright kind shows. People with handwriting that slopes at this angle make ideal mothers and fathers, devoted to their children and ready to make any sacrifices for them. In fact, after the children come they are apt to lose some of their affection for each other ; to become " mother " and " father " rather than to remain married sweethearts. But they are loyal and constant husbands and wives, so if you marry a man whose writing is of this type you should feel " safe " with him.

If your own handwriting slopes at this same angle, you will be happy married to a man of a similar disposition. Such a match is often an ideal one. But for you to marry a temperamental man—one whose writing slopes far forward or far backward—is running a risk, for he will need a sweetheart all his life, and will feel dissatisfied and jealous if he thinks that you put the children before him—as you probably will. He will want to be first in your heart and your thoughts always, and you, though you may not realise it yet, will be inclined to put the children first.

People who write with this slight slope are usually fond of a country life, of animals and pets as well as children ; the men make good farmers and gardeners, the women excellent housekeepers.

Handwriting that slopes more definitely (11)—as that of most people does—shows a nature well-balanced in the sense of affection, loving but not carried away by love. If " his " writing has this angle, you may feel fairly sure of a good lover and good husband.

A more pronounced forward slope denotes the temperament that lets the heart rule the head, and an exaggerated one (12) indicates an excessively emotional and passionate disposition. Unless there are other signs to counteract it, think well before you marry a man with handwriting of this type.

Other Signs

NOW for some other general indications.

Do not think that untidy writing, with carelessly-formed letters, is a sign of lack of education or intelligence. By no means. The handwriting of many very clever people is extremely difficult to read. Writing of this type often shows great personality, and means that the writer thinks so quickly that he cannot get his words down on paper fast enough ; he has no time to bother about forming his letters correctly. Very well-shaped letters are a sign of a calm, leisurely temperament and a mind that works slowly, though accurately.

Eager and enthusiastic 13.

If "he" joins his words together (13) he is eager and enthusiastic, and should go far in life, though he will probably be careless about details.

Impulsive 14.

Unevenly spaced letters—some close together and others far apart in the same word (14)—are a sign of impulsiveness.

If there are spaces between groups of letters, breaking a long word up

Easily distracted 15.

into, apparently, several short ones (15) it is an indication that the writer has little power of concentration; his mind is easily distracted and he lacks the steady, stick-to-it determination that is usually needed to win lasting success in life.

Sympathetic 16.

If his letters are well-rounded (16) it means that he is kind,

Meanness 17.

Firmness 18.

sympathetic and—if the slope of the writing agrees—affectionate.

Narrow, angular letters, set very close together (17) are usually a sign of meanness.

Stubborn 19.

If his writing is plain, with strong, straight lines in it (18) his character is firm and reliable. The merely stubborn and obstinate man's writing is cramped (19) and the downstrokes are noticeably much heavier than the upstrokes.

Large capital letters (20) com-

Ambition and Personality 20.

pared with the small ones, are an indication of pride and ambition, usually combined with a strong personality. If, in addition, the capitals are very flourishing (21) it often means vanity and conceit. But if "he" uses small, plain

Vanity and Conceit 21.

capitals (22), he is a simple, unaffected, straightforward soul.

Very plain capitals, almost like printed ones (23), indicate a practical nature; engineers, and men engaged in similar work, often use capital letters — particularly " E's "—of this kind.

Simple And Unaffected 22.

Practical 23.

Writing in which the letters vary greatly in size belongs to the moody, discontented person.

Particular Letters

IN addition to these general signs, there is a great deal to be learnt from the way "he" forms certain letters of the alphabet.

Sometimes the meanings of these may seem to contradict what you have learnt from the general character of his handwriting, but actually this only means that the main features of his disposition are modified by other traits. To read his character rightly you must take these modifying influences into account.

24. *Charitable*

A. When the top of the small "a" is left open (24) instead of being closed, he is generous.

25. *beware*   26. *believe*

B. A very narrow, squeezed-up small "b" (25) usually shows a cautious, even timid, character.
A small "b" that finishes with an outward curve as in (26) belongs to the kind of person who will believe anything he is told, and is easily "taken in."

27. *Devotion*

28. *Detached*

D. If he uses a capital "D" as in (27), the curve turning back before it reaches the downstroke, he is kind, affectionate and generous. But a capital

"D" like (28) with a flat base and the curve brought right over the downstroke, shows a reserved and perhaps cold temperament.

29. *Refined*   30. *dancing*

A man who always uses the Greek small "d" (29) usually has refined and cultured tastes and a great love of beauty.

A small "d" such as (30), with the stroke swinging forward instead of back, shows a love of pleasure and gaiety. The writer will be a cheery, jolly companion.

F. Very elaborate capital letters are almost always a sign of a florid character, and "F" (31) betrays this most of all. A highly decorative capital "F" is an indication of lack of taste and refinement.

31. *Florid*

G. A capital "G" with a short, straight final stroke (32) instead of a loop, is a sign of a precise

32. *Grand*   33. *finest*

and careful mind. If this straight stroke is long, it stands for firmness of will and decision.
A small "g" such as is shown in (33)—something like a long figure 8—is a sign of efficiency and capability, and of tact. It belongs to the man who is a "good mixer" and can get on well with most people, however unlike himself in tastes and disposition they may be.
A "G", large or small, in which

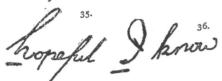

34.

there is a forward hook at the bottom instead of a loop (34), means that the writer is very generous. The same applies to a " j ".

35.

36.

H. The man who makes his small " h's " with a very tall loop (35) is likely to be a hopeful dreamer, always counting on things he has no reasonable grounds for expecting. He is not very practical, and has no great sense of humour.

I, J. A capital " I " or " J " with a large loop (36) is usually a sign of pride or vanity.

37.

imagination

The dotting of a small " i " or " j " can reveal a great deal of character. If " he " puts his dot neatly over the top of the letter, he has a careful and orderly mind. If the dot follows a long way after the " i " (37) it is a sign of imagination and impulsiveness. If it is a dash rather than a dot (38) it reveals a great sense of humour.

39.

Folly *Book*

38.

K. A long loop to a small " k " (39) means very much the same as the same feature in a small

" h ", but this kind of " k " is found particularly in the writing of deeply religious, rather visionary people.

40.   41.

L. If he makes his capital " L's " with a large loop (40) he is fond of money.

M, N. A capital " M " such as (41), commencing with a backward curve, belongs to the type of man who thinks a great deal about appearances and social position.

42. *Amenable*

If " his " small " m's " and " n's " are well rounded (42) he is affectionate and sweet-tempered.

43. *Undaunted*

If they are very angular (43) it is a sign of courage, ambition and great skill in some direction.

44. *Ordinary*

O. A perfectly rounded " O " (44), large or small, stands for lack of imagination and personality. Generally speaking, the more irregular the " o " the greater the individuality of the writer.

P. If he makes a small " p " with a very long downward stroke or loop (45) he is probably good

45.

at games and fond of the open
air.

46. *Appearances*

47. *particulars*

R. A small " r " which is large in
proportion to other letters (46)
shows a great regard for what
other people think.
An " r " with a long upstroke
to it (47) indicates a careful,
particular, even finicky disposition.

48. *Interests*

S. If he makes two or more kinds
of small " s " in the same word
or sentence (48) it is a sign of
versatility ; he is the kind of
man with many interests who
can turn his hand to almost anything, and do it well.

49. *Little will* 50. *Put it off*

T. The crossing of small " t's " is a
very important sign ; it reveals
even more than the dotting of
" i's." No cross-bar at all, or a
very small one (49), is generally
a sign of small will-power—
unless the rest of the writing is
powerful ; in this case, it suggests some hidden weakness.
The cross-bar that does not
reach, or only just reaches, the
upright (50) belongs to the man
who would rather put off till to-
morrow the job he ought to do
to-day. A long cross-bar (51) is
a sign of decision and resolution,
and the heavier it is, the greater
the strength of character.

51. *Strength*

A curved cross-bar (52) is unusual and may stand for a self-
indulgent character that has
been brought well under control.

52. *control* 53. *Great*

It is generally found in those
rather curious natures that
seem a mixture of weakness and
strength. A long cross-bar that
thickens towards the end (53)
often belongs to the aggressive,
dominating, selfish man.

54. *Determination*

If the cross-bars to his " t's "
slope downward as in (54), he
has a tremendously strong, determined character and will
make his way through life
against all odds. He is not,
however, necessarily a " hard "
man ; he may be very affectionate, and gentle with women
and children. The " t " made as
in (55) can usually be read as
standing for quiet persistence.

55. *Persistent*

These hints will give you quite a
good basis for reading " his "
character from his handwriting.
Women's handwriting, of course,
follows the same general rules as
these laid down for men's, but
curiously enough it seldom " gives
them away " so completely as a
man's writing does.

" GLYPH."

CHAPTER X

Say It with Flowers

The meanings of flowers—Special birthday flowers—The day you find the first flower of the season—Beliefs about birds — Animals — Insects — The language of stamps, etc.

SWEETHEARTS naturally write each other love-letters, but messages may be sent—sometimes by a third person who is not in their happy secret —or sentiments exchanged without the written, or even the spoken, word, and it is here that the language of flowers—one of the sweetest and most charming languages in the world—will be found valuable.

Every flower has a meaning, and it is possible to say " I love you," or " Do you love me ? " or to send a greeting, a message of hope or encouragement, by the simple means of a spray of blossom or a single flower rightly chosen. Here are the meanings of all the better-known flowers, many of which you may find growing in your own gardens or by the wayside.

Almond. This lovely blossom, coming so early in the year, means " hope," and a girl giving a spray to her boy friend could by this means tell him that there is a chance for him to become more than a friend, for as an old poet puts it :

" *The hope, in dreams of a happier hour,*
That alights on misery's brow,
Springs out of the silvery almond flower,
That blooms on a leafless bough."

Apple blossom. This signifies " I have heard of you," and could be given by a girl or a young man who has at last achieved an introduction for which they have been waiting.

Asphodel. This flower has rather a sad meaning, for it signifies regret for a lost love, and to wear the asphodel means to mourn.

Aster. This flower gives a girl a chance of showing she has changed her mind, for it means " afterthought " and, given to a boy she had sent away, might bid him hope once more.

Azalea has a lovely meaning for it says : " True till death."

Bachelor's Buttons. The name of this flower will tell that it means " a single life," and in some country districts a boy who had fallen in love with a girl would wear a " button " in his coat. If it kept fresh it was a sign the girl returned his affection, but if it faded then he was doomed to be a bachelor.

Balsam. This flower may be worn by the girl who is not yet ready for love, since it means " touch-me-not."

Bay-leaf. This signifies : " I change but in death," and would be a beautiful message to send to an absent sweetheart.

Belladonna (Deadly Nightshade). Owing to its poisonous berries this may not seem a very pleasant blossom, yet, in the flower language, it is very useful, for it means " silence," and to those lovers who wish to keep their romance a tender secret between themselves, may be very helpful at times.

Bergamot. Any girl receiving this may regard it as a compliment, for it means " sweetness."

Bilberry. Warning may be given by means of this plant, for it means " treachery," and can thus convey a message that a mischief-maker is near.

Bird's-eye. This tells those who receive it to be on the alert, for it signifies " watchfulness."

Bluebell. This pretty flower means " fidelity."

Box. Endurance.

Boy's Love (Southernwood). This fragrant plant means " a jest " and in olden times was sometimes given by a girl to a boy whom she considered too young for serious love-making.

Branch of Currants. Anyone being offered this may feel flattered, for it means : " You please all."

Briar Rose. This flower was often worn by those whose love affair was not going smoothly, for it signifies " pleasure and pain."

Broom. A fitting flower for the shy lover, since it means " humility," or " I am not worthy to aspire to you."

Buttercup. A charming little flower, but with an ugly meaning, for it signifies " ingratitude."

Calceolaria. A flower that should be pressed and treasured, for it means : " Keep this for my sake."

Campanula. " Gratitude."

Candytuft. A sweetheart would hardly be pleased to be offered a buttonhole of these pretty little flowers, for their meaning is " indifference."

Canterbury Bell. This should be a favourite with true lovers, since it signifies " constancy."

Carnation. This lovely flower has various meanings, according to the colour. One to whom love had come at first sight might well wear a red flower, for this means : " Alas, for my poor heart." A girl may dash her boy's hopes with a yellow carnation, since this signifies " refusal," while woe to the boy who is offered a striped one, with its meaning of " disdain."

Cedar Leaf. A real lover's message may be sent with these, since they say : " I live for thee."

Celandine. This is for the lover who hopes, for it means " joys to come."

Chestnut Blossom. One who has been misrepresented may well choose this flower, since it says to the loved one, " Do me justice."

China Aster (double). This flower should be a favourite with sweethearts who have come to an understanding, for it whispers : " I share your sentiments."

Chrysanthemum (red). This bears the loveliest message in the world, for it says : " I love you."

Clarkia. This is hardly a ballroom flower, yet it is there it should be found, since it asks : " Will you dance with me ? "

Clover (white). A simple little blossom to give to the friend who is going away, for it says : Remember me."

Clover (four-leaved). The boy who is too shy to tell his love can say : " Be mine," with this.

Columbine. Here's a flower for the faint-hearted, since it means : " Resolved to win."

Convolvulus. Those whom Cupid has chained should like this, for it signifies " bonds."

Coreopsis. " Love at first sight."

Cornflower. A flower we should all be glad to wear, since it stands for " kindness."

Crocus. If you have had a tiff with your boy, this little flower may bear a message for you, since it means " reconciliation."

Daffodil. All girls would like to see this flower a favourite with their boy friends, for it stands for " chivalry."

Dahlia. This beautiful flower has a beautiful meaning — " Friendship."

Daisy. This humble little blossom

has always played a large part in the language of flowers. In olden days, when a lady was not sure about her feelings for her knight, she wreathed wild daisies in her hair, and these told him : " I will think of it." If she accepted him, he had daisies engraved on his shield, and these proclaimed : " I share your love."

Dog-violet. This means what all sweethearts crave : " Faithfulness."

Eglantine (sweetbriar). This means : " I wound to heal," and stands for the mingled pleasure and pain of love. Here is a beautiful little verse about it :

" *From this bleeding hand of mine,*
Take this sprig of eglantine ;
Which, tho' sweet unto your smell,
Yet, the fretful brier will tell,
He who plucks the sweets shall prove
Many thorns to be in love."

Elder. Blossoms of this signify something we do not like to feel : " remorse."

Even-leaved Ash. This is a lucky leaf, as we can tell from this old rhyme :

" *An even-leaved ash,*
And a four-leaved clover,
You'll see your true love,
'Fore the day is over."

Fennel. This plant is said to bring its wearer " courage."

Fern. This means what we should all like to feel we possess, " fascination."

Forget-me-not. This has always been a lovers' flower, and its name is its meaning. Legend tells us that it got its name from a sad incident. Two lovers were strolling by a river when the girl expressed a wish for some of the little flowers which grew by the edge of the water. Her companion began to pluck them for her, overbalanced and fell in. The current was strong and as he was swept away he flung the flowers he had gathered at her feet and cried : " Forget-me-not."

Foxglove. This is supposed to be the fairies' flower, but it has not a fairy meaning, since it stands for " insincerity."

Geranium. This flower has several meanings according to its colour. The oak-leaved variety stands for " true friendship," a scarlet flower for " comfort," and a white one for " innocence."

Gillyflower. This is a real " friendship " flower, for all friends like to feel they are united in " bonds of affection," which is the meaning of this old-fashioned blossom.

Golden Rod. This is a good flower to send to the backward wooer, for it signifies " encouragement."

Hart's-tongue. " Longing " is the meaning of this pretty fern.

Hawthorn. Though this fragrant blossom is so often considered unlucky, in the flower language it signifies " hope."

Hazel. Here is a plant for those who regret a quarrel. It says : " Let us be reconciled."

Heartsease. If you wish to tell a friend you think of him, give them this flower, which means : " You occupy my thoughts."

Heather. This stands for " courage," and white heather carried by a bride brings good fortune.

Heliotrope. " Devotion," may be expressed by a gift of this lovely flower.

Hollyhock. This tall flower has a very suitable meaning, for it signifies " ambition."

Honesty. The meaning of this flower lies in its name.

Honeysuckle. A meaning as sweet as the flower itself, for it expresses " generous and devoted affection."

Hyacinth. Another flower which means " affection."

Ivy. This plant has always stood for constancy and fidelity. In some countries it is a symbol of " wedded love."

Jasmine. This should be for happy lovers, since it signifies " transport of joy."

Jonquil. Anyone who loves could choose this flower, which murmurs : " I desire a return of affection."

Laburnum. A flower which would appeal to the jilted, for it means " forsaken."

Laurel. The leaves of this shrub stand for " glory," which is the reason the victor's crown was always twined with them.

Lavender. It seems strange that so charming a bloom should bear the ugly meaning " distrust," but there is an old belief that a certain poisonous snake always hid in the lavender bushes, hence they were to be distrusted.

Lilac. A meaning as sweet as its perfume : " First thoughts of love."

Lily. The chosen flower of brides, it signifies " purity and sweetness."

Lily of the Valley. This flower might well be worn by the girl who is going to meet her sweetheart after a long absence, for it means "return of happiness."

London Pride. Not to be worn on serious occasion, since it stands for "frivolity."

Love-in-a-mist. The ways of love are often a little mystifying, and this charming little flower signifies "perplexity."

Love-lies-bleeding. "Hopeless, but not heartless," is the message of this flower.

Maiden-hair. "Secrecy" is the word whispered by this delicate fern.

Marigold. A bright flower with a dark meaning, for it expresses "grief."

Mignonette. A great compliment may be conveyed by this, for it says: "Your qualities surpass even your charms."

Mistletoe. We all know what is associated with this plant, but its real meaning is: "I surmount difficulties."

Moss Rose. Here is a sweet way of making a proposal, for this lovely flower is "a confession of love."

Mountain Ash. This means "prudence," and was in earlier times supposed to be a guard against witchcraft.

Myrtle. There is no wonder that brides so often carry this in their bridal bouquets, for it expresses "love."

Narcissus. The unselfish will not choose this, for it means "self-love."

Nettle. This has a meaning very suited to it, for it says: "You are cruel."

Periwinkle. A flower once used in the making of love potions. It signifies "early friendship."

Petunia. "Never despair," says this gay blossom.

Pimpernel. Sweethearts may find this tiny flower useful, for it murmurs: "I will arrange a meeting."

Pink. "Pure love" is expressed by this old favourite.

Poppy. This is a flaunting flower, and we need not be surprised that it means "extravagance."

Pyrethrum. This might be favoured by the girl whose sweetheart doubts her, for it says: "I have not changed; you wrong me."

Rhododendron. A flower broken from this bids you "beware."

Rose. The queen of flowers could not mean anything but "love," while the old-fashioned but fragrant cabbage rose is "a messenger of love."

Sage. "Esteem" is expressed by this herb.

Salvia. This flower bears the sweet message: "I think of thee."

Scilla. This flower aims at reconciliation, for it whispers: "Forgive and forget."

Snapdragon. This signifies "presumption."

Snowdrop. As this is one of the first flowers of the year it is fitting that it should express "hope."

Sunflower. "Adoration" is the meaning of this flower.

Thrift. A flower with a pleasant meaning, for it expresses "sympathy."

Tulip. Most girls would appreciate the message conveyed by this flower, for it stands for "a declaration of love."

Violet. Since this little flower hides in its leaves we can understand why it expresses "modesty."

Wallflower. This sweet, old-fashioned flower expresses a beautiful virtue: "fidelity in adversity."

If, by good fortune, your sweetheart should find a four-leaved clover and present it to you, you may take it as a sign of the greatest luck and happiness. Here is a beautiful legend attached to this little plant:

Three beautiful sisters, Faith, Hope and Charity, came to visit the earth, and wherever their footsteps pressed there sprang up the fragrant clover blossoms. But after them came an even more wonderful being whose name was "Love," and it was for him that there sprung the four-leaved clover.

The flowers your sweetheart gives you may have a secret meaning apart from those attached to each particular kind.

If there are more flowers than buds, you may take it as a sign that you will be married within a year, but if there are more buds than flowers, marriage may be some way away yet.

A withered or a misshapen flower means that someone is trying to make mischief between you and your sweetheart, so it warns you to beware.

Should your boy bring you white flowers, it signifies that his love is deep and true, but that you must be careful to live up to the high ideal he has formed of you. Blue flowers promise a happy married life, but yellow ones warn of jealousy, and bid you beware of false friends.

Birthday Flowers

AS for each birthday there is a lucky stone, so there is a lucky flower, and here are the names of the flowers which, worn in your birth month, will bring you good fortune.

January. Snowdrop.
February. Violet.
March. Daffodil.
April. Primrose.
May. The white lily.
June. Wild rose.

July. Carnation.
August. White heather.
September. Michaelmas Daisy.
October. Rosemary.
November. Chrysanthemum.
December. Ivy.

The First Flower

MOST of us who live in the country like to look for the first flower of the season, and the day on which we find it may help us to foresee our future, for if it is found on:

Monday, it brings good luck.
Tuesday, it shows success in money matters.
Wednesday, it means that your wedding day is not so very far away.
Thursday, you will have to work hard.
Friday, it foretells a surprise gift of money.
Saturday, it bids you be watchful during the day.
Sunday, it promises you great good fortune.

You may learn the initials of your future husband from the first spring flowers you see when you go for a country walk. For instance, if you see violets and primroses, his initials will be V.P. or P.V.—the order does not matter.

Birds

JUST as there is a language of flowers, so there is a meaning attached to seeing or hearing certain birds, and those who like to  study the subject may learn something of what fate has in store for them.

Cock. If you hear the farmyard rooster crowing in the afternoon, it bids you look out for an unexpected visitor, but if he crows in the night you may hear of illness.

The rooster was often used in a favourite method of prophecy concerning love affairs or wedding dates.

Several girls, all naturally interested in their wedding day, would enter a barn and each hide a ring under a little heap of corn on the floor. Then the rooster was brought in, set in the midst of the corn, and left to make his choice. The owner of the ring under the corn he ate first would be married before the year was out.

Cuckoo. When you hear the cuckoo for the first time in the year,

listen carefully and make sure if the call comes from the left or right. To hear it from the left indicates a slight loss; from the right a pleasant surprise. To hear the cuckoo while standing on soft ground is a sign that your way in life will be easy, but if you are standing on hard ground, then you will have to work.

One old belief tells us that what you are doing when you hear the cuckoo is what you will do for the rest of your life, but this may be taken to have a wider meaning. Thus, if you are doing housework, you will spend most of your life caring for your own home ; if you are nursing a baby, motherhood will be yours, and so on.

One superstition tells us that a girl may learn the year of her wedding by listening to the cuckoo when she hears it for the first time in the year. Directly she hears the first call she should kiss her hand to the bird and say :

" *Cuckoo free, in the tree,*
  Tell me when I'll wedded be."

The number of times the bird calls after that, denotes how many years must go by before the wedding takes place.

In one country, on hearing the cuckoo for the first time, to jingle money and run a short distance is believed to bring good luck.

Magpie. This has long been regarded as a bird of prophecy, and the old rhyme tells us :

" *One for anger,*
   Two for mirth,
  Three for a wedding,
   Four for a birth,
  Five for silver,
    Six for gold,
  Seven for a secret
   That shall never be told."

An old country proverb warns us that :

" *He who takes a magpie's life,*
   Will rue the day he took a wife."

Nightingale. If you should hear the nightingale before the cuckoo this is a most fortunate omen, and is a sign that your love affair will run smoothly. If, by happy chance, your sweetheart should be with you when you hear it, then you must clasp hands and stand in silence while you count thirty, and your love will end in marriage for, as a poet tells us :

" *The liquid notes that close the eye of*
   day,
  First heard before the shallow
   cuckoo's bill
  Portend success in love."

Owl. Sorrow is foretold by the hooting of an owl, but if you can make the sign of the cross before the sound dies away, the misfortune is averted.

Peacock. The screech of this bird is not considered lucky, and the feathers should never be brought into the house.

Pigeon. Should a pair of pigeons fly over a house it foretells a wedding in the family.

Robin. This little songster has always been looked upon as sacred, and there are several old rhymes to this effect :

" *The robin and the wren,*
They are God's cock and hen.

" *He that hurts a robin or a wren*
Will never prosper among men."

To have a robin's nest near the house foretells good luck, and to kill one after it has so nested is to court disaster. A girl who hears a robin singing on her window-sill may listen with content, for this foretells happiness in love.

Seagull. If you live by the sea, or if your boy should chance to be a sailor, you will no doubt have heard some of the old beliefs about these birds. In some parts of the world the souls of men drowned at sea are said to take on the shape of seagulls, and, therefore, to kill or wound one is thought to bring ill-fortune.

Swallow. Swallows nesting on a house will bring good luck to its inmates, but should they be molested and thus forsake their nests, the luck will go with them. Indeed, it is considered very unlucky to interfere with any sitting bird and thus cause her to leave her nest.

To kill a **Swan** or a **Kingfisher** is held to be equally unlucky, but in this, as in other instances, the killing must be intentional and not

accidental for the ill-luck to come to pass.

Woodpeckers are lucky, but if you kill one after it has nested in the garden you will lose something you value. The same belief is held regarding a raven.

When you start on a journey, take notice and see if there is a flock of birds flying towards you. If they turn to the right your journey will be lucky, if to the left, there may be a disappointment in store for you.

Animals

THERE are also age-old superstitions about certain animals.

Cat. Most people know that a black cat is lucky, and in the North of England for a boy to give his sweetheart a black kitten is held to bring luck to their courting, while in the Highlands the gift of a dog before marriage is held to have the opposite effect.

If a black cat enters the house of its own accord, be sure to make it welcome, for if it is driven away it may take a week's luck with it. A white cat, coming uninvited to a house, is said to foretell the illness of someone in the family.

To kill or drown a cat means ill-luck for nine years. Sailors believe this supersition so firmly that, though it is held to be bad luck to find a cat on a vessel, they will on no account throw it overboard, as this would add to the ill-fortune.

Frog. Should a frog hop into the house, drive it forth gently. If you kill it under your roof there is misfortune in store for you.

Hare. If, when you are out for a walk, a hare runs straight across your path, you may expect a disappointment. If seen running past houses, it is said to foretell a fire in one of them. In olden days girls who were going to meet their sweethearts always ate hare first, as it was said to make them beautiful for a week.

Horse. To see a black-and-white horse is lucky, and if you can wish before you see its tail, your wish will be fulfilled.

If you see a white horse, and then afterwards meet a person with red hair, you are going to have a piece of very good news.

Pig. To meet a pig when you are out walking is unlucky, but if you meet another before you go home the misfortune is averted.

Snake. Most people imagine these are unlucky, but this is not so. In the East, serpents are looked upon as the symbol of wisdom, and if you should see one of the harmless grass snakes which may be found in this country, it shows that you are going to be successful in money matters.

Insects

EVEN insects are held to foretell good or bad luck.

Bees. These are lucky, and if you have a romance you wish to keep secret, be sure to tell the bees, if there is a hive near you, as this is said to help to preserve your secret.

To see a swarm of bees is lucky, but, as this old rhyme tells us, the luck varies according to the month in which it is seen :

" A swarm of bees in May
Is worth a load of hay,
A swarm of bees in June
Is worth a silver spoon,
A swarm of bees in July
Is not worth a fly."

Cricket. To hear a cricket singing in the house betokens good luck to all the family.

Glow-worm. If, when you are walking with your sweetheart, you see a glow-worm in your path, this is a sign that your love affair will prosper, but be sure not to kill it or you will kill your luck.

Ladybird. This little creature is lucky, and if one settles upon you it should never be driven away. The earlier in the year it comes, the greater the luck, while if it settles on you in the morning it means a visitor before the day is out.

Moth. To see one on your clothes foretells that you will have a gift, but should a death's head moth fly in at the window it foretells an illness. Should it fly out again of its own accord the illness will not be severe.

Spider. Though these are not usually welcome in a house, they should never be killed, for they bring good fortune, as we can guess from the old rhyme.

" If you wish to live and thrive
Let a spider run alive."

The ordinary spiders bring good fortune, but little red ones are particularly lucky. Should one settle on you, on no account brush it off as it means a present of money for you very shortly.

The Language of Stamps

WHILE on this subject we may mention the language of postage stamps. Here is the " code " :

A stamp placed at the bottom right-hand corner of an envelope asks : " Why are you so distant ? "

At the same corner, but upside-down, it says : " Yes."

If placed cross-wise in the same place it says : " No."

At the top left-hand corner, the stamp, upside-down, sends the sweetest message a lover can receive, for it murmurs : " I love you."

If it stands cross-wise in the same place it is a disappointing message, saying : " I am in love with another."

Correctly set in the top left-hand corner it reads : " Good-bye for the present, dear."

Sideways, in the top left-hand corner, it says cruelly : " I hate you."

In the top right-hand corner, the correct position, but placed upside-down, the stamp says : " All is over between us."

By placing the stamp on the right-hand side of the name, over the address, you say : " I am longing to see you. Please write soon."

Placed sideways at the bottom left-hand corner it means : " I like you, but as a friend."

On the left-hand side of the name, placed upright, it sends a charming message, for it whispers : " You have all my love."

If placed upside-down, the message is very different, for it reads : " I am engaged to be married."

And here are the meanings attached to the different colours of sealing-wax :

Black stands for sorrow.
Blue means loyalty.
Brown stands for thoughtfulness.
Green says " Hope."
Grey indicates friendship.
Orange means deep regard.
Pink tells of love.
Ruby means luck.
Rose is for tender affection.
Vermilion means indifference.
Violet stands for sympathy.
White tells of a proposal.

" FLORA."

CHAPTER XI

"Bumps" that Betray

*How to tell character from the shape of the head—The " bumps,"
their positions and meanings—How to discover if a characteristic
is developing or not.*

THE study of the "bumps" of the head—or to give it its scientific name, Phrenology—is a most fascinating subject.

If you pass your fingers slowly over your head, you will find there many bumps, some large, some small, some hardly noticeable at all. These are not just a freak of nature, but have a very definite meaning, for they are a guide to your general character, showing, by their size, which instincts are well developed in you and which are only slight.

These bumps in your skull, you see, are a reflection of the brain beneath. Those parts of your brain which are well developed, and therefore bulge a little above the rest, have their effect upon the skull, which to some extent is moulded on the brain. So that, as the brain holds the key to all our hopes, our desires, our capabilities and ambitions, when we know exactly what each bump stands for, the shape of the head can be a true guide to a person's character.

Besides being a useful guide to character, this study of the bumps of the head can be a great help in other ways. It can tell you whether you are suited to the kind of job you are doing, or if some other type of work is more in your line. In this way you can gauge your own talents and disposition, and know, if a certain opportunity is offered, whether or no you would be wise to take it. You can, of course, help other people in this way also when you are able to read their bumps.

For instance, anybody whose bump of colour-sense is strongly in evidence should do well in any artistic calling, dress-making or

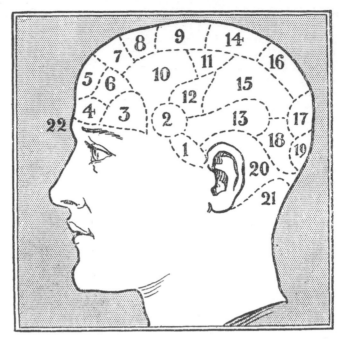

This chart shows you the areas of the head in which occur the "bumps" described.

other work in which colour plays an important part. The bump of invention, when nicely developed, shows, of course, one who should do well in any job which calls for mechanical ingenuity.

A fair-sized bump of logical reasoning points to the fact that work requiring a cool, level, business-like head is most suitable. Well-developed bumps showing love of children, patience and sympathy are ideal equipment for those who are thinking of starting out on a nursing career.

It is not always a good thing for bumps to be very large. Over-developed bumps are sometimes a sign that you have rather more of a certain characteristic than is good for you. Thus, if your bump of determination is very large, it may mean that your will power is so strong that it amounts to stubborn-

ness and obstinacy, which, you will agree, is not greatly to be desired !

In the same way, if this bump is slight it might mean a weak will and one who is easily led, so that in many cases a nice, moderately-sized bump, neither too large nor too small, is the best sign of all.

You need not worry a lot, though, if you should find some bumps very unfavourable for you, because it is definitely possible for us to improve, to a great extent, any defects. We can help the "little bumps" to develop more and the big ones to "keep their place," as it were, for our bumps by no means remain the same size throughout our lives. Developing or checking their growth, of course, rests with yourself.

It is even possible sometimes to discover for ourselves whether we are successfully developing a small bump into a larger one. When running your fingers lightly over the head, bumps which feel slightly warm to the touch are growing. If these are bumps you have been hoping to enlarge, you will know by this means how well you are succeeding !

The professional phrenologist, of course, makes a life-time study of people's heads, but for the ordinary person, a simple indication of the position of the " bumps," and what they indicate, is enough to form quite a good estimate of the characters of their friends.

The diagram on page 120 shows you the position of each " bump," and here is an account of what each stands for.

The " Self " Bump, just by the ear.   The " Music " Bump is above one eye.

1. The Bump of "Self"

This bump occurs just in front of the ear, by the upper part of it. If there is little trace of it, you are unselfish, generous and kind-hearted, with a love of doing those little things for others which count for so much.

The larger the development of this bump, the more does " self " sway your actions and thoughts. Fondness of the good things of life are indicated, too, with love of pleasure and entertainment and little thought for others.

2. The Bump of Invention

The inventive bump comes a little in front of and above the " self " bump, and when it is fairly prominent—not too big or too small—it shows a love of making things, putting things together and generally an excellent constructive ability.

A deep interest will be taken by such a person in anything mechanical, and nothing would suit him better than work in which there is a chance to make full use of his ability to invent and construct.

Where the bump is slight or non-existent, inventive powers are very low, but if *very* prominent, there is a danger of these powers taking too big a hold on the mind, so that other thoughts and aims are over-shadowed—a case of " too much of a good thing " which may have an ill effect on results.

3. The Bump of Judgment

This is a very useful bump to have in correct proportions. It lies just above the eye, towards the rear of it. It shows good judgment in all things—the ability to make wise decisions, to weigh matters up carefully and justly, to judge sizes and values and to distinguish very quickly between wrong and right.

A strong inclination towards method and orderliness in everything is also indicated in the bump.

A slightly formed or entirely absent bump naturally means that these characteristics are not too strongly marked, while the large bump sometimes signifies harsh judgment in which the quality of mercy is lacking.

4. The Bump of Music

Just in front of the latter bump is the bump of music, which obviously stands for love of all things musical. There is a strong artistic sense, which is directed almost wholly towards beauty in music.

If you have this bump nicely developed you are exceedingly quick at learning to play most musical instruments, and will seldom grudge time for practice. You will probably make a good music-teacher as well as a performer.

5. The Bump of Argument

This bump is just above No. 4, on the brow, and shows, when well-developed, an argumentative nature. There is a fondness for contradiction, and a great reluctance to " giving in." If you have a good-sized bump you will enjoy arguing, and take a great deal of convincing. You will often go well out of your way to find a subject for argument, and will pick things to pieces with your criticism.

Where the bump is absent or very slight, you can be sure the possessor will be easily convinced and not too obstinate in argument, but when the bump is big—beware !

6. The Bump of Humour

This bump indicates a capacity for appreciating humour and wit. It is above and a little behind the eye, and is usually just covered with hair. To possess this bump nicely developed, but not too large, shows that you have a deep fund of humour, are very jolly and the best of company, especially at a party.

It is a bump of imagination, too, and you should get on well in any job requiring imagination and far-seeing vision.

Little or no sense of humour is present where the bump is not well-developed, and there is a tendency to be a little slow in grasping things. With an over-developed bump you may expect too frivolous a sense of the funny side of life—one who seldom takes anything seriously enough.

7. The Bump of Beauty

A well-formed bump here belongs to one quick to appreciate beauty when it meets the eye. Love of beautiful scenery is very deep ; mountains, the sea and anything impressive in its grandeur will strike a chord in the heart of a friend with this bump, while pretty, dainty clothes appeal to her strongly.

She will have a lovely home ; a delight to the eye and with nothing to jar or mar its perfect taste. Love of flowers is strong, too.

The larger the bump, the deeper the sense of beauty.

8. The Bump of Generosity

Generosity and a charitable nature are the virtues of this bump. If it is very large, generosity is often carried to extremes ; if yours is large you will give away your last penny if it means helping some poor creature, and your generosity may be taken to such lengths that folk take advantage of you.

Where the bump is moderately developed, you will find a person

" Argumentativeness " —on the brow.   The " Beauty " Bump.

who is an excellent friend, anxious to do her best for everybody, and a willing helper in any charitable cause.

9. The Bump of Kindliness

Here is a bump which shows the kindest of hearts and a nature full of tenderness and sympathy. It is on the top of the head, near the middle. You can be certain that a friend with such a bump will make a very good and loyal pal, and one who will be at her best when help and sympathy in sadness or sorrow is needed.

A poorly developed bump indicates a lack of kindliness, while if it is very big it shows great unselfishness and the power to make big sacrifices.

10. The Bump of Enthusiasm

If you have this bump well-developed, you will throw yourself into anything you take up, whether work or play, with your whole heart and soul, and with a sincere determination to carry it through conscientiously.

You have, as well, that type of enthusiasm which quickly communicates itself to others, and inspires them to follow your example. In this way you make a splendid leader.

If this bump is accompanied by a good bump of determination and perseverance, you have it in your power to achieve almost any ambition you set yourself to attain.

The bump of enthusiasm cannot be too large.

11. The Practical Bump

This bump shows a practical nature; very matter-of-fact and with not a great deal of imagination. Anyone possessing it will be an excellent manager, able to organise cleverly and see that things are

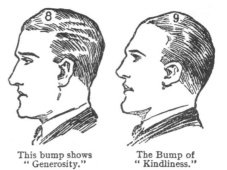

This bump shows "Generosity."   The Bump of "Kindliness."

carried out on common-sense lines. Orderliness and method are well to the fore, while a cool, level head in any emergency is indicated.

A very slight bump shows lack of these things; an over-developed one a nature that has little sympathy or appreciation of anything but cold, hard facts.

12. The Bump of Ambition

A well-developed bump here shows a person who means to get on at all costs; ambition is strong, and every effort will be used to "get there."

Such persons have plenty of common sense, and use it to the fullest extent to help them to their goal. They are fond of money, but only as a means to help in their ambitions.

13. The Bump of Energy

When this bump is well in evidence on your head you are one of those people who are "always on the go"; even when your body is at rest, your mind is busy with new plans and ideas.

You are a wonderful leader, your inspiring example bringing out the last ounce of energy from those who follow you.

There is a tendency towards secretiveness in this bump, especially if it is over-developed.

This bump shows "Energy."   The " Determination " Bump.

14. The Bump of Determination

Here is the bump which shows our will-power. When moderately developed, it denotes a strong will, firmness, and an abundance of perseverance and determination ; you will not easily be turned aside from anything you have set out to do ; doggedly you will follow it up to the end, unless unavoidable circumstances prevent you.

A small bump is a sign of a rather weak will ; one who is easily led. If the bump is very large, strength of will may be carried to such lengths that it becomes stubbornness and a selfish ruthlessness.

15. The Bump of Cautiousness

Folk who have this bump well-developed are usually very careful where they tread in their walk through life. They are cautious in the extreme ; they look, not only once, but twice before they leap.

They have good heads for business matters, but are liable to miss opportunities through being overcautious, though sometimes this trait will stand them in good stead.

Where the bump is very pronounced indeed, a suspicious nature is indicated. Complete absence of a bump in this region shows recklessness.

16. The Bump of Dignity

This bump, when you have it moderately developed, indicates self-respect and dignity. There is just the right measure of pride in your make-up—neither too much nor too little—and enough self-respect and dignity to earn admiration and respect from other people. You should make an excellent leader and organiser.

Too big a bump is a sign of pride and haughtiness, with a touch of conceit. Too small a bump signifies one who is timid and reserved, content to keep in the background rather than assert herself.

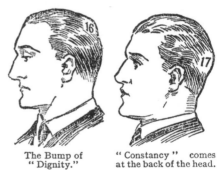

The Bump of "Dignity."   " Constancy " comes at the back of the head.

17. The Bump of Constancy

A good, well-developed bump here is much to be desired, and the bigger it is, the better. It denotes constancy in love and in friendship. If you have this bump nicely in evidence you make the finest of friends, and the best of lovers.

It will take a good deal to sway you from the object of your affections—you will never be the one to break friendships, and in marriage your love is undying once it is given.

A strong sense of loyalty is indicated, too.

18. The Bump of Reason

People who have this bump well developed have excellent powers of reasoning, and can weigh up difficult problems in a careful, methodical way which leads them to the correct solutions.

These folk look at things from a logical point of view, and their common sense is well above the average. Excellent business abilities are theirs, and a fine power of concentration. Over-development of this bump suggests too much attention to minor details and a tendency to miss the big things.

19. The Love-of-Children Bump

At the back of the head, rather low down, is the bump which stands for love of children—the better

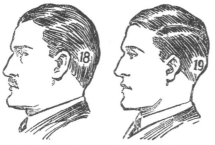

The Bump of "Reason."   "Love of Children" is shown here.

developed this bump is, the stronger are these instincts.

Anyone with a good bump here makes a splendid parent. She is attracted to the little ones as by a magnet, whether they be her own or other folk's, and can play with them for hours.

Patience in great measure is another virtue of hers—a very necessary one where children are concerned, too ! Sympathy and tact are strong also.

20. The Bump of Courage

When this bump is large, little daunts the possessor ; she knows no fear, and will undertake to brave the greatest perils with unfaltering heart. Such courage is sure to take

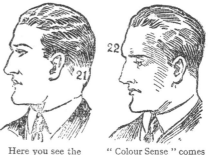

Here you see the Bump of "Love."   "Colour Sense" comes between the eyes.

her far in the world. Too big a bump of courage is not good, for it indicates foolhardiness.

21. The Bump of Love

Here is a most important bump—the bump of love, which is situated at the base of the skull, where it joins the backbone. Well in evidence, but not too large, it shows that you are capable of the truest kind of love, deep and lasting, and willing to make any sacrifice for the loved one.

A sympathetic and tender heart is also indicated ; unselfishness, too.

The bump of love should not be too big, for then it may mean that a little fickleness is present. If it is very small, or not to be found at all, coldness and an unsympathetic nature may be suspected.

22. The Bump of Colour

This bump, just between the eyes and a little above them, shows colour-sense. Where the bump is well-developed, love of colour is very strong.

Naturally, the artistic sense is present in good measure, and painting is likely to attract more than anything else, though such folk will be at home in any calling where their colour-sense and artistic talent can have plenty of scope.

"CEREBRO."

CHAPTER XII

Luck in Love

*How to ensure good luck in your love affair—Lucky omens—
Mascots to keep love true—Foretelling the future by flowers—
Charms for St. Valentine's Day and Hallow-e'en.*

COURTSHIP days are a delightful time, yet the heart of the true lover is often beset by doubts and fears, and always there is a desire to peep into the future, to try to learn if the course of true love is to run smooth, or what difficulties may be encountered.

Here is a list of omens which may help sweethearts to learn what Fate has in store for them.

Clothes. If your apron-string becomes untied of its own accord it is a sign that your sweetheart is thinking of you. A man should never give his sweetheart a black silk scarf; if he does they will certainly be parted.

Coins. For your sweetheart to give you a threepenny bit with a hole in it is very lucky, but should you lose it, you will lose luck with it. If you come across a crooked sixpence, cut it in half, give half to your sweetheart and keep the other half yourself. While you keep the pieces your love will flourish, however you may be parted, and if, when you come together again, the pieces fit perfectly, it is a sign you have both been faithful.

Ears. Should your ear tingle, someone is talking about you—" left for spite, right for love "—an old saying tells us, and if you mention aloud the name of the person you think may be speaking of you the tingling will cease if it is the right name.

Finger Nails. If you want to see your sweetheart, cut your nails on a Friday for, according to an old rhyme :

" *Cut them on Monday, you cut them for news,*
Cut them on Tuesday, a new pair of shoes,
Cut them on Wednesday, cut them for wealth,
Cut them on Thursday, you cut them for health,
Cut them on Friday, a sweetheart you'll know,
Cut them on Saturday, a journey you'll go,
Cut them on Sunday, you'll cut them for evil,
For all the week long you'll be ruled by the devil ! "

Fruit Stones. When you are eating stone-fruit close your eyes and wish. If the number of stones is even your wish will come true.

Hair. Though a lock of hair is often treasured by sweethearts, this is not considered really lucky. " Keep hair, keep care," an old saying tells us, but if the hair is worn in a ring, or a locket of gold, this averts any ill-fortune.

Hands. If your right palm itches you are going to receive a present ; if your left palm, you may be asked to give one.

In the Garden. Should a deep red rose bloom in your garden before June, it foretells a wedding in the family. If you find an ash leaf with an even number of fronds, you are going to get a surprise about your sweetheart. Should you have quar-relled with your sweetheart and can find a four-leaved clover, wear it against your heart and you will become reconciled.

In the Street. Should you meet a load of hay, wish before it is out of sight, and you will get your wish. To meet a load of straw bids you to be watchful during the day, or you may lose something you value.

If you see a dropped glove, do not pick it up or it will bring ill-luck, but if your sweetheart is walking with you and he picks it up, you will get a present within a week. To pick up a dropped handkerchief is always risky, since you may be picking up its owner's bad luck. Pins, however, should always be picked up, for :

" *See a pin and let it lie, you're sure to want before you die ;*
See a pin and pick it up, all the day you'll have good luck."

Should a butterfly fly across your path, it shows your sweetheart is thinking of you, and the same is true if you see a bee.

Letters. Should you go to the pillar-box and there meet the postman you may expect an interesting piece of news. If you get two letters from the same person by one post, you may expect a piece of good fortune before the day is over. Be careful not to lose a love-letter or you may lose some of your love with it.

Lovers. It is unlucky to kiss on a staircase, or to look into a mirror together. A love-letter should never be written in red ink, or there will be a quarrel. An engagement is luckiest if announced on a Saturday.

Mistletoe. If you wear a bracelet of this wood it is a charm against false friends, but be very careful you do not tread a berry beneath your feet or ill-luck may come to you.

Mole. To have a mole on your person is considered lucky, but the meaning varies according to the position of the mark. Above the left eye it indicates a flirt, or one who is a great favourite with the opposite sex. Above the right eye promises wealth and a happy marriage. On the nose signifies success in business, while on the cheek indicates happiness. On the chin shows that you will be happy in choosing your friends, and on the ear indicates contentment. On the shoulders shows that you have fortitude, and on the arms that happiness will come to you. On the hands shows that you are able to take care of yourself, and on the neck that you have a patient nature.

Moon. It is better to get engaged when the moon is waxing than when it is waning, and the ring should be first put on when the moon is full.

Photographs. While sweethearts like to exchange photographs, it is not considered lucky for them to be photographed together before marriage, as this may foretell a parting. In no circumstances should they address each other as "wife" or "husband" before the knot is tied.

If you are having a photograph taken to give to your sweetheart, it is luckiest to sit for it on a Friday.

Stairs. Should you stumble upstairs it is a sign that your wedding day is nearer than you imagine.

Stars. If you are wishing something about your sweetheart, try to count seven stars seven nights in succession, and your wish will come true.

Sneezing. Here are two old rhymes concerning sneezing:

" Once a wish, twice a kiss,
Three times a letter,
Four times something better ! "

" Sneeze on Sunday before you break
your fast ;
You'll see your true love before the
week is past."

If you sneeze on Saturday it foretells an unexpected visit from your sweetheart on Sunday.

Speaking. Should you and your sweetheart be talking and you happen to speak the same word together, link little fingers and wish. Your wish will come true before the year is out.

Table Lore. Never give your sweetheart a knife, for it may cut the friendship between you. If there are two knives crossed, uncross them by removing the under one first, or you may quarrel. Should you drop a knife on the floor it tells of a visit from your sweetheart. Should you be handed a cup with two spoons in it, your wedding day is nearer than you think. Should you have poured him out one cup of tea, and your sweetheart pours himself out another from the same pot, you may expect your marriage to be blessed with children. Do not let him help you to salt, or it may fulfil the old saying: " Help me to salt, help me to sorrow."

PLATE 9

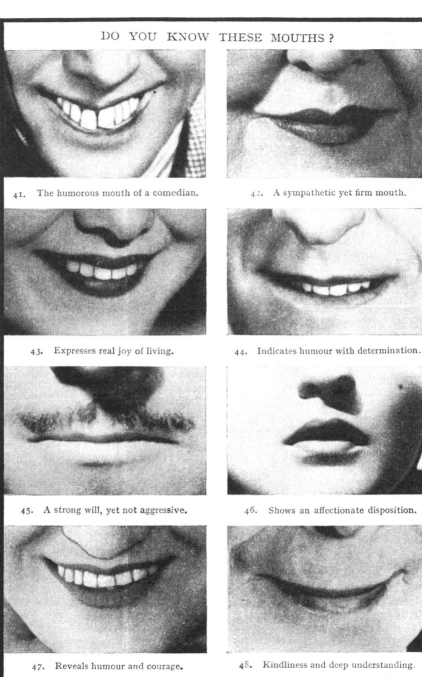

DO YOU KNOW THESE MOUTHS?

41. The humorous mouth of a comedian.

42. A sympathetic yet firm mouth.

43. Expresses real joy of living.

44. Indicates humour with determination.

45. A strong will, yet not aggressive.

46. Shows an affectionate disposition.

47. Reveals humour and courage.

48. Kindliness and deep understanding.

PLATE 10

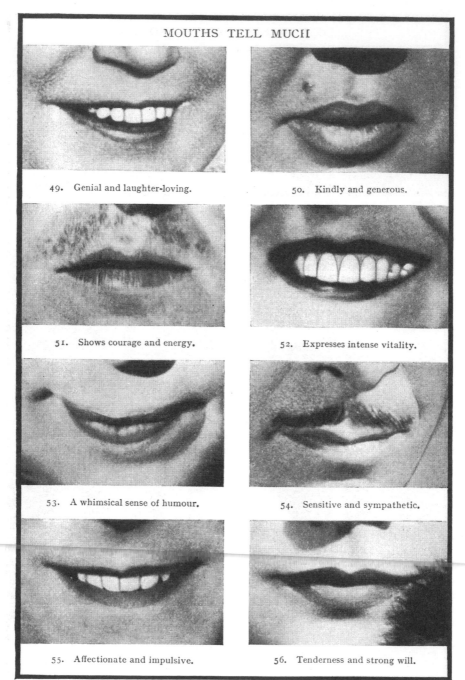

MOUTHS TELL MUCH

49. Genial and laughter-loving.

50. Kindly and generous.

51. Shows courage and energy.

52. Expresses intense vitality.

53. A whimsical sense of humour.

54. Sensitive and sympathetic.

55. Affectionate and impulsive.

56. Tenderness and strong will.

PLATE 11

DO YOU KNOW THESE NOSES?

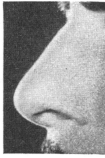

57. This promi-
nent nose expresses
force of character
and great thorough-
ness.

58. This one re-
veals a love of
beauty and excellent
taste.

Goldwyn.

59. The owner of
this unusual nose
has a very marked
personality.

*Metro-Goldwyn-
Mayer.*

60. Much under-
standing and deter-
mination are shown
here.

61. This nose in-
dicates tender-
heartedness and
sympathy.

*First National
British.*

62. A great sense
of humour is reveal-
ed by a nose of this
shape.

63. Here is another
nose of the " humor-
ous " type, with
much personality.

64. Pride and re-
serve, with a capac-
ity for intense feel-
ing.

Warner.

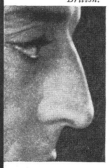

65. A strong will
that refuses to be
beaten is revealed
here.

66. An unusual
nose, indicating in-
dependence of
thought.

Paramount.

67. An easy-going,
tolerant disposition,
kindly and gen-
erous.

68. Much charac-
ter, conscientious-
ness and firmness of
will are in this nose.

PLATE 12

PERSONALITY IN NOSES

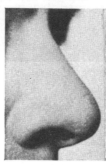

69. This rather long nose speaks of painstaking thoroughness in all things.

70. A highly sensitive nose, indicating delicacy of thought and feeling.
Metro-Goldwyn-Mayer.

71. The nose that tells of a kindly, good-natured disposition.

72. There is much determination in this nose, but not of the aggressive kind.
Paramount.

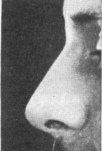

73. Here is every indication of an affectionate, tenderhearted disposition.

74. An unusually delicate nose for a man; it indicates sensitiveness.
Fox.

75. A nose that reveals personality and a great capacity for hard work.

76. Here cheerful courage and candid downrightness are shown.

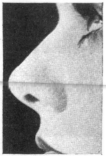

77. The shortness of this nose is a sign of an unaggressive disposition.

78. A love of the beautiful, of colour and harmony, are indicated here.

79. A sensitive disposition allied with force of character and a certain pride.

80. The dominant nose of a man who will succeed in whatever he undertakes.
Paramount.

When you are tasting a fruit for the first time that year, wish, and your wish will be granted before the year is out. If you are talking to a man you love, do not sit on the table, or you will never become his wife.

Washing Hands. If you and your sweetheart wash your hands in the same water, be sure to make the sign of a cross over it, or you may quarrel before the day is out.

Mascots

ALL through the ages people have attached faith to charms or mascots of various kinds, and whatever may be our belief in the power of mascots, it is certainly true that a real faith in one does help to make us lucky, because it puts us in the frame of mind to expect luck and to be ready to seize it when it comes.

Select your mascot carefully, and then believe in it. To be really lucky, mascots should be given, not bought ; if they are found it is luckier still.

Here is a list of mascots most favoured at the present time :

Black Cat. A tiny figure of a black cat is supposed to bring good fortune to the wearer ; if it has green eyes it is luckier still.

Cat's Eye. This stone, which is the result not of nature but of the jeweller's art, is said to be a charm against all unkind thoughts on the part of others. In olden times it was worn to keep off witchcraft.

Coal. A piece of coal carried on the person is said to bring luck in money matters, but the coal must be found in the street and not taken from your own coal cellar.

Horseshoe. This is very lucky if found in the road, and the older the shoe the greater the luck, while the number of nails in it indicate for how many years the luck will hold

good. Tiny horseshoes of gold or silver may be worn as brooches or pins, but remember that whether placed over a door, or worn as an ornament, the horseshoe must be placed with the open ends uppermost or the luck will run out.

Scarab. This is a mascot to be chosen with discretion, for it may prove very lucky or very unlucky according to the disposition of the wearer. It requires a very thorough knowledge of charms to choose a scarab mascot.

Serpent. A ring or a bracelet in the form of a serpent is a very ancient charm, for the serpent was said to bestow wisdom and clear-sightedness, and to have the gift of healing.

Solomon's Seal. A very ancient charm said to preserve the wearer from harm, and to ensure success in money matters.

Stones. A jacinth and an amethyst are very lucky, and a black opal brings a gift of gold with it, but the stone must be bought, for to give a black opal is unlucky.

Swastika. This word means "well-being," thus the sign of the swastika is supposed to bring health and content.

Once you have chosen your mascot, carry it always with you and, if possible, wear it on the left

side of your body. Do not drop it if you can possibly avoid doing so, or you may drop your luck, and remember that a mascot which has brought others good may be of no use to you, for according to the planet under which we were born so will a mascot work for us, so take a little thought in selecting your charm, ask your sweetheart to give it to you for your next birthday present, and then believe in it !

Foretelling the Future

IN every age lovers have wished to peer into the future, to see if the loved one returns their affection, and if his love will be true. Here are a few of the simpler ways which are said to help sweethearts to learn how their romance is likely to progress :

Flowers and Plants

Bluebell. If you can turn a bluebell inside out without breaking it, it signifies that your lover will be faithful to you.

Daisy. Midsummer Eve is a real lover's hour, and if you place beneath your pillow a daisy root dug up that night as the clock chimes midnight, you will dream of your future husband.

If you wish to know if your sweetheart loves you, pluck a daisy and then pull out the petals one by one saying : " He loves me, he loves me not " at each petal. Whichever comes last tells of his affections.

Fern Seed. This is supposed to be a powerful spell, but it can be practised only on Midsummer Eve. At the hour of midnight you must catch some of the fern seed, which grows on the back of the leaf, as it falls, but you must catch it in a white handkerchief, as on no account must you touch it by hand. If

you can thus obtain the seed, success in love and money is said to be yours. If you carry the seed about with you, the courtship will be happy.

Ivy. In olden times girls who wished to know the name of their future husband plucked a spray of ivy at dawn on New Year's Day and carried it near their heart. The first young man who spoke to them was destined for their husband :

" *Ivy, ivy, I thee pluck,*
 And in my bosom I thee put,
 The first young man who speaks to me
 My own true lover he shall be."

Love-in-a-mist. The girl who wishes her sweetheart to be faithful to her should grow this pretty plant in her garden. As long as she tends it carefully he will prove true, but should she neglect it, he is likely to change, and if through her neglect the flower dies, his love will die, too.

Pansy. Count carefully the lines on the petal of a pansy which you pluck, or which is given to you— you must not buy it—here is what their number foretells :

Four—your wish will come true.

Five—there's trouble ahead, but you will overcome it.

Six—a surprise is coming to you.

Seven—you have a faithful sweetheart.

Eight—he may be fickle.

Nine—you will go over the water to wed.

It is luckier for the lines to incline towards the right, and if the centre line is the longest, be sure to announce your engagement on a Sunday.

Find His Name

THERE are many old super-stitions which are said to tell a girl the name of her future sweet-heart, and here are a few of the more simple ones.

Cut twenty-six tiny squares of cardboard and write the letters of the alphabet upon them. When you go to bed place the squares face downwards in a basin of water. In the morning those letters which have turned right side up are the initials of your future husband. Sometimes a whole name is spelled out.

Peel an apple very carefully without breaking the peel, toss it over the left shoulder, and the letter it forms will be the first letter of your sweetheart's name.

Melt a spoonful of wax in an old spoon, pour it quickly into cold water, and note the letter it forms.

You may be able to foretell something of your future if you try this with molten lead. Take a little strip of lead—the solder used for mending kettles will do very well—melt it in an old teaspoon, and then drop it into a bowl of very cold water. Note the shape into which it forms. If it resembles a bouquet, it means you will be married much sooner than you think; if a ship, then you will cross the water, or marry a sailor; if a gun, then your sweetheart will be a soldier, while if it is a cross, then your husband will be connected with the Church. If the lead forms trees you will live in the country, but if there is a suggestion of houses, your future will be passed in a town.

Charms for St. Valentine's Day

GOOD St. Valentine is the patron saint of lovers, and there are many old charms which, practised on this day, are said to tell something about your sweetheart or sweetheart-to-be.

If, on St. Valentine's Eve, a girl gathers five bay leaves, and, on going to bed, pins one to each corner of her pillow and one in the centre, she will dream of her future husband.

Another old superstition tells us that the first single man friend a girl meets on St. Valentine's Day will marry her.

Another charm is much more difficult to carry out, and the girl who has the courage to follow it deserves her wish. She must boil an egg hard, take out the yolk, fill its place with salt and then eat the egg just before going to bed. She must neither speak nor drink after it, and then her sweetheart will come to her in a dream.

Another old charm which will bring a dream sweetheart is known as " The Dumb Cake," and three girls are required to carry this out. Two girls make the cake, two girls bake it, and the third breaks it into three pieces and places one piece under the pillow of each girl, but not one word must be spoken during the making, the baking, or the placing of the cake. If these observances are carried out faithfully, the girls are said to dream of their future husbands.

If you wish to know how your love affair will progress, cut an apple in half and count the pips. If there are an even number, you will be married soon ; if one pip is cut through you will quarrel with your sweetheart ; if two pips are cut then you will be a widow.

An easy charm of olden days was worked with a ball of red worsted. This had to be tossed out of the window at midnight, the girl holding an end of the wool. When the ball touched the ground the girl wound it back again round her fingers, and as she drew the last bit over the window-ledge the vision of her sweetheart appeared to her.

Charms for All Hallow-e'en

ALL HALLOW-E'EN, or the eve of All Saints' Day, is held to be very favourable for love charms, and here are a few of those still widely practised in many parts of the country, especially in Scotland.

A girl who wishes to know what her future husband will be like, takes a candle and an apple into a dark room just before midnight. Standing before a mirror she cuts the apple into small pieces, throws one piece over her right shoulder, but without looking behind, and then eats the rest, combing her hair as she does so. As the clock strikes, the face of her future husband will appear in the mirror.

If a girl had two admirers she stuck an apple pip on each cheek, giving each pip the name of one of her friends. The pip which fell off first showed that the sweetheart whose name it bore was fickle.

The same charm may be tried with chestnuts. Name each chestnut, place them on the bars of the grate, and murmur this rhyme :

" *If you love me, pop and fly,*
If not, lie there silently."

If the chestnut pops and flies towards her, he whose name it bears is thinking of her. If it burns away he will not be true.

Here is an old Scottish charm believed in by many Scots lassies. On All Hallow-e'en girls must go into the garden in couples, and with their eyes fast closed—they then pull the first plant they touch and, from its nature, so they foretell the kind of sweetheart they will have during the next twelve months. If the plant is straight, he will be honest and true ; if crooked, then he will be false. If the heart of the plant is hard, his heart will be hard, but if soft, then he will be tender-hearted. The amount of money he has is indicated by the amount of earth which clings to the root of the plant.

" JULIETTA."

THE ROAD OF LIFE

PLAY this game and find what destiny lies before you. Take a pack of playing cards and turn up the first. If it is a 7, you " move " seven divisions of the road ; if a 5, five divisions, and so on. Aces count 1 and all court cards 10. Then turn up the second card and move on in the same way. If one of your moves finishes on (A) it means " You have a false friend " ; if on (B) " Your plans will be hindered " ; (C) " Beware of a dark man " ; (D) " Unexpected luck " ; (E) " A chance meeting will lead to an engagement " ; (F) " A rise in position " ; (G) " You will take an important step " ; (H) " Doubts and difficulties " ; (I) " Your industry will be rewarded " ; (J) " A journey, with good luck at the end " ; (K) " A misunderstanding, but it will be cleared up " ; (L) " You will discover his true nature " ; (M) " A great surprise " ; (N) " News from over the water " ; (O) " You are in for a gay time " ; (P) " Beware ; someone means harm to you " ; (Q) " A fair man will prove a friend in need " ; (R) " You will be faced with a difficult choice " ; (S) " You will receive a proposal of marriage " ; (T) " Wedding bells will ring for you."

CHAPTER XIII

" Confessions "

An amusing " party " game—How to read your friends'
characters from their favourite colours—Flowers—Film favour-
ites—Recreations, etc. etc.

chart on the opposite page, and ask your victim to confess her (or his) tastes in each column. Then put down the numbers of the items she (or he) has chosen. If the answer to any question is, " I don't like any of them," put down a O.

For instance, if her favourite colour among those given is pink (4), favourite flower wallflower (4), favourite male film star Tom Walls (9), her favourite woman film star Gracie Fields (8), country she would visit Australia (1), favourite occupation swimming (6), and the woman she would like to be Lady Diana Manners (9), you consult the list, find the set of numbers that correspond, and read out your friend's " character." It has not been possible to include all the combinations of the seventy numbers—they would run into thousands and fill a book in themselves ! —but the most likely ones have been selected. If you cannot find a set that corresponds exactly with your " victim's," choose the nearest.

THIS game is for amusement only ; it is not intended to be a serious method of character reading, and you and your friends will find it great fun. At the same time, it is based on sound psychological principles, and you will be surprised how often it " hits the mark."

It is quite simple. Just take the chart on the opposite page, and ask

Ask your friends these questions and write down the numbers of their answers. Then find the corresponding set in the following pages.

WHICH OF THESE COLOURS DO YOU LIKE BEST ?

1. Pale Blue.
2. Mauve.
3. Light Green.
4. Pink.
5. Yellow.
6. Scarlet.
7. Crimson.
8. Dark Green.
9. Dark Blue.
10. Purple.

AND WHICH OF THESE FLOWERS ?

1. Violet.
2. Lily of the Valley.
3. Primrose.
4. Wallflower.
5. Geranium.
6. Rose.
7. Carnation.
8. Tulip.
9. Begonia.
10. Heliotrope.

WHICH OF THESE FILM ACTORS DO YOU MOST ENJOY SEEING ?

1. George Arliss.
2. Ronald Colman.
3. Gordon Harker.
4. Ralph Lynn
5. Douglas Fairbanks (Senior).
6. Jack Holt.
7. Jack Hulbert.
8. Jack Buchanan.
9. Tom Walls.
10. Wallace Beery.

AND WHICH OF THESE FILM ACTRESSES ?

1. Florence Arliss.
2. Janet Gaynor.
3. Katharine Hepburn.
4. Mary Brough.
5. Alison Skipworth.
6. Jessie Matthews.
7. Cicely Courtneidge.
8. Gracie Fields.
9. Mae West.
10. Greta Garbo.

WHICH COUNTRY WOULD YOU MOST LIKE TO VISIT ?

1. Australia.
2. South Africa.
3. Norway.
4. The United States.
5. Italy.
6. India.
7. Egypt.
8. Japan.
9. China.
10. The South Sea Islands.

WHICH OF THESE RECREATIONS DO YOU PREFER ?

Girls.	*Men.*
1. Needlework.	1. Cricket.
2. Reading.	2. Reading.
3. Tennis.	3. Tennis.
4. Cycling.	4. Gardening.
5. Boating.	5. Rowing.
6. Swimming.	6. Swimming.
7. Hiking.	7. Hiking.
8. Dancing.	8. Dancing.
9. Skating.	9. Football.
10. Motoring.	10. Motoring.

WHICH OF THESE NOTABLE PEOPLE, IF ANY, WOULD YOU MOST LIKE TO BE ?

Women.

1. Lady Oxford.
2. Miss Ishbel MacDonald.
3. Miss Ethel M. Dell.
4. Dame Laura Knight.
5. Dame Clara Butt.
6. Miss Dorothy Round.
7. Miss Gladys Cooper.
8. Mrs. Amy Mollison.
9. Lady Diana Manners.
10. Greta Garbo.

Men.

1. Sir Oswald Mosley.
2. Sir Malcolm Campbell.
3. Signor Marconi.
4. Sir Alan Cobham.
5. Don Bradman.
6. F. J. Perry.
7. Alex James.
8. Jack Petersen.
9. Douglas Fairbanks (Senior).
10. Jack Hylton.

Girls

1, 1, 1, 1, 0, 1, 0 :
You are rather an old-fashioned girl, with simple tastes and a practical disposition, shy and sweet-natured. You have scarcely yet begun to dream of romance.

1, 1, 2, 5, 8, 1, 5 :
You are very quiet and unassuming, and not in the least demonstrative, but you are very, very kind and capable of a deep, life-long love and boundless sacrifice. You are, indeed, too ready to give in to other people, and you should beware of your trust and generosity being wasted on unworthy objects.

1, 4, 1, 2, 6, 1, 0 :
You are quite clever and capable really, but you do not think half enough of yourself. You are too ready to believe that other people know better than you, because they are more self-confident and self-assertive. You should try to stand up for yourself and your opinions more.

1, 4, 2, 2 or 9, 0 1 or 2, 1, 0 :
You like simple ways ; " love in a cottage " is your idea of happiness. You are good-natured and even-tempered.

1, 5, 8, 1, 0, 3, 2 :
You are very conventional, with a great regard for what other people think and say ; you dislike demonstrative affection, and men will probably think you are cold.

1, 9, 3, 9, 7, 5, 0 :
You have a very placid disposition, and are not too disposed to exert yourself. You are fond of pleasure, but expect it to be provided for you rather than to go out and find it. You are, however, appreciative of all that is done for you.

2, 1, 2, 2, 5, 2, 3 :
You have too sympathetic a heart ; you become far too upset by other people's troubles—even the imaginary troubles of characters in books, plays and films. But you have a sweet disposition, if a little sad, and men will find you very comforting.

2, 1, 3, 4, 3, 8, 9 :
You are rather moody ; gay and sad by turns, for no apparent reason, and a little discontented ; men find you a little difficult to understand, and you will be happiest married to one with a very sympathetic temperament and a great deal of patience.

2, 2, 1, 1, 3, 2, 2 or 3 :
You are studious, serious and thoughtful, and not very affectionate ; you think more of making a career for yourself than of love and marriage.

2, 10, 2, 3, 5, 1, 7 :
You have a great love of beauty in every form ; you may be rather a dreamy person, and not too practical, but you can find a delight in lovely things that more worldly-wise folk miss.

3, 1, 2, 2 or 3, 4, 2, 3 :
Your husband will be a lucky man, for you will not only cook his meals and darn his socks conscientiously, but you will be a partner in whom he can confide, and you will do your best to help him on.

3, 2, 9, 9, 6, 10, 9 :
You are rather a quiet, shy little thing, but inwardly you think

you would love to " kick over the traces " and do something dashing and unconventional. You are not very likely, however, to make your dream come true.

3, 3, 1, 1, 1 2 or 4, 3, 6 or 8 :
You are a lover of open country, of animals and birds and all wild things ; you prefer comfort to appearances.

3, 4, 6, 7, 4, 3, 1 or 2 :
You are quiet but capable and with a practical business head. If you are not exactly the type to thrust your way on in the world, at least you are well able to take care of yourself.

3, 5, 10, 2, 1 or 2, 7, 2 :
You have very simple tastes and wishes, and no very great ambitions. You will be happiest living a simple country life, for anything in the nature of stress or strain is actually bad for you.

3, 8, 6, 4, 4, 4, 2 :
You are one of those efficient, thorough and conscientious people; you like everything neat and tidy and in order ; you appreciate politeness and correct behaviour.

4, 2, 1, 1, 0 1 or 2, 1, 0 :
Cheerful and contented, you are the sunshine of your home ; it will be some time before you are tempted to leave it.

4, 3, 4 or 7, 4 or 7, 0 or 4, 8, 0 or 1 :
You are so apt to see the funny side of things that you will have difficulty in making people take you seriously.

4, 4, 9, 8, 1 or 2, 6, 9 :
You are a happy-go-lucky girl, taking things as they come and making the best of them ; you meet your troubles with a smile and a stiff upper-lip, confident that they will turn out right in the end. Money and possessions do not mean a great deal to you ; the things you appreciate are kindness and friendship.

4, 6, 3 or 4, 4 or 5, 4, 2, 0 :
You have a fund of cheery common sense and a great sense of humour ; you will get on well with men, but it may be some time before you meet Mr. " Right."

4, 7, 5, 6, 10, 7, 8 :
You are a jolly, breezy girl, a " good pal " to your men friends, and loyal to your girl pals. You will probably not marry very early, but when you do, if you choose wisely, you will be very happy.

4, 7, 7 or 8, 7 or 8, 0 or 4, 8, 9 :
You are fond of fun and gaiety ; at present you are apt to take life and lovers lightly, and prefer having a good time to undertaking responsibilities.

4, 9, 7, 7, 8, 8, 1 :
Lighthearted and gay, you are fond of social life and conversation ; you have a quick, alert mind and are good at witty repartee. When you marry you will love entertaining, even if only in a small way, and your parties will go with a swing.

5, 3, 1, 1, 3, 9, 2 :
You are quiet in manner and reserved, but you have a will of your own, and once you have made up your mind you do not change it easily. But you do not

thrust your opinions on other people ; you are content to let them go their way if they will let you go yours.

5, 6, 7, 8, 8, 8, 7 :
You are fond of fun and amusement, but you are by no means a mere butterfly. You have a firm will and a shrewd sense of the value of things.

5, 7, 5, 8, 1 or 2, 7, 9 :
You have an affectionate disposition, but you do not let your heart rule your head. You have little patience with weaklings, and would never care for a man you could not respect in every way.

5, 8, 6, 4, 4, 7, 9 :
You are ambitious, self-reliant and ready to stand on your own feet. You will be happiest with a husband who will treat you as an equal partner. You will not put up with being " bossed," yet you will have little respect for a man who will allow you to " boss " him.

5, 9, 8, 6, 9, 10, 9 :
You have rather expensive tastes, and are fond of dress and show. You will not be happy as a poor man's wife, though you have the strength of mind to face adversity, if it comes, with courage.

6, 6, 2, 5, 7, 8, 7 :
You have an affectionate disposition and a longing for romance. You rebel against the dreary humdrum of everyday life, and want change, colour and movement. You should not marry and " settle down " too early, but at the same time, do not let discontent master you.

6, 6, 6, 5, 6, 10, 7 :
You have an affectionate disposition, but rather a hasty temper, though you are just as quick to relent and to forgive. You would never cherish a grudge or do anyone a deliberate ill-turn.

6, 7, 3, 7, 8, 10, 1 :
You will probably find in life that your heart and your head are often at war. You are very intelligent and good at your work, take an interest in it and are anxious to get on. At the same time you have a warm heart, and business life and worldly success alone will not content you.

6, 8, 7, 6, 6, 8, 9 :
You are a popular girl, full of life and fun, and thoroughly enjoy a gay time, but you think a good deal of yourself and are a little ready to take offence.

6, 9, 9, 8, 1 or 2, 10, 8 :
You are a dashing, up-to-date girl, full of courage and energy. You are rather impulsive, and a little impatient of slowness of any kind, in thought, speech or action, but you are very generous and good-hearted.

7, 4, 2, 3, 1 or 2, 2, 3 :
You have a very affectionate nature, and a very unselfish one. When you love you will give your whole heart, and no sacrifice you may be called upon to make for " him," will be too great. Money and position will mean little to you, so long as you have plenty of love.

7, 6, 8, 6, 6, 8, 9 :
You are very popular with men, and at present, at any rate, you like to have plenty of them around you. You do not take any of them very seriously—but a day will come when you meet Mr. " Right," and then you will forget all the others.

7, 7, 3, 5, 5, 4, 5 :
You have a very tender and sympathetic heart ; you cannot bear to see pain and suffering, and cruelty and injustice rouse you to indignation. You are eager to help to put things right, at whatever cost to yourself.

7, 7, 5, 9, 1 or 2, 10, 8 :
You are one of those people who are alive to the finger-tips ; whatever you do, you throw your whole heart and soul into it. You have plenty of courage and enterprise, and have no use for cautious people and weaklings. Beware of being too impulsive, especially in love.

7, 8, 10, 9, 9, 10, 1 :
You have a very strong personality, and love to exercise your power over others—especially men. You delight in making them fetch and carry for you. But you would not be deliberately unkind, and you are capable of very deep, intense and lasting affection.

7, 9, 5, 6, 4, 9, 9 :
You are ambitious ; you want to be rich and distinguished, and you have gifts and force of character that should help you to reach your goal. But you are not the cold and calculating type, and beware lest your deep feelings run away with you.

7, 10, 2, 10, 3, 1 or 2, 10 :
You have an intensely affectionate disposition, and your emotions are far more profound than people suspect. You are serious and thoughtful, disliking frivolity and flippancy ; you will not give your heart readily, but when you do, you will " count the world well lost for love."

8, 1, 1, 1, 3, 2, 1 :
You are reserved and unassuming, and people often under-estimate the quiet strength of your character. You are thoughtful and studious, rather slow to act, but very sure. You take life seriously, though by no means sadly.

8, 2, 1, 2, 4, 2, 2 :
You are in your element when at work. You are efficient, reliable, conscientious and keep your head in emergencies. You are not of a very affectionate disposition, and no romantic lover is likely to sweep you off your feet. You are rather indifferent to appearances.

8, 4, 2, 5, 3, 5, 3 :
Men find you comforting. You may not be demonstratively sympathetic, but you are a good listener, and your calmness and wise advice soothes them and restores their faith in themselves. You love a country life, and dislike towns.

8, 6, 2, 3, 0, 3, 5 :
You have a sweet, placid disposition, and a kind heart rather than an affectionate one. You are fond of children and animals, and your mother-instinct is strong. You like to protect, soothe and comfort the sick, sad and weary.

8, 7, 6, 8, 5, 6, 1 :
You do not attract men readily, but you will make a splendid wife to the one who learns to understand and appreciate you. You will check his impulsiveness, inspire him to work hard, and guide him with your calm, sound judgment.

8, 8, 9, 7, 6, 5, 4 :
You are not in the least assertive, but quietly, smoothly and tactfully you usually contrive to get your own way. You have your own ideas on life, and are not easily diverted from any purpose you form. You are very even-tempered and can be relied upon to keep your head in an emergency.

8, 10, 2, 10, 10, 5, 5 :
" Still waters run deep " is a proverb that applies particularly to you. Outwardly you are calm and serene, you hate fuss and flurry ; but you have great depth of feeling. You are steadfast in your friendships and loyal to your ideals, but you do not easily

forget an insult or an injury. You do not care very much for men, but when you meet the right one you will give him an intense, unselfish love that will endure for life.

9, 1, 4, 4, 3, 8, 10 :
You are something of a puzzle to your friends. At times you seem gay and pleasure-loving, at others you are gloomy and abstracted. Actually you are burdened by melancholy thoughts at times, and try hard to escape from them.

9, 1, 10, 1, 3, 1, 2 :
You take life far too seriously and think too much in a groove. You are clever, conscientious and determined, but you would get on better if you gave yourself more recreation and amusement and so widened your interests.

9, 3, 2, 2, 5, 3, 7 :
You do not wear your heart on your sleeve, and are quite incapable of flirtation or deliberately trying to attract a man. But you have a sweet, though rather serious, nature, and a wealth of affection deep inside you. You are loyal, patient and brave, and though you guard your heart carefully, once you give it, it will be with all your soul, and for ever and a day.

9, 4, 9, 8, 1 or 2, 6, 9 :
You are very capable and intelligent, but you have not enough faith in yourself. You would like to do big things, but have not the confidence to attempt them. You need the companionship of someone brisk and cheerful to laugh away your doubts.

9, 8, 5, 10, 9, 10, 10 :
Your feelings are not easily aroused, but they are exceptionally deep and strong. You are rather jealous and very possessive and will resent your lover or husband having any interests that he does not share with you. You are easily wounded, but seldom reveal the fact; you are rather too apt to brood over your wrongs, real or imaginary, and let them rankle. You do not make friends easily, and seldom have more than one at a time.

9, 10, 2, 2, 10, 5, 5 :
Unless you bestir yourself, you will waste your talents. You have great capabilities, and a firm character, and your friends find you a rock to lean on, but you do need rousing to push yourself on. In love you are far from cold, but you may miss a golden opportunity by being too distant and reserved. You find it difficult to show your affection.

10, 1, 2, 2, 1 or 2, 2, 3 :
You have a very affectionate disposition and a simple and trusting nature. You are inclined to believe the best of everyone, and many disillusionments, though they will wound you deeply, will not entirely shake your faith in the goodness of human nature. You will be wise to listen to the advice of others in your love affairs, and you should not marry without knowing a man well, but with an affectionate, loyal, considerate husband you should be wonderfully happy.

10, 2, 1, 3, 3, 1, 2 :

You have very high ideals and live up to them whole-heartedly. You will take life seriously and give your best. But you are difficult to please, critical of others, and deeply hurt when they seem to fail you. You will set your lover on a pedestal and will be grieved if he fails to stay on it. You have, however, your own hidden weakness, and the knowledge of it should soften your judgment of others.

10, 6, 3, 8, 4, 8, 7 :

You are rather unconventional and make friendships that to others may seem difficult to understand. But you have a kindly heart and a quick instinct for summing up human nature. You have no use for shams and pretences. You take people as you find them, and make the best of them as they are, without being critical. You are fond of fun, but have a serious side to your character as well. You will very probably make a match that your friends consider unsuitable, and surprise them by being ideally happy with the man of your choice.

10, 7, 2, 9, 7, 5, 10 :

You are very affectionate indeed, and your dreams are all of romance. You will probably have a succession of love affairs—for you are irresistibly attractive to men—and to you, at any rate, they will all be serious affairs, for you cannot love lightly. At last, however, you should find peace and happiness with some-one who approaches your ideal.

10, 8, 9, 9, 1 or 2, 9, 1 :

You have a very strong and vigorous nature. Whatever you turn your hand to you carry through determinedly, and when you set your heart on a thing you usually win it sooner or later. You will demand a great deal from your lover or husband, and he may find you exacting, but you will reward him with a deep, powerful love and unswerving loyalty.

10, 9, 8, 10, 6, 10, 9 :

You have an almost passionate desire for comfort, beauty, wealth and position, and may be seriously tempted to sacrifice love for these things. You will not, however, make your decision without considering it very carefully, for you do nothing in haste. Certainly "love in a cottage" has no attraction for you and would only mean disillusionment and unhappiness.

10, 10, 2, 2, 5, 2, 4 :

You are inclined to live in a world of dreams, to see things not as they are but as you would like them to be. This may bring you some rude awakenings in life— but you have the happy knack of relapsing into your dreams again and finding comfort in them. You will idealise your lover, but if he is the right man you will be quite content to see him through rose-coloured glasses all your life.

Men

1, 1, 2, 2, 0, 4, 0 :
He is rather a stick-in-the-mud, and is not likely to go very far in life, but he has no vices. If you are content with a safe, peaceful, humdrum life, he may suit you very well.

1, 2, 5, 3, 0, 2, 0 :
He is a serious young man, with simple, old-fashioned tastes. He will expect his wife to dress neatly, behave very correctly, cook well, keep his socks darned, and study his tastes and wishes.

1, 4, 5, 5, 1 or 2, 4, 1 :
He is capable and has ideas, but he suffers from a lack of self-confidence. A wife who understands him and knows how to give him faith in himself may push him on, but she may have to fight some of his battles for him.

1, 5, 5, 1, 4, 1, 5 :
He is terribly conventional, and attaches far too much importance to what the world thinks. He is not very likely to strike out a line for himself, but will probably do well in some settled job. He will be kind to his wife, but not easy to please.

1, 7, 2, 2, 7, 3, 9 :
He has an affectionate disposition and would rather like to be a romantic lover, but does not quite know how! He is a thoroughly " good sort," though, and a girl who never pines to be swept off her feet by tempestuous wooing could be very happy with him.

1, 10, 10, 10, 10, 10, 9 :
He would be rather a " gay dog " if he could, but he hasn't the courage. He thinks a good deal of himself, but a girl will find it quite easy to twist him round her finger.

2, 1, 1, 1, 3, 2, 1 :
He is rather clever, and of a serious and studious turn of mind, but he lacks the driving force that gets a man far up the ladder of success. He is gently affectionate, but not demonstrative.

2, 3, 5, 2, 1 or 2, 4, 5 :
He likes a country life and will never be really happy in a town. His tastes are simple, and he is easy to please.

2, 6, 1, 5, 6, 6, 1 :
He is a " good sort," kind-hearted and sympathetic, always ready to " help lame dogs over stiles." He may be a little too easy-going, but his wife will find him a considerate and attentive husband.

2, 7, 2, 10, 8, 5, 1 :
He has an affectionate disposition and does not forget the little compliments, the little attentions, that mean so much to a girl. He is sensitive, though, and easily cast down, and is at his best with a girl who will be careful not to hurt his feelings and will cheer him up.

2, 8, 8, 7, 5, 8, 10 :
He is fond of parties and amusements, and will only care for a girl who shares his tastes. He is not likely to neglect his work for his pleasures, though, and will probably do well in a small way.

2, 10, 1, 10, 10, 5, 0 :
He is rather a dreamer, and apt to put off till to-morrow the things he ought to have done the day before yesterday, and is apt to blame life because he does not get on ! He needs a bright, brisk girl to wake him up.

3, 2, 8, 6, 0, 8, 10 :
He is not very clever nor has he much strength of character, but he is a pleasant, good-tempered companion.

3, 3, 5, 2, 1 or 2, 7, 9 :
He is simple in his tastes and very even-tempered, and likes a quiet, placid life ; he is unsuited to the rush and hurry of towns.

3, 5, 6, 2, 0, 7, 3 :
He is careful and conscientious, but a plodder ; he will never " set the Thames on fire," and is too ready to " knuckle under " to stronger personalities, but he is quite easy to get on with.

3, 8, 5, 9, 1 or 2, 9, 7 or 8 :
A shy lover this, and not at all a passionate one ; in fact, he is not really very interested in girls as yet.

4, 3, 4, 4, 4, 3, 9 :
He is a cheery soul, and a good companion, and reasonably affectionate, but he has no very great depth of character.

4, 6, 3, 7, 9, 10, 9 :
This is a jolly lad, with a great sense of humour. In fact, he sees the funny side of things so much that you will probably not realise that he can be a very devoted lover.

4, 7, 2, 6, 4, 9, 7 :
He is a cheery lover, full of life and laughter and enthusiasm ; you may think he has too little sentiment, but he can be very tender at times.

4, 7, 8, 8, 8, 8, 10 :
He is good fun, and very good-natured, but he thinks far more of enjoying himself than of getting on in the world. He is a satisfactory lover, but not an exciting one.

4, 8, 9, 8, 4, 6, 8 :
He is ambitious, and though not a grim struggler for success, he takes the hard knocks of life without complaining, and comes up smiling to meet the next.

5, 3, 5, 8, 1 or 2, 7, 2 :
He is a free and easy lad, with a scorn for " dressing up " and appearances generally. To be happy with him you need to be rather happy-go-lucky.

5, 6, 3, 5, 6, 2, 1 :
He is very kind-hearted, and seldom fails to respond to a tale of woe. You will find him thoughtful and considerate, but not more so to you than to anyone else.

5, 7, 2, 10, 7, 10, 8 :
He has an affectionate disposition, but a jealous and possessive one. If he sees his girl with another man there will probably be serious trouble, and he will be rather an exacting husband.

5, 9, 1, 5, 4, 1 or 9, 3 :
He means to get on in the world, and as he is clever, too, he will probably be able to give his wife all the comforts of life, but he is not a tender lover, and his wife will probably complain that he neglects her for his work and his men friends.

5, 10, 1, 9, 5, 5, 0 :
He is rather selfish and quite lazy ; not at all inclined to put himself out for you, but rather expecting you to wait on him. He is shrewd, though, and may make a good deal of money, but not through hard work. He is most likely to be attracted by a handsome, worldly girl.

6, 1, 1, 2, 1 or 2, 1 or 9, 5 or 8 :
He seems rather quiet and shy, and does not know very much about women, but he is capable of a warm-hearted love for the kind of girl who appeals to him—the quiet, modest, old-fashioned type.

6, 2, 1, 5, 3, 2, 1 :
He has very little use for girls. He is a deep thinker and full of high ideals. He burns to right wrongs, and to fight for justice and fair play, and would gladly sacrifice himself for a good cause. A girl is only likely to interest

him if she shares his ideals and is ready to give herself whole-heartedly to whatever cause he is championing.

6, 5, 5, 5, 3, 9, 9 :
He is a real "man's man," full of pluck and "go," but he can be a splendid lover, too, and as a husband will be a sure shield against the hard knocks of life, and loyal through everything.

6, 7, 2, 9, 8, 6, 9 :
He is a great "ladies' man," and knows just how to appeal to them. Many girls find him irresistible. He is not, however, a mere male flirt, and is capable of forming a very real, true affection —probably for a girl who does not particularly admire him.

6, 7, 9, 8, 6, 7, 9 :
You will find him something of a stormy lover. He is intensely affectionate, but his temper is easily aroused. Be careful never to keep him waiting, or to disagree with him, or you will be sorry.

6, 9, 9, 10, 6, 10, 2 :
He is extravagant and fond of show ; if he takes you out he will spend money like water to impress you, and if you really care for him you will be wise to restrain him. He is by no means weak-willed, though, and will learn to be more careful of money when he settles down.

6, 10, 9, 5, 5, 10, 2 :
He suffers from a restless, impulsive disposition. He hates to be kept in a groove, and he is likely to do unwise things for the sheer sake of a change. If you are of the placid type, life with him will be rather dizzying.

7, 6, 1, 2, 8, 6, 0 :
He is soft-hearted, and full of compassion for the unfortunate. Pour your troubles into his willing ear and you will find him very sympathetic and consoling.

7, 6, 8, 8, 8, 10, 10 :
You may think him rather gay and pleasure-loving, but he has deeper emotions than you realise. He is very kind, and as a lover is always thoughtful and considerate.

7, 7, 2, 10, 7, 5, 9 :
He is a romantic lover, masterful and passionate, and will probably rather sweep you off your feet. But he is sincere, and will devote himself to you alone, and give up anything for your sake.

7, 8, 10, 9, 10, 9, 8 :
He has a passionate nature and a temper that is easily roused and not too easily quelled. He is impulsively generous, broad-minded, and can be influenced by appeals to his better nature, but he likes his own way, and opposition only makes him more determined.

7, 9, 5 or 6, 9, 4, 1 or 9, 4 :
Here's a man who is likely to get on in the world, and will not let anyone or anything stand in his way. He will be very affectionate when he is in the mood for affection, but love will only play a secondary part in his life.

8, 1, 6, 3, 5, 4, 3 :
He is very reserved, and takes a great deal of knowing. You will find him rather strait-laced, with very fixed opinions, yet not intolerant. He is the last man in the world to criticise you or interfere in your affairs, but if you ask his advice and help you will be surprised what a comfort he will be.

8, 2, 3, 4, 8, 5, 3 :
He thinks a good deal of himself, and looks down on girls with lofty male superiority, as if he considers them amusing little creatures, but scarcely worth a man's serious attention. But one day he will fall in love, badly, and then your sex will be avenged !

8, 5, 1, 5, 3, 2, 1 :
He is rather an old sobersides, and
not an exciting lover, but as a
friend he is well worth having. He
is calm, shrewd and very discreet
and reliable. If you take your
troubles to him he will probably
tell you that you've been a " silly
little fool "—but he will give you
the wisest of advice.

8, 6, 2, 5, 7, 0, 0 :
He is quiet in manner, and you
might not think there was very
much in him, but he has great
strength of character, and a
kindly heart. He will not be a
romantic lover, but a quietly
devoted and self-sacrificing one.

8, 7, 8, 10, 5, 6, 2 :
Here is a lover who will trust you
implicitly, never believe a word
against you, and stick to you
through thick and thin. He will
put up with the worst treatment
you can give him, not meekly,
but in patient strength.

8, 8, 10, 8, 1 or 2, 5, 8 :
" It's dogged as does it " is his
motto. He is not brilliant, but
he has more forcefulness than
the mere plodder. Once he takes
up a thing he will not let go until
he has seen it through to the end.

9, 1, 1, 5, 3, 1, 5 :
He is a good friend to any girl,
staunch and reliable and not
critical—but a lively girl may
find him depressing, because he
will look on the " black side."

9, 1, 4, 7, 3, 5, 8 :
He suffers badly from depression,
and unless you have a very bright
disposition and a strong character, he will probably make you
unhappy. But if you can be a
cheery influence in his life, he will
be eternally grateful and do all
he can in return.

9, 4, 8, 10, 8, 3, 6 :
He is shy, and has not a very
high opinion of himself. He will
probably love you devotedly in
silence, and never show his
feelings towards you, unless you
give him definite encouragement.

9, 6, 4, 10, 5, 2, 1 :
He is acutely sensitive, and you
will probably often wound his
feelings without realising it, because he is never peevish or
complaining. For this reason he
may seem melancholy, but he
responds to kind treatment.

10, 1, 5, 6, 1 or 2, 1 or 9, 5 or 7 :
He is one of those strong, simple
natures. He is shrewd in his
dealings with men, but a girl
can twist him round her little
finger. He will idealise you, and
you must never betray his trust.

10, 6, 9, 9, 7, 8, 10 :
He will make a very satisfactory
lover, loyal and devoted, unselfish and very affectionate. You
may even find his public demon-
strations of affection embarrass-
ing ! But his companionship is
delightful, for he is eager and enthusiastic and throws himself
wholeheartedly into whatever he
is doing.

10, 7, 2, 9, 5, 6, 9 :
He will be a passionately devoted
lover, willing to give up everything for the girl of his heart, but
expecting the same from her in
return. His emotions are deep
and strong, and though a frivolous girl may attract him, they
are not likely to be really happy
together.

10, 9, 9, 10, 7, 7, 4 :
His is a very strong nature, for
good or ill. Once he has settled
on a line of action he will go
through with it recklessly, regardless of consequences. He is not
easily influenced, but a woman
who is strong-willed enough may
either make or mar him.

" VERITY,"

CHAPTER XIV

Improve Your Luck

How to make the most of your personality—The good points in your appearance—Your walk—Your voice—Charm—How to overcome shyness—The power of thought, etc.

A girl who wishes to improve her personality—and what girl does not ?—must start by taking honest stock of herself, by trying to see herself as she really is, and as she appears to others. When she has come to a sincere conclusion, then she can decide on what steps she is going to take to help herself to acquire charm, poise and fascination.

First, concentrate on your appearance, and do not be too down-hearted if you have to admit that you are not very pretty. Good looks are certainly a great asset, but if you look round your own circle of friends, you will see that it is not always the prettiest girls who are the most popular, or who make the most successful marriages.

You will most certainly have at least one good point. You may have fine eyes, a good skin, nice features, pretty hair, a good figure, a graceful carriage, or a beautiful voice.

WHILE fate, or luck, or chance may play a great part in our lives, heaven helps those who help themselves, and we can improve our fortunes by cultivating and developing our personalities, by making the most of our good points and toning down our bad ones. Many a girl considered " lucky " is merely one who has taken pains to make herself charming and attractive.

Any one of these is an asset, and should be cared for and studied. If you have lovely eyes, you may help to bring out their colour by choosing your dress effects carefully, you can improve the lashes and brows by a little simple beauty treatment, and most important of all, you can refrain from the frowning, discontented expression which, more quickly than anything, will bring lines and wrinkles and thus ruin the loveliest eyes.

A good skin is always attractive, and should be guarded carefully. Soap and water, fresh air, plenty of fruit and fresh vegetables, rest and exercise are Nature's way of keeping a lovely complexion ; you may also help by taking very great care to choose the right make-up, by using it very sparingly, and by protecting your skin from scorching sunshine and cold, roughening winds.

If you have good, regular features, you have an advantage over the girl who is no more than " pretty," for you will be able to select styles of hairdressing, and wear fashions, that are unsuited to her. Study your type and then " dress the part." The smart or striking-looking girl will always attract more attention than the merely pretty one.

We all know how much really lovely hair is admired, and while you cannot choose the colour of your hair, you can improve its natural colour and sheen by choosing the right hair-wash, by brushing it well—the brush is the cheapest and most effective hair-beautifier of all—and then by selecting the style of hairdressing which best suits you. And never mind if that is not the one which is the most fashionable at the moment ! The loveliest hair does not look at its best when arranged in a style unsuited to the head.

A good figure is quite as great an attraction as a pretty face, and if you are naturally well-proportioned and graceful you have a great asset. The right exercises will help to keep you shapely, and the right clothes will help to show off the natural, graceful lines of your figure.

A good carriage and graceful walk usually go with a good figure, but may be acquired with patience and practice, and are well worth the time and trouble spent on their acquisition.

A beautiful speaking voice is an immense attraction, and many a man has first been drawn to a girl because her voice charmed him. Remember, all charming voices are quiet and sweet in tone. A loud, shrill voice is always ugly, and a harsh voice will detract greatly from the charm of the prettiest girl.

If your voice is not all you would wish it to be, try reading aloud to yourself. Listen most carefully to the tone of your voice, and when you find a shrill or harsh note creeping in, correct it, aiming always at a quiet, even note, but avoiding the flat, colourless voice of an uninteresting personality. Listening to good actresses in good plays or films will help a great deal, for you will hear the kind of voice which is best worth imitating.

Charm

CHARM, that nameless fascination which will bring a girl friends, lovers and success, is a quality difficult to describe in words. It is much more important than looks, for a charming woman will always outshine a merely pretty one, and with care, patience and determination charm can be cultivated.

If you will consider the attractions of the girls people call charming, you will find that one of their most outstanding qualities is their ability to seem interested in those about them. This interest may not always be quite genuine, for it is hardly possible for the ordinary girl to feel interested in everyone she meets, but she who wishes to cultivate charm must certainly appear to take more interest in those about her than she does in herself, and above all she must be a good listener—especially if she wishes to attract the opposite sex.

Some girls do not quite understand just what is meant by a good listener. It means much more than just to sit silent while another person speaks. The good listener looks at the person who is talking to her, follows what they are saying with attention, and by her remarks shows that she is genuinely interested in the subject of conversation.

Men in particular appreciate a good listener. If a man is introduced to a girl who listens to all he says with interest, and replies attentively, he will most probably take away with him a far more lasting impression than he would of a pretty girl who sat silent and looked as if she was thinking of something else all the time.

The good listener must know how to encourage her companion to talk, and to talk about the things which interest him most. She herself may not be interested in those things, but if she can make her companion feel that she is, then she has learned one of the most important lessons in the art of being charming.

A man who is naturally talkative will enjoy being listened to with attention, while the shy, rather reserved man will be drawn out and encouraged by the feeling that he is talking to someone who is really interested in him and his doings.

The girl who wishes to be charming must cultivate a good memory. If she can remember little facts about people she has met, what they said to her, and what they told her about themselves, and thus show them that they made an impression upon her—a thing we all like to feel we have done to people we meet—she will have gone a long way to acquiring a reputation for charm.

To be able to judge character, even if only to a slight extent, is a great help, for it enables a girl to tell what will most interest her companion, and if it is a man, how best to interest him in her should she wish to do so. She will be able to judge if he is the type of man who wants to be taken very seriously, or who appreciates good-natured "ragging," or who is craving for sympathy and understanding.

From these remarks, it may be thought that the charming girl must be a little insincere. Not a bit of it! Naturalness and simplicity are the keynotes of charm, but to these must be added a real interest in people, a genuine friendliness and a desire to please, and it is very difficult to please and interest people unless we know, or take the trouble to learn, something about them.

While the "charming" girl is usually the centre of attraction, she loses half her charm if she makes obvious efforts to hold people's attention. She must always be ready to recognise another girl's attractions—"cattiness" and charm never go together—to keep cheerfully good-tempered, nor take offence easily, and, in homely language, to take the rough with the smooth. The girl who can be charming only when everything goes well, will find that her "charm" does not exert a very binding spell.

The Shy Girl

THE girl who is shy in company, who finds it difficult to talk to strangers, and who is never at her ease in a crowd, may think her shyness will always be a handicap, but this need not be so. To many men, shyness in a girl is an added charm, and in any case she can do a great deal to overcome this drawback.

Shyness is really self-consciousness. The shy girl is silent and ill-at-ease because she thinks others are noticing her, criticising her, talking about her. In this she is usually mistaken, for as a very wise man once remarked : " Do not think others are thinking about you ; they are not. They are like you, and are thinking about themselves ! "

The best way for a girl to overcome her shyness is to think not of herself but of others. When she is in company and finds it difficult to start a conversation, as the shy girl usually does, let her think of the person to whom she is talking, and try to guess what will interest him. Once she starts him talking on one of his favourite subjects she need only listen sympathetically, and her companion will be favourably impressed by her.

To enter a room full of strangers is, for the shy girl, always something of an ordeal, but it will help her enormously if she can say to herself : " I am just one of the crowd. No one is thinking particularly of me, or noticing me more than I am noticing them. I will just be myself."

The shy girl dreads meeting fresh people, but one of the best ways of overcoming this dread is to meet as many fresh people as possible, and many a girl has lost her uncomfortable shyness by joining a tennis, social or dance club, and mixing freely with the other members until she is quite at ease with them.

The Power of Thought

WHATEVER may be your belief in mascots and talismans, in omens and portents, nothing can exert so powerful an influence upon your future as your own attitude of mind.

Wise men who have studied the occult sciences, and who have devoted their lives to gaining knowledge of the unseen forces which govern our destinies, tell us that we can so control and order our thoughts that they will attract love, luck and happiness.

To attract happy things you must have a happy, cheerful outlook. The old saying which tells us troubles go where they are expected is true, and in the opposite sense, good luck goes where it is looked for.

In no circumstances should you allow yourself to drop into the habit —a very easy one to develop—of looking upon yourself as an unlucky person, or one to whom trouble is sure to come.

" Things always go wrong with me ! " we hear people say, and by expecting trouble they prepare themselves to attract it.

Try to train yourself into the opposite line of thought. When you rise in the morning smile cheerfully at yourself in the mirror and say : " I'm going to be lucky to-day ! " Just by this simple practice you have put yourself into the right frame of mind to attract good fortune.

Select your mascot or talisman with care—other chapters of this book will have told you the best way to select your most suitable charm—wear it, or have it about you constantly, and believe in it.

Remember, the most powerful talisman becomes useless if it is worn by a person who has no faith in its powers.

Banish resolutely from your mind all dark, gloomy, pessimistic thoughts, and concentrate on all that is cheerful and hopeful. Don't dwell on " failure," look forward to " success." Look determinedly on the bright side and you will find that your side will become bright.

As it is with luck, so it may be with love. Never allow yourself to think : " Why should he love me ? " Say rather : " Why *shouldn't* he love me ? " and you will thus be ready to receive love when it comes. It is the bright, cheery, hopeful girl who attracts affection, for she helps people to believe in themselves and thus they come to believe in her.

The girl who inspires a man, whose company makes him feel more fit to play his part in the world, is the one he is likely to ask to be his partner in life.

Remember, your thoughts—the thoughts which come most easily to you—make an atmosphere, or as clever people call it an " aura," around you. Each thought of the same kind strengthens that atmosphere, and makes it more powerful to attract either good or bad luck, so make up your mind that you will think only the bright, cheerful, hopeful kind of thoughts such as will bring bright things to you. Practise doing this steadily for a month and you will be surprised to find how much it has helped you.

" AURORA."

CHAPTER XV

Lucky Birthday Forecasts

Will you be lucky in love ?—Will you be wealthy, or will your greatest riches be in happiness ?—The date of your birth will tell you what Fate holds in store.

Jan. 4th. You will have to fight hard for what you most desire in life, but you will get it in the end.

Jan. 5th. Yours will be a long and happy life.

Jan. 6th. You will have enemies, but your good friends will outnumber them.

Jan. 7th. The longer you live, the more will luck exert itself on your behalf.

Jan. 8th. There will be plenty of love in your life, but you must cherish it to keep it.

Jan. 9th. You will be lucky in most of the things you set out to do.

Jan. 10th. The little things in life may go wrong for you, but not the big things.

Jan. 1st. You will be rich, not in money, but in love.

Jan. 2nd. Happiness in love will come only after many disappointments.

Jan. 3rd. Money will come to you in the latter half of your life.

Jan. 11th.	A very happy married life will be yours.
Jan. 12th.	You may not have wealth, but you will certainly have health and happiness.
Jan. 13th.	Take care you do not fly too high in your aims.
Jan. 14th.	You are likely to have many love affairs, but your final choice will be a wise one.
Jan. 15th.	You are destined to find your greatest happiness with a home and children of your own.
Jan. 16th.	Many ups and downs fill your life—be hopeful and there will be more "ups" than "downs."
Jan. 17th.	Love may call for sacrifices from you, but you will never regret making them.
Jan. 18th.	Try not to expect too much from life, for you may have disappointments.
Jan. 19th.	Hard work will be your lot, but it will be well rewarded.
Jan. 20th.	Spring should be the luckiest time of the year for you.
Jan. 21st.	Never despair, for luck will usually smile for you when things are darkest.
Jan. 22nd.	There will be plenty of romance in your life.
Jan. 23rd.	Love will bring you good luck as well as happiness.
Jan. 24th.	Big responsibilities will be yours.
Jan. 25th.	You will seldom want for money, but you will have to work hard for it.
Jan. 26th.	Many friends will be yours; it rests with yourself how many of them you keep.
Jan. 27th.	You will have many problems to decide in life, and the greatest of them will be a love-choice.
Jan. 28th.	Nothing is beyond your reach if you try hard enough for it.
Jan. 29th.	Yours will be a long life and a happy one, with plenty of love in it.
Jan. 30th.	Marriage will change your life from dullness to gladness; children will gladden it still more.
Jan. 31st.	Success can be yours, but to attain it you must learn perseverance and patience.
Feb. 1st.	You may not make a great deal of your own life, but you will live to see your children do well.
Feb. 2nd.	Money will come to you at a time when you most need it.
Feb. 3rd.	Luck will be on your side in most things, but not in speculation.
Feb. 4th.	Your sweetheart will need your help if he is to succeed; especially after marriage.
Feb. 5th.	The longer you live, the higher you are likely to climb.
Feb. 6th.	Some of your "castles in the air" will col-

Feb. 7th. lapse, but the most cherished ones have great possibilities. Very happy family life will be yours.

Feb. 8th. Jealousy may spoil things for you, but it will not keep you from eventual happiness.

Feb. 9th. Good luck is likely to come in greater measure after you are thirty.

Feb. 10th. You will be particularly lucky in some specially important venture.

Feb. 11th. Your talents could take you a long way if you will only use them rightly.

Feb. 12th. Big responsibilities are coming your way; you will need to keep a level head.

Feb. 13th. You are likely to have more than one love in your life.

Feb. 14th. Some disappointments are in store, but happier things will follow.

Feb. 15th. Great ability is yours and will take you far.

Feb. 16th. There will be few remarkable happenings in your life; quiet content will be yours.

Feb. 17th. Plenty of opportunities will come your way; take care you make the most of them.

Feb. 18th. You will encounter many changes; mostly for the better.

Feb. 19th. Disappointments in love will be yours, but happiness will not be denied you.

Feb. 20th. Influential friends will prove of enormous help to you.

Feb. 21st. Success in work, and happiness in love, are in store for you.

Feb. 22nd. Enemies may hinder you, but good friends will help you through.

Feb. 23rd. You will have money, and will live to a great age to enjoy it.

Feb. 24th. Your children will help you a great deal as they grow up.

Feb. 25th. You are likely to travel far.

Feb. 26th. Great possibilities in life could be yours if you will only make use of opportunities.

Feb. 27th. Few things will be denied you if you go " all out " for them.

Feb. 28th. You may be inclined to under-estimate your abilities. Cultivate greater confidence.

Feb. 29th. Not knowing just what you want may be a great drawback to you in life, but you will get *somewhere*.

March 1st. More than the usual measure of happiness will be meted out to you.

March 2nd. Seek to control your rather restless nature, or you may never get what you want.

March 3rd. Love will be the most powerful influence in your life, altering everything for you.

March 4th. Your life will hold an abundance of luck.

March 5th. The man you marry will find his way to

success and prosperity through your help.

March 6th. Do not despair if things go wrong for you early in life ; everything will be in your favour later.

March 7th. You will lose many opportunities in life through lack of confidence, but will make good in the end.

March 8th. Your greatest happiness will come with middle age.

March 9th. A happy home, with loving children, will be yours.

March 10th. Life's road holds many obstacles for you, but luck has a strong influence in your favour.

March 11th. Money troubles will come, but will solve themselves in an unexpected way.

March 12th. You will need to be very careful in the choice of a marriage partner. Guard against impulsiveness.

March 13th. Success and even fame are within your reach if you use your abilities wisely.

March 14th. Your life will hold much pleasure, but do not let it spoil your work.

March 15th. Worry will be your greatest load in life ; and most of the troubles will never happen !

March 16th. Do not aim too high ; your best sphere is in a home of your own.

March 17th. Many difficult problems will confront you, but marriage will solve most of them.

March 18th. You have a great influence over others ; use it wisely.

March 19th. Your greatest happiness will be in home and husband.

March 20th. There will be plenty of variety in your life, and many ups and downs.

March 21st. You will achieve many things by persistency alone.

March 22nd. You will find love in an unexpected quarter.

March 23rd. Your children will prove a blessing to you when you grow old.

March 24th. Love of adventure may lead you into queer places.

March 25th. Do not expect too much luck in life until you are past thirty-five.

March 26th. A loving husband will help you over your worst difficulties.

March 27th. Take care not to let opportunities pass you by through being too cautious.

March 28th. You will be most successful after you have learnt one or two lessons in life.

March 29th. You can achieve wonderful things in life if you have the right partner by your side.

March 30th. Too much attention to detail will cause you to miss the biggest things in life, unless you take care.

March 31st. You may never be rich, but you will always have sufficient for your needs.

April 1st. You will be lucky in love, and in most other things as well.

April 2nd. Quiet, humble surroundings will bring you the greatest happiness.

April 3rd. You may lack money, but not love.

April 4th. You may never realise your ambitions, but you are sure to get a good way along the road.

April 5th. Focus your energy in the right direction and it will work wonders for you.

April 6th. With care in the choice of a life partner marriage will be wonderfully successful for you.

April 7th. Friends will flock round you wherever you go. You will always be popular.

April 8th. Your children will be clever and successful.

April 9th. Restlessness may spoil your chances if you do not combat it.

April 10th. A long life will be yours, with plenty of love on the way.

April 11th. You are likely to do well in life if you have plenty of chances of using your originality.

April 12th. Take care that pride does not become a handicap to you in life.

April 13th. You may fail in little things, but in the big things you will be surprisingly successful.

April 14th. You will reap a rich harvest from hard work.

April 15th. You will not know the greatest measure of happiness until love comes into its own.

April 16th. Many good friends will come your way; but a few false ones.

April 17th. Your old age will be filled with deep content.

April 18th. You may be the victim of jealousy and mischief-making, but they will not rob you of happiness.

April 19th. A happy, peaceful old age will be your reward for hard-working youth.

April 20th. Luck is on your side, but it will let you down occasionally.

April 21st. Children will come to mean a great deal to you in your life.

April 22nd. You will win what you most desire through dogged perseverance and patience.

April 23rd. You will not know your happiest days until you have passed through a big crisis in your life.

April 24th. You will never have more money than is really necessary for your complete happiness.

April 25th. There is a long, rough road before you, but something well worth the winning is at the end of it.

April 26th. Your happiness will increase with the years.

April 27th. You need a marriage partner with a stronger will-power than your own for perfect happiness.

April 28th.	You have the power within you to help you to great heights if you wish.
April 29th.	Life will demand many sacrifices of you, but it will reward you well for them.
April 30th.	Marriage will bring you good luck.
May 1st.	There will be plenty of joy and good cheer in your life.
May 2nd.	Mischief-makers will have a big influence on your life ; keep a cool head and you will come to no harm.
May 3rd.	You will go far towards success, but you may make a few enemies on the way.
May 4th.	Neither poverty nor wealth will be your lot—just a happy, contented medium.
May 5th.	Nothing very startling will affect your life. Your home should be a happy one.
May 6th.	Ambitious and determined, it will not be *your* fault if you do not climb to the top of the tree.
May 7th.	Loving children will help you enormously.
May 8th.	Many difficulties lie in your path, but you will surmount them with ease.
May 9th.	Marriage will bring you the greatest happiness it is possible to know.
May 10th.	Recklessness may land you in trouble, but will never work you real harm.
May 11th.	An exceptionally lucky fate is on your side.
May 12th.	You will be wise not to marry until after you are twenty-five.
May 13th.	You will not make many friends, but those you have will be real ones.
May 14th.	Many sweethearts will come your way, but you will quickly know Mr. " Right."
May 15th.	Given country air and a happy home, you will live to a fine old age.
May 16th.	Jealousy may rob you of many things unless you try hard to keep it in check.
May 17th.	You can win what you want if you do not lose heart.
May 18th.	Take care how you spend money if you wish your life to run smoothly.
May 19th.	Do not let fondness for the good things of life stand in the way of more important matters.
May 20th.	You will not find real content until after marriage.
May 21st.	All the worries, if any, in your life, will be mostly of your own making.
May 22nd.	Plenty of ups and downs for you, but keep your heart up and trust your luck.
May 23rd.	You will need to cultivate tact if you wish to get on in life.
May 24th.	A very contented and long life will be yours.

May 25th. Success for your sweetheart will only come after marriage, when he has your help.

May 26th. Too independent a spirit may spoil your chances if you are not careful.

May 27th. A big choice in your life will mean a great deal to you. It will need careful thought.

May 28th. Friends will help you more than you help yourself.

May 29th. You will have to keep your temper to keep your friends.

May 30th. Things will come right for you if you learn to exercise patience.

May 31st. You have it in your power to achieve almost anything you set out to do.

June 1st. Only marriage can give you your greatest happiness.

June 2nd. You are likely to have many important changes in your life.

June 3rd. Over-cautiousness may cause you to miss valuable opportunities unless you are wiser.

June 4th. The reward of your efforts will not come until later in life.

June 5th. Try to look before you leap and you will land on safer ground.

June 6th. " To-morrow will do " may be your undoing if you let it get too great a hold on you.

June 7th. One can be *too* generous, and this virtue may cost you dear unless you keep it within bounds.

June 8th. Plenty of friends will be yours, but obstinacy may lose you many good ones.

June 9th. Given certain other necessary qualities, you have just the right temperament for success in film or stage work.

June 10th. Too trusting a nature may lead you into difficulties and disappointments. Try to strike a happy medium.

June 11th. Marriage will help you a good deal more than you think.

June 12th. Beware of being taken in by too much flattery, and take care not to let pride get too great a hold on you.

June 13th. Impulsiveness may lead you into taking unwise steps.

June 14th. You will win all you most desire in life, but only after many disheartening setbacks.

June 15th. Marriage will bring you a quiet, contented, peaceful life, full of happiness.

June 16th. Fortune will smile on you just when you need her most.

June 17th. More than one love affair will be yours before you settle down.

June 18th. You will have health and strength in full measure for the greater part of your life.

June 19th. Do not be in too much of a hurry to marry; the longer you leave it, the greater will be your chances of happiness.

June 20th. Money will come to you later in life.

June 21st. A very lucky day to be born on.

June 22nd. A happy, comfortable home will be yours after marriage.

June 23rd. Money matters in which you are concerned should turn out well for you.

June 24th. Misunderstanding may hamper you on your way through life.

June 25th. You will not be really happy unless there is a good deal of variety in your life.

June 26th. Plenty of opportunities will come your way, but you may miss them. Be on the look-out.

June 27th. Do not get disheartened when things go wrong; you will get what you want in the end.

June 28th. Do not expect too much good luck in your life—but it will come when it is needed most.

June 29th. Many difficulties will confront you, but you have the power to overcome them.

June 30th. Do not neglect other folk's advice. It will help you more than you believe.

July 1st. Not many chances in life may come your way, but you will seldom fail to make the most of those that do.

July 2nd. You may lose friends through being too domineering.

July 3rd. You are rather impulsive, but usually it will take you on the right course.

July 4th. Try not to be too reserved, and you will make more friends.

July 5th. Most of your greatest happiness in life will come through a good home and husband.

July 6th. You will be luckier after marriage than before.

July 7th. Your children will help you on.

July 8th. The things you wish for may not come, but you will have compensations.

July 9th. If you concentrate on only one thing at a time, you will do it far better.

July 10th. Try not to be too sensitive; it may prove a great drawback to you.

July 11th. It is possible you may find many disappointments just because you expect too much.

July 12th. Be careful you do not rush into marriage; it is essential for you to find just the right partner if you wish for complete happiness.

July 13th. Do not let impatience spoil your ability to give of your best, for you have great talents.

July 14th. Think always before you act and you will go far.

July 15th. A lucky birthday, and especially so if the day was a Friday.

July 16th. You will have to overcome many difficulties before you know true happiness.

July 17th. The latter half of your life will be the luckiest.

July 18th. Real love will console you for many disappointments.

July 19th. Your energy will help you to many good things in life if you use it wisely.

July 20th. Your home and your married happiness will be the envy of many of your friends.

July 21st. Wonderful luck will help you out of many a difficulty.

July 22nd. Do not be too reckless or you may walk into trouble. Cultivate the habit of looking before you leap.

July 23rd. You will keep youthful in mind and body for a longer time than most people.

July 24th. You have the ability to do many things, but are inclined to be disheartened too quickly.

July 25th. Many people will admire you, and many love you.

July 26th. You may suffer through thinking too much for others before yourself.

July 27th. You will attain most of the things you set out to do.

July 28th. Do not expect too much luck before your thirtieth birthday.

July 29th. Misfortunes will not defeat you ; they will only strengthen your endeavours.

July 30th. You will make enemies who will try to rob you of happiness, but they will not succeed.

July 31st. Unhappiness in married life is a danger to you if you do not guard well against it when making your choice.

August 1st. Success will only come to you through tremendous perseverance and will-power.

August 2nd. You will have to guard against putting pleasure before work.

August 3rd. You may lose friends through being outspoken, but you will keep the best of them.

August 4th. Marriage will bring out all that is best in both yourself and your partner.

August 5th. Responsibilities will be yours ; you will need a very level head.

August 6th. You may lose happiness through lack of faith.

August 7th. A lucky day for those born on a Monday.

August 8th. You have the great asset of being clever— but one can be too clever. Remember that !

August 9th. Some big change will occur in your life which will alter your fortunes considerably.

August 10th. Being very adaptable, you should do well in any calling you care to follow.

August 11th. More confidence in yourself will make things better for you.

August 12th. You are likely to be more successful as a home-maker than anything else.

August 13th. Plenty of friends will flock round you all through life, and there will be many to help you, too.

August 14th. You will never be very rich, but to one of your nature, you will be all the happier for that.

August 15th. You may be called upon to make many sacrifices as you go on, but you will find much happiness as a result.

August 16th. Many talents are yours—make sure of choosing the one most to your own advantage.

August 17th. There will be plenty of love in your life, and plenty of luck, too.

August 18th. Take care that, in looking too much after details, you do not miss seeing the big things that life will offer you.

August 19th. Your life will be a quiet, uneventful one with much happiness.

August 20th. Get as much open air and healthy exercise as you possibly can. By doing so you will live to a great age.

August 21st. So strong is your personality that many will follow whither you lead, so choose the path carefully.

August 22nd. Though many troubles will beset you, you will shake them off with ease.

August 23rd. A very lucky marriage should be your lot.

August 24th. Real happiness will only come to you with marriage.

August 25th. If you were born on a Wednesday, you will be lucky indeed.

August 26th. There will be money troubles, but they will eventually solve themselves in a surprising way.

August 27th. You should follow your impulses, for they will generally lead you aright.

August 28th. True love will come to you from a quarter least expected.

August 29th. Too reserved a nature may keep you back from many things if you do not try to correct this fault.

August 30th. Deep contentment will be yours, though never great riches.

August 31st. Married life will suit you better than any other job.

Sept. 1st. You are likely to marry young, and live to a great age.

Sept. 2nd. Love of children will bring you great rewards through them.

Sept. 3rd. Marriage will bring you greater happiness than you realise.

PLATE 13

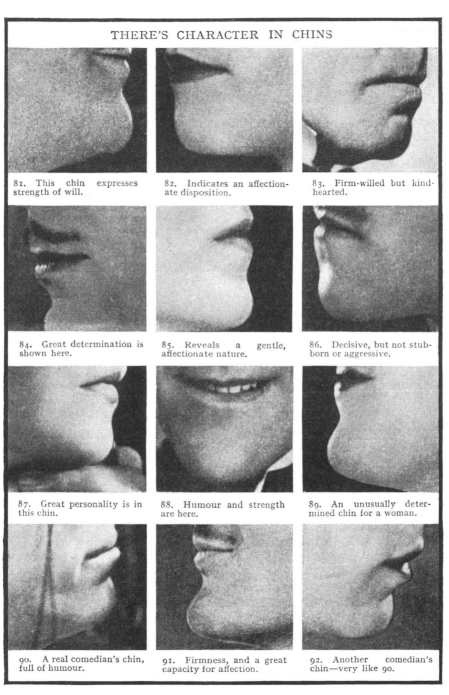

THERE'S CHARACTER IN CHINS

81. This chin expresses strength of will.

82. Indicates an affectionate disposition.

83. Firm-willed but kind-hearted.

84. Great determination is shown here.

85. Reveals a gentle, affectionate nature.

86. Decisive, but not stubborn or aggressive.

87. Great personality is in this chin.

88. Humour and strength are here.

89. An unusually determined chin for a woman.

90. A real comedian's chin, full of humour.

91. Firmness, and a great capacity for affection.

92. Another comedian's chin—very like 90.

PLATE 14

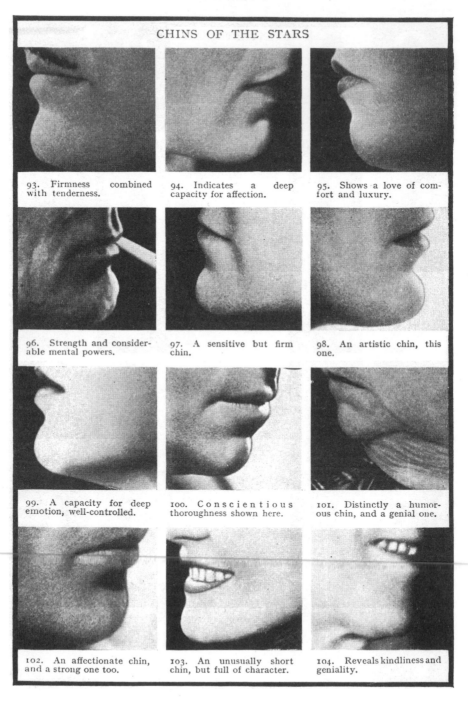

CHINS OF THE STARS

93. Firmness combined with tenderness.

94. Indicates a deep capacity for affection.

95. Shows a love of comfort and luxury.

96. Strength and considerable mental powers.

97. A sensitive but firm chin.

98. An artistic chin, this one.

99. A capacity for deep emotion, well-controlled.

100. Conscientious thoroughness shown here.

101. Distinctly a humorous chin, and a genial one.

102. An affectionate chin, and a strong one too.

103. An unusually short chin, but full of character.

104. Reveals kindliness and geniality.

PLATE 15

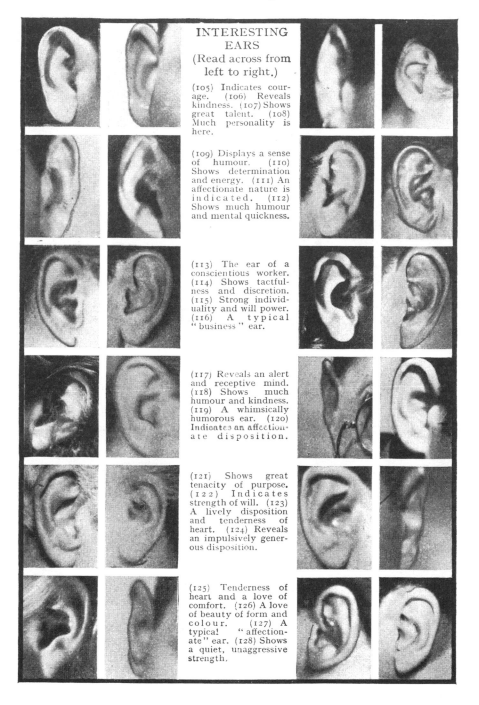

INTERESTING EARS
(Read across from left to right.)

(105) Indicates courage. (106) Reveals kindness. (107) Shows great talent. (108) Much personality is here.

(109) Displays a sense of humour. (110) Shows determination and energy. (111) An affectionate nature is indicated. (112) Shows much humour and mental quickness.

(113) The ear of a conscientious worker. (114) Shows tactfulness and discretion. (115) Strong individuality and will power. (116) A typical "business" ear.

(117) Reveals an alert and receptive mind. (118) Shows much humour and kindness. (119) A whimsically humorous ear. (120) Indicates an affectionate disposition.

(121) Shows great tenacity of purpose. (122) Indicates strength of will. (123) A lively disposition and tenderness of heart. (124) Reveals an impulsively generous disposition.

(125) Tenderness of heart and a love of comfort. (126) A love of beauty of form and colour. (127) A typical "affectionate" ear. (128) Shows a quiet, unaggressive strength.

PLATE 16

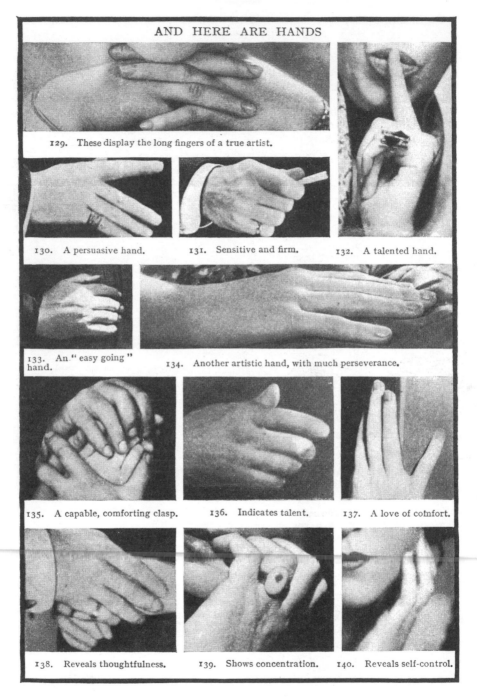

AND HERE ARE HANDS

129. These display the long fingers of a true artist.

130. A persuasive hand.

131. Sensitive and firm.

132. A talented hand.

133. An "easy going" hand.

134. Another artistic hand, with much perseverance.

135. A capable, comforting clasp.

136. Indicates talent.

137. A love of comfort.

138. Reveals thoughtfulness.

139. Shows concentration.

140. Reveals self-control.

Sept. 4th.	A very lucky birthday, especially for those born on a Wednesday.	Sept. 17th.	There will be plenty of luck in your life, but it will come only at certain periods.
Sept. 5th.	Luck will exert a favourable influence for you in money matters.	Sept. 18th.	You will have many a disappointment, but the pleasures in your life will more than make up for them.
Sept. 6th.	Your dearest wishes are likely to come true in unexpected ways.	Sept. 19th.	Love will bring luck for you with it.
Sept. 7th.	You will work hard all your life, but you will reap rich rewards from it.	Sept. 20th.	Many people will want to be your friend, but you must choose wisely, or unhappiness will follow.
Sept. 8th.	Shyness may bar you from many pleasures unless you do your best to master it.	Sept. 21st.	Scandal about yourself may trouble you, but it cannot harm you.
Sept. 9th.	You will have many sweethearts to choose from.	Sept. 22nd.	Country life will bring you the greatest happiness.
Sept. 10th.	Happiness for you will come in greater measure as your life goes on.	Sept. 23rd.	Money will come to you in a surprising way.
Sept. 11th.	Luck will help you many times when all else has failed.	Sept. 24th.	Will-power will help you to accomplish many things that may seem out of reach.
Sept. 12th.	You are rather inclined to be too hasty—this fault may trip you up dangerously unless you curb it.	Sept. 25th	You will be exceedingly lucky at a time when you most need it.
Sept. 13th.	Worry—mostly over nothing—is likely to be your greatest enemy in life.	Sept. 26th.	There will be plenty of romance in your life.
Sept. 14th.	With a practical, not too emotional partner your married life should be a great success.	Sept. 27th.	Without true love in your partner, you will never make a success of marriage.
Sept. 15th.	Yours will not be too easy a life, but your children will help you over many a hurdle.	Sept. 28th.	Your generous nature will foster deceit in others—take care not to be imposed upon.
Sept. 16th.	You will find your greatest happiness in making other folk happy.	Sept. 29th.	Guard against a tendency towards rashness, for people are inclined to follow where you lead.

Sept. 30th. Home life will suit you better than a worldly career.

Oct. 1st. There is a danger of your marrying in haste. Be warned against it, for it may lead you to repenting at leisure.

Oct. 2nd. Don't give up hope because the things you try for do not come at once. Cultivate patience.

Oct. 3rd. Friends will help you a great deal in life.

Oct. 4th. Perseverance will help you to your goal.

Oct. 5th. Yours will be an exceptionally happy home.

Oct. 6th. You have a very useful fund of energy if it is only directed into the right channels.

Oct. 7th. You may expect many disappointments before you at last win happiness in love.

Oct. 8th. You will get on well in any kind of social life.

Oct. 9th. You are likely to rise in the world.

Oct. 10th. Wonderful luck will come in unexpected ways.

Oct. 11th. Other folk will help you on more than you help yourself.

Oct. 12th. Adventure may often lead you far from home.

Oct. 13th. You will receive a great deal of help from your best friends if you treat them in the right way.

Oct. 14th. Marriage will bring you many of the good things of life.

Oct. 15th. You may expect your greatest stroke of luck after you are forty.

Oct. 16th. You will have to achieve your greatest desires before you attain real happiness.

Oct. 17th. A very lucky birthday for those born on a Thursday.

Oct. 18th. Great riches in money are not for you—but a wealth of love will be your lot.

Oct. 19th. Treat things more seriously and they will yield better results for you.

Oct. 20th. Hard work will bring you many things you have always wished for.

Oct. 21st. You will be very successful in a social sphere.

Oct. 22nd. The latter half of your life will contain many comforts which were lacking before.

Oct. 23rd. You should do very well in any calling connected with music.

Oct. 24th. A long and happy life will be yours.

Oct. 25th. You need plenty of variety in your life for your greatest happiness.

Oct. 26th. Marriage will bring you abundant love both from husband and children.

Oct. 27th. You have many talents — follow the one which promises the richest reward.

Oct. 28th. Take care that your generous nature is not

	imposed upon too much.
Oct. 29th.	Your children will help you a great deal.
Oct. 30th.	You will have to fight very hard for all you want, but nothing will stop your getting it.
Oct. 31st.	Unless you stand up for yourself, you will find yourself for ever taking a back seat.
Nov. 1st.	Marriage is your best career in life, though you may not believe it at first.
Nov. 2nd.	You will find you have a wonderful influence over others. You can help to make the world a much better place if you use this power wisely.
Nov. 3rd.	You may lose many friends through moodiness, but the worth-while ones will always stand by you.
Nov. 4th.	Big emergencies will find you at your best. Your married life will be happiest when you have children to care for.
Nov. 5th.	A very lucky day to be born on. Money and success should be yours in plenty.
Nov. 6th.	To do your best, you should marry a man with a commanding nature, and one who loves deeply.
Nov. 7th.	Your happy-go-lucky nature may bring you up against many difficulties, but few things will ever worry you.
Nov. 8th.	A clever head will get you on, and, when

	you marry, will help your husband to success.
Nov. 9th.	You may meet trouble through disregarding advice from others.
Nov. 10th.	A very lucky birthday. Luck should be on your side at every turn.
Nov. 11th.	You will have plenty of girl friends, and few men, but the one you love will hold your affection for all time.
Nov. 12th.	Very popular with both sexes, you will be a great success in any social sphere.
Nov. 13th.	Do not expect a great deal of good fortune until fairly late in life.
Nov. 14th.	Whatever you win in life will have to be by your own endeavour.
Nov. 15th.	Many trials will come your way, but you will get over them by dint of pluck and perseverance.
Nov. 16th.	You will find plenty of romance in your life.
Nov. 17th.	A lucky birthday indeed, especially for fair people.
Nov. 18th.	Unless you guard against it, fondness for pleasure may rob you of excellent opportunities.
Nov. 19th.	Your life will run very smoothly, and especially your love affair.
Nov. 20th.	This birthday is most lucky for Sunday-born folk.
Nov. 21st.	Moving about will not agree with you. Your best happiness will be

found in your home-town.

Nov. 22nd. A clever brain may lead you to be too sure of yourself. Do not let it run away with you !

Nov. 23rd. Cultivate more caution, or you may run into danger.

Nov. 24th. You will win love only after a hard fight.

Nov. 25th. Yours will be a lucky life, especially in the latter half of it.

Nov. 26th. Your home-life will be very happy.

Nov. 27th. A job with plenty of responsibility will suit you better than anything.

Nov. 28th. You are likely to have much more health than wealth.

Nov. 29th. Your love affair may be marred by mischief-making, but it will turn out well in the end.

Nov. 30th. Try to live out of doors as much as possible, in the interests of your health.

Dec. 1st. You will help others on in life much more than you help yourself.

Dec. 2nd. You will make a wonderful and dearly-loved wife and mother.

Dec. 3rd. Fortune may frown on you, but it will not rob you of your happiness.

Dec. 4th. You need plenty of romance in your life to make it truly happy.

Dec. 5th. You must use extreme caution in the choice of a marriage partner, or you may find disappointment.

Dec. 6th. You have plenty of talents, but should use them wisely. Heed the advice of those who know better than you.

Dec. 7th. Money will come your way in plenty.

Dec. 8th. Try not to be too restless, for it may have an adverse influence on your life.

Dec. 9th. A very lucky birthday for all.

Dec. 10th. Cultivate patience and you will achieve all the things you most desire.

Dec. 11th. Many friends and many sweethearts will come your way.

Dec. 12th. Love and luxury will be yours if you go the right way to work to win them.

Dec. 13th. Not a great deal of wordly luck for you, but plenty of love.

Dec. 14th. Only in married life will you find your greatest happiness.

Dec. 15th. You may not seem to be successful, but the work you do will bring rich results in the end.

Dec. 16th. Don't worry over disappointments ; they are for your own good.

Dec. 17th. An extremely lucky day for those born on Saturday.

Dec. 18th. You will never lack help from friends and children when you most need it.

Dec. 19th. Marriage will bring you many joys and comforts which you have long desired.

Dec. 20th. You may have a long wait, but love will come into your life at last, bringing with it a wealth of happiness.

Dec. 21st. Your children will make your old age a time of complete happiness and comfort.

Dec. 22nd. Not very much luck for you until later in life.

Dec. 23rd. The man you marry will be of a type you least expect.

Dec. 24th. Recklessness is your weakest point, but your luck will hold surprisingly.

Dec. 25th. You will have to make many sacrifices, but will reap the greatest happiness from them.

Dec. 26th. Your dearest hopes will be realised if you only exercise patience.

Dec. 27th. You will have to work hard for your happiness.

Dec. 28th. There are plenty of disappointments in store for you, but plenty of happiness, also.

Dec. 29th. Those you love most will help you most when the need arises, as it is likely to.

Dec. 30th. You will always be looked up to, and will have a tremendous influence over your friends.

Dec. 31st. A great love will be yours, and you will have the opportunity to help your husband to wonderful heights.

" DATA."

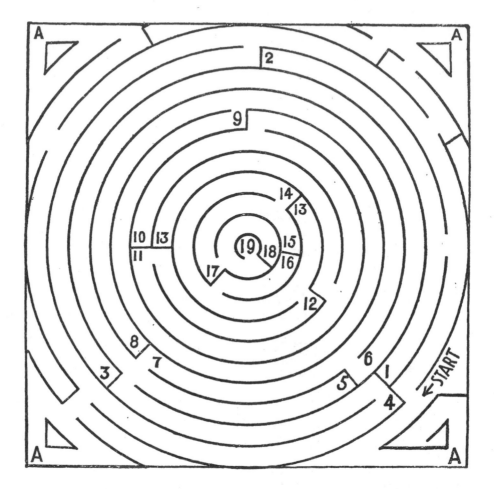

THE MAZE

'THIS is quite an amusing little game. Take a pencil, a knitting needle, or something similar, and try to trace your way to the centre of the maze. The letters and numbers show incidents that Fate has in store for you in the immediate future. If you find yourself in any of the corners marked (A) it means "you are wasting your time and efforts in a position that will not lead to anything." If you come to a point (1) it means "You will experience a setback"; (2) means "An enemy is plotting against you"; (3) "You will suffer injustice, or an undeserved misfortune"; (4) "A choice lies before you, but your decision will be the right one"; (5) "Don't think any more about him, he is not worthy of you"; (6) "You will find that you need not have worried after all"; (7) "A pleasant surprise is coming to you"; (8) "Beware of a false friend"; (9) "Your good luck will hold"; (10) "You will receive a letter with unexpected news"; (11) "A proposal of marriage; think it well over"; (12) "Someone you little suspect is helping you"; either (13) "You seem beset by troubles," but (14) "They will soon pass"; (15) "Someone will try to part you from one you love"; (16) "Take care not to quarrel, or you will regret it"; (17) "You mean well, but your actions may be misunderstood and cause trouble"; (18) "A disappointment in love"; (19) "You will obtain your heart's desire."

CHAPTER XVI

Your Lucky Number

*Every number has a meaning—How to find your own number by
your birthdate—And by your name—People whose numbers are
in harmony with yours.*

THE study of numbers and
of their effect on our daily
lives dates back into the
dim past.

The wise men of old devoted
much time and thought to the subject, and their untiring research is
responsible for much of our knowledge to-day.

They discovered that every number—from One to Nine—has a
meaning of its own, and each has
its particular influences in one way
or another. They found, also, that
every person has his or her own
special lucky number, based on the
day, month and year of birth, and
that that number was favourable to
that person in many ways, if made
use of whenever possible.

Another discovery of the ancients
was that the letters of the alphabet
have corresponding values in numbers. By this means we can find
the numerical value of our own
names, information that we can
often turn to advantage in our
daily lives.

Often our lucky number tends to
influence us in certain directions
against opposite tendencies given

us in other ways—such as those endowed by our zodiac sign.

First of all, we will take the nine numbers and what each stands for.

1 is the greatest of all the numbers, because it stands for leadership, power and confidence. If your lucky number is 1 you should do great things in life, for its influence causes you to push forward to success in every undertaking.

It confers courage of the highest order. Self-reliance is another of its great boons, for it helps you to be independent of others and rely entirely on your own powers.

2 has influences which are in some ways the reverse of those of Number 1. Its tendency is to make you reserved and satisfied to keep in the background ; even, in some cases, timid. It gives you a quiet, contented temperament, and bestows patience in good measure.

Another influence is a desire for peace. Affection and deep, constant love will be yours, too, while love of children and home life helps to make wonderful mothers of women dominated by this number.

It gives an ideal temperament for those who wish to follow the nursing profession, or desire to become teachers or governesses.

To some people the number 2 gives a dual personality, with conflicting desires and interests, making them hard to understand. Often it implants wonderful powers of intuition which at times almost amount to " second sight."

3 gives, above all things, joy and cheer to the fortunate possessor of it as her lucky numeral. It not only bestows a happy, cheerful nature, but gives you the power of communicating happiness to others, making you a fascinating and entertaining companion, and one much sought after where parties and other functions are concerned.

The number gives faithfulness and loyalty as well, and the power of deep, constant love, while a fondness for all kinds of music is another of its gifts.

4 is one of the most fortunate of numbers, and has a great influence towards success and the fulfilment of ambitions.

The number stands mainly for Work, and confers great energy and driving-power, with the will to win at all costs. People with this as their lucky number make splendid managers, foremen and organisers. They are reliable too, and seldom make a wrong move. Generosity is another gift, together with a sincere, honourable nature that shrinks from anything underhanded or mean.

5 is often known as the Soul Figure. Being the central figure of the nine, it is typical of the centre of the universe—the very heart and soul of it.

Naturally, it endows you with great depth of soul, strong emotions and a great power for loving. You have the warmest of hearts and the tenderest of sympathies ; because of your emotions you are inclined, at times, to be moody—joyful one day and depressed the next, but full of hope and inspiration when it is required of you.

The number sometimes gives a tendency towards love of ease and comfort, and a fondness for travel.

6 is the Love number, being associated with marriage, love of humanity and love of children. It stands also for home happiness and deep contentment with family life, and if it is your number you can find the greatest pleasure in the humblest and simplest of joys.

You can usually see the bright side of life when the clouds are at their blackest, and can give cheer and comfort to those in need of it.

You are upright and honourable, and are fond, above all, of peace. A better friend or marriage partner could not be found.

7 stands for virtue in the highest degree. Its influences are all for good, bringing noble aims and ideals and purity of thought and deed. Unselfishness and unlimited powers of self-sacrifice are conferred by this number, while it implants in your heart wonderful understanding and sympathy.

A love of all things beautiful, especially where Nature is concerned, is a strong point. If you come under this number you are probably a dreamer, and are frequently happiest when alone.

8 is in many respects similar to Number 1, standing for power, confidence and success. People coming within its influence can be firm, forceful and far-seeing, and if you are one you have great will-power and self-confidence.

Other influences are towards cool, practical common sense and the ability to reason things out carefully ; able leadership and a gift for organisation.

Although outwardly seeming hard and unyielding at times, you Number 8 folk are just and considerate, having thought for others as well as for your own aims.

9, the last of the numerals, stands for deep, wholly unselfish love, for wisdom and for sympathy and understanding. You who are influenced by it live, not for yourselves, but for others, and will do your level best to leave the world a better place for your presence.

You have faith and trust in full measure, and your understanding of human nature makes you ideal comforters in sorrow and pain. You make splendid nurses.

How to Find your Lucky Number

IT is quite easy to discover your lucky number from the day, month and year of your birth.

Each of these three sets of figures must be reduced to a digit by adding the numbers where necessary. For instance, if you were born on the 23rd of the month, the 2 and 3 must be added together, and become five. The whole three final figures of your day, month and year of birth are then added together, and, the total being reduced again to a single digit, you arrive at your lucky number.

Let us take, for example, someone born on the 29th of April, 1911.

Her day of birth, added together, comes to 11. This must be added together yet again, because no final figure must be higher than nine. We thus get the figure 2.

April, the fourth month, gives us 4, which being a single digit remains as it is.

The year of birth, 1911, comes to 12 when added the first time. Adding together again, we find the figure 3.

We now add all three final figures together—2, 4 and 3, which gives us 9. That is the lucky number for anybody born on that particular day.

To make it still clearer, here is another birth-date worked out in the form of a sum.

We will take the 19th of September, 1917.

Day of Birth :—19 = 9 + 1 = 10 . . 1 + 0 = 1
Month : —9 . . . . = 9
Year:—1917 . . 1 + 9 + 1 + 7 = 18 . . 1 + 8 = 9
$$\overline{}$$
19 = 1 + 9 = 10 . . 1 + 0 = 1
$$\overline{}$$

Therefore, the lucky number in this case is 1.

You can use your lucky number in all sorts of ways. In games of chance, in which you have to pick a number ; in choosing a number in a raffle—in fact, you can pin your faith to it in all kinds of circumstances.

Of course, you must not expect it to help you always—nothing can be so certain as that—but your number will exercise a fortunate influence on your behalf that will help a great deal in swaying the balance of luck your way.

Your luckiest days of each month are the days which, when added together, form your lucky number. For instance, if your number is 9, the 9th, 18th and 27th are the best days for you. If it is 1, the 1st, 10th, 19th and 28th are your fortunate days. It is a good idea to make plans for important events or undertakings of your own on your lucky days.

The Number in Your Name

EACH letter of the alphabet has its own number value, and by learning these we can find the numerical value of our names, and those of other people. In this way it is easy to find if folk are likely to be in harmony with us, either as friends, work-mates or sweethearts.

The numerical values run, beginning with A, from 1 to 9 and then repeat themselves throughout the alphabet, so that some letters have the same number as others. Thus :

A	J	S	equal	1
B	K	T	,,	2
C	L	U	,,	3
D	M	V	,,	4
E	N	W	,,	5
F	O	X	,,	6
G	P	Y	,,	7
H	Q	Z	,,	8
I	R		,,	9

Knowing this table, it is now a simple matter to give the correct number to each letter of your names, and, adding them all together and reducing the total to a digit, as with the birthday lucky number, find your harmonious figure.

You must use *all* your full Christian names, if more than one, as well as your surname.

As an example, take the name Jenny Brown, and see how this is cast.

J   1
E   5
N   5
N   5
Y   7

B   2
R   9
O   6
W   5
N   5
———
50....5+0=Name-number, 5.

Simple, isn't it ? It is now easy for Jenny Brown to find the name-numbers of her friends, or perhaps her sweetheart, and discover if they are the same as hers. Those with the same numbers are harmonious, and therefore should get on wonderfully well together.

This does not mean, of course, that you cannot be in harmony with someone whose name-number is not the same as yours, but only that those are the people with whom you are *best* in tune.

Apart from this .

If your name-number is 1 you will be fairly well in harmony with someone whose number is 4 or 8, and to a rather less extent with a number 3.

If you are a 2, you will be happier with a 3, a 5, a 6 or a 7 than with a 1, 4, or an 8.

If you are a 3, you will find few people with whom you cannot be more or less in harmony.

If your name-number is 4 you will get on best with a 1 or an 8.

A 5 person is best in harmony with a 2, 6, 7, or 9, a 6 with a 2, 5, 7 or 9, a 7 with 5, 6, or 9, and a 9 with 5, 6, or 7.

An 8 person is best in tune with a 1, 2, 4, or 8.

It is possible, of course, for friends or sweethearts to get on well even if their numbers clash, but it is often a great help when they harmonise, for the influence exerted by the two numbers working together has a tremendous power towards not only love and friendship, but good luck too.

If your name-number should turn out to be the same as your birthday number, then you should be lucky indeed, through life !

"NUMERO."

LUCKY LOVE GIFTS

FATE sends a message with each present given you by a male admirer, and from this list you can easily tell what *his* gifts mean to you.

Gloves show he is a man you can trust.

Jewellery is a sign that good luck will favour your love affair.

A **Scarf** suggests that you will have to wait some time for marriage.

A **Handbag** means that nothing more serious than little tiffs will mar your married life.

A **Fur** indicates that you could not have a better protector than the giver.

A **Book** denotes success for your husband.

An **Umbrella** shows that your sweetheart's first thought will always be for you.

A **Watch** shows that his love will last as long as life.

A **Clock** is a sign that your married life will hold many changes, but much domestic happiness.

CHAPTER XVII

The Lucky Dream-Book

*A useful dictionary of dreams from A to Z—" Contrary "
dreams—Dreams of success—Dreams of travel—Dreams of love
—Dreams of married happiness, etc.*

This is where a study of dreams is helpful, for that part of the mind which is known as the subconscious works in a very strange and secret way, so that our dreams may be regarded as in the nature of parables. That is to say, persons, places and events are often represented to us in our dreams as entirely different from what they are in our waking hours, but from the earliest days wise men who have spent a lifetime in the study of dreams have, to a certain extent, been able to classify and interpret our dreams. Here you will find an account of the meaning of the dreams which come to us most frequently.

MOST people have, at times, been puzzled by their dreams. We dream something clearly and vividly, and yet the dream is so mixed, and often so foolish, that we tell ourselves it cannot mean anything at all. Or we have a bad dream, in which unpleasant things happen to us, and when we are awake the influence of the dream still persists and we feel afraid that something unpleasant actually *will* happen to us.

Those who are worried and troubled by bad dreams should remember the old saying which tells us that dreams go by contrary, that : " to dream of a funeral is to hear of a wedding," and " dream of the dead and you'll hear of the living " ! Often, therefore, correctly interpreted, a bad dream may indicate good fortune on its way.

Sometimes we find it difficult to recall the whole of a dream, and here the list of dreams which follows may be found very helpful, for by fixing the mind on one object of the dream the whole may become clear.

If we wish dreams to come true, they should not be repeated to anyone else, though Friday's dreams are an exception to this rule, for :

" *Friday's dream on Saturday told,*
Sure to come true, if ever so old."

Remember, that it is the main fact—the subject which occurs most often in a dream—for which you should look when searching for the meaning.

Abroad. To dream you are going abroad means that you will receive a present, but if you dream you are travelling in foreign lands, be careful over business transactions, or you may lose money.

Accident. If, in your dream, this happens to yourself, you have a false friend, but if it happens to someone you know, you are going to get a letter from them containing good news.

Air. If, when you take a dream walk, the air is bright and clear, it is a very good sign, and shows that you will be successful in what you are about to undertake ; or if you are starting on a journey, then it will be a very pleasant one. Should you walk in a fog, there are difficulties ahead of you requiring courage and caution, but you will surmount them.

Should you see anything suspended in the air above you, it is a sign that your position is going to improve.

Airship. This is a good dream for sweethearts, for it shows that unexpected happiness is on the way.

Almanac. If you are flirting, and dream of this, take heed, for it is a warning to be true to your sweetheart.

Almonds. To dream you are eating these shows that you will encounter a time of want followed by great prosperity.

Alms. If these are asked of you, and you refuse them, you will hear of illness ; if you give them, great joy is coming to you and a particular friend.

Alone. While to dream that you are alone in the world may seem a sad dream, it is one of those which go by the contrary, for it signifies that your friends will always be true to you.

Altar. This means a great piece of good fortune or, possibly, a wedding. Should you uncover it in your dream, it means a most unexpected proposal.

Amber. This foretells a letter from over the sea.

America. This is warning against false friends who will not, however, have power to harm you.

Anchor. A sailor will fall in love with you.

Angel. To dream that you see an angel is very good, and shows that you will hear very good news. If you dream that you yourself are an angel, this is even better, for you will obtain your heart's desire. If, however, you see an angel who does not approach you it warns you against some course of action you are planning. If the angel flies over your house it is a sign that a great blessing will come to it.

Anger. Another " contrary " dream, for it shows the person with whom you are angry to be a true friend. Should your anger be caused by someone you do not see, it foretells a slight quarrel with your sweetheart.

Angling. It is going to cause you a great deal of trouble to get what you want, but you will win it in the end.

Animals. If you see a great many of these in a dream, a stroke of luck is coming to you very shortly.

Ant. A temptation will befall you, so prepare to resist it.

Ant-hill. You will hear of an accident to a friend.

Ape. Do not believe all that is told to you, especially if it is by a man friend.

Apparel. To dream of new clothes denotes happiness and prosperity. If they are white, you will shortly be present at a wedding. If they are black, someone you know is going to recover from an illness. If they are scarlet, it means money, or increased responsibility. To dream of men's clothes shows that you are going to make a new friend.

Appetite. To dream that you are hungry denotes that a friend is going abroad.

Apples. To eat them warns of a quarrel with your sweetheart. Should you pluck them from a tree, it denotes a happy married life with many children.

Apples of Gold. This is an exceedingly lucky dream, and promises great happiness and much love.

Apricot. You are going to be taken to a place of amusement.

Apron. An unexpected gift of money.

Arab. This is a warning of danger that, however, you will overcome.

Arbour. A pleasant dream signifying an unexpected meeting with your sweetheart.

Arch. To dream you are passing under an arch denotes a romantic adventure with a very happy ending. To pass over one shows advancement in business.

Argument. Should you dream you are arguing with anyone, it shows you will overcome an enemy.

Army. An army denotes a journey, which will be long or short according to the number of the soldiers.

Arrow. There is a danger of a quarrel with someone you love, so beware.

Ashes. You will hear of illness.

Asylum. Another " contrary " dream which denotes success in your undertakings.

Aunt. You are going to have a secret romance.

Avenue. To dream you are walking down an avenue of trees denotes success in your love affair.

Baby. All dreams of babies are good. To see many of them together means riches, and that you have one, future prosperity. Should you dream you are wishing for one, you will have a stroke of good luck before the year is out. If, however, the baby is crying, there will be some difficulty to be overcome before you get your wish.

Bagpipes. Love is coming to you.

Ball. If you yourself are dancing, this is a good dream, but if you are not dancing, then you will have a dispute with someone over money matters.

Balloon. To dream you see a balloon means you are likely to " go up " in the world !

Banns. To hear these being called denotes a disappointment in love.

Banquet. It may not be your present sweetheart whom you will marry.

Barefoot. Your endeavours will be crowned with success.

Bath. To dream that you are bathing in clear water denotes recovery from an illness, but if the water is muddy you will hear of an accident. To bathe in the sea denotes coming prosperity, while to get into an empty bath promises a happy ending to your romance.

Bed. To dream of an unmade bed denotes a change of residence ; a tidy, well-made bed, that you are going to settle down.

Bees. This is a lucky dream, for it means a speedy marriage ; should they sting you, beware of enemies.

Bells. To hear a peal of these signifies that you will shortly be invited to a wedding. If yourself ring the bell the wedding will be your own.

Birds. Someone dear to you will soon be made very happy.

Blossoms. Your sweetheart is going to ask you an important question.

Blow. If you dream someone strikes you, a service will be rendered you.

Boat. After marriage you will settle overseas.

Books. Marriage will raise you in the world.

Boots. New boots signify success in love ; old ones that you may incur a disappointment.

Briars. You have enemies. If you walk through the briars unscratched you will triumph over your false friends.

Burden. You will have to work for others.

Buried. This unpleasant dream is very lucky, and as much earth as is laid on your coffin, so much money will you have in the near future.

Butterflies. You will shortly receive an invitation to a dance.

Cabbage. Look forward with interest to meeting a fair man.

Cage. You will be offered the opportunity of making a change in life, but think well over it, for it is not all it seems.

Camel. You are likely to travel abroad, and your travels bring money to you.

Candle. If you light it, an undertaking you are planning will be successful. If it goes out, someone is trying to cross you.

Cap. If, in your dream, you put one on, be careful in your love affairs.

Cards. Should you be a player, the course of true love may not run smoothly for a time. To see cards is lucky—hearts mean love, diamonds money, clubs happiness, but spades foretell a disappointment.

Cat. To dream of a black cat means luck ; of a white one that your sweetheart is true to you. To see many cats bids you beware of false friends.

Cathedral. This denotes a crisis in your life. If you enter the cathedral you will pass through a crisis to happiness.

Cemetery. Another lucky dream. To be walking in one foretells you will be successful in your undertakings. Generally speaking, it may be said that any dream which concerns death and funerals signifies just the reverse, and when these " bad " dreams occur you may expect to hear good news.

Cinema. You will be asked to a party.

Climbing. If you dream you are climbing upwards, your circumstances in life will improve, or you will marry above your station.

Clock. This foretells luck, but if you hear it strike you may hear a piece of bad news concerning a friend.

Comb. If you dream you are combing your hair, someone is trying to steal your sweetheart from you.

Cooking. You will hear of a wedding very soon.

Corpse. Another " bad " dream which is very lucky. You may look for success in love.

Cradle. You may hear of the illness of a friend whom you have not seen for some time.

Crown. Your friends are true to you.

Crying. An unexpected pleasure during the day.

Daffodils. Very good. If you are ill this is a sign you will recover.

Dahlia. Your sweetheart will succeed in life.

Daisy. Your sweetheart is true to you.

Dandelion. Beware of a false friend.

Dentist. To dream you are having teeth drawn, signifies you will lose some small article.

Devil. You will succeed in your undertakings.

Diamonds. You will hear of the engagement of someone very near and dear to you.

Digging. If you dream you are digging and turn up what you are digging for, you will get your wish. If the ground is barren, your wish will be unfulfilled,

Dishes. To break them signifies loss, but to see silver dishes means a gift of money.

Doctor. Do not believe all that is said to you in the day following this dream.

Dog. To dream of a dog is lucky, and a white dog denotes marriage, while if you should dream of a mad dog you may expect a very joyful surprise.

Dove. You will receive news of a wedding.

Drink. To drink clear water is good, but if you are drinking muddy water be careful lest you quarrel with your sweetheart. To drink milk signifies approaching prosperity.

Drowning. There is pleasure coming to you.

Duck. Watch your tongue carefully.

Dwarf. You will probably marry a very tall man.

Eagle. Consider this dream carefully, for much depends on how you saw the eagle. If it is flying overhead, you will succeed in your plans, or an unexpected honour will be offered you, but if it alights on your head there will be great difficulties.

Ear-rings. You will gain another admirer.

Eating. Much depends on the nature of the dish. Cheese is good, so are apples, while to eat grapes denotes money coming to you, but to eat meat foretells a quarrel.

Echo. You are going to be told a secret.

Eels. Watch lest you lose an opportunity of advancement.

Eggs. If you are buying eggs, you will marry your sweetheart, and your union will be blessed with children. If the eggs are broken, take care or you will lose something you value.

Elderberries. To dream of picking these, promises you a meeting with your sweetheart.

Elephant. You will rise in the world.

Elm. You will overcome a difficulty which now lies before you.

Elopement. Your engagement is likely to be broken, and you may marry another.

Emerald. This warns you of the jealousy of a dark woman.

Employment. If you are seeking work, your new job will be hard.

Enemy. You will make a new friend.

Engagement. You will be told a secret that will surprise you.

Engine. You will hear of the illness of a relative.

Errand. If you are sent on one, your love affair will have a happy ending; if you send someone else on an errand, you may break your engagement.

Escape. Take care, danger threatens you!

Examination. To dream you are sitting for one, denotes that someone is very interested in you.

Explosion. You will hear news that will greatly surprise you.

Face. To see a smiling face is lucky, but if you see your own in a mirror, take care lest you fall out with your sweetheart. To wash your face signifies sorrow for a wrong done.

Factory. You will make a change of employment much sooner than you expect.

Falling. Your affairs will mend.

Family. Should you dream you have a large family, your husband will be well-to-do.

Fan. Should anyone be fanning you, you will meet a new admirer, but if you fan yourself your jealousy may be aroused.

Farewell. To say farewell to a person you know, denotes that they are in trouble.

Farthing. There is a gift of gold for you.

Father and **Mother.** To dream of your parents denotes that a new interest is coming to you.

Fear. A " contrary " dream, for it shows you will be brave when necessary.

Feather. If white, then money is coming to you. If black, you will hear of illness.

Ferret. Your admiration is misplaced.

Fiddle. To hear one being played, indicates good fortune. If it is silent your sweetheart is not serious in his intentions.

Field. Your husband will be very affectionate.

Figs. A present is coming to you.

Fingers. If you dream of your own, beware how you meddle in the affairs of others.

Fire. Should you see one burning, you will marry the man you love. If the house is on fire, you will pass through sorrow to joy.

Fish. There are difficulties ahead for you.

Flag. To carry this denotes that a better position is to be offered you.

Flowers. If you are picking them, your undertakings will be profitable. If they are white, there is a small difficulty to be overcome; if yellow, your sweetheart is jealous, while red means that there is a pleasure in store for you.

Flying. A very good omen. You will surmount all difficulties.

Foot. There is someone who will do you harm, if possible.

Forest. If you are lost in one, think carefully over your plans for the future. Your present idea is not the right one.

Fork. You have a false friend.

Fortune-telling. Should you dream you are having your fortune told, you may expect a proposal.

Fountain. Clear water denotes prosperity ; dirty, that you will meet trouble.

Fowls. You admire a flirt.

Fox. Beware, your confidence will be betrayed !

Friends. You are worrying without reason.

Frogs. You will get your wish if you can overcome your timidity.

Frost. You are suspecting your sweetheart unjustly.

Fruit. If in season, this is lucky, but " Fruit out of season, trouble without reason." Should you be selling fruit, you will come into money.

Funeral. You will hear of a wedding.

Gale. Take care, or you will quarrel with a friend.

Gallows. A very lucky dream, promising happiness in love.

Game. There is hard work before you.

Gaol. You are loved in secret.

Garage. There is a journey before you.

Garden. Your position in life will improve, but you must make up your mind to act with courage.

Geese. You will have an unexpected visit from a friend. Should the geese cackle, there is a present for you.

Gems. Take care, or you may lose something you value.

Giant. There is an adventure at hand.

Gift. Do not be too ready to talk about your private affairs.

Gipsy. There are many changes ahead of you.

Glass. An old friend is thinking of you.

Gloves. You will safely overcome a difficulty.

Goat. Very lucky, especially if the goat be white.

Gold. A " contrary " dream, for you will lose money. If your dress is embroidered with gold, there is pleasure in store for you.

Gong. You are probably going to be asked to be a bridesmaid.

Gooseberries. Your family may be a large one.

Grain. Your husband will be prosperous.

Grapes. White ones are lucky, but if they are black you will lose something.

Grass. If the grass is green, this is good, but if it is withered, you will not get your dearest wish.

Grave. Happiness in love for you.

Green. Your life will be a long one.

Guests. You will have a disappointment.

Guns. If you hear these in a dream, beware of quarrelling with your sweetheart or your love affair may end unhappily.

Gymnasium. Take care that you do not overtax your strength.

Hail. Not a lucky dream, for you will incur a disappointment.

Hair. If you are brushing it, your sweetheart is true ; if combing it, he is inclined to be fickle. If it falls out, you will lose a friend. If you dream of a bald-headed man, you will have a pleasant surprise.

Hammer. Your pride is interfering with your happiness.

Hands. If your right hand, you will be given a present of money ; if your left, you will pay money away.

Harp. If this is being played, you will overcome a difficulty.

Hat. Someone is hoping for news of you.

Hawk. You will not obtain your wish without trouble.

Hay. Your sweetheart needs encouraging.

Head. To dream of your own head, denotes that you are treating a friend unfairly. Should you dream you have a headache, you will fall desperately in love.

Heather. A lucky dream, foretelling luck from a journey.

Heaven. Your life will be long and peaceful.

Hell. You have false friends.

Hills. There are difficulties in front of you, but with courage you will surmount them.

Hive. If this is empty you may expect a disappointment; if full, you will hear of some scandal.

Hog. You will inherit money.

Home. To dream of this when you are away from it, shows that someone dear to you is hoping for news.

Honey. You will shortly fall in love.

Hops. A most unexpected sum of money will come to you.

Horse. A good omen, especially if you are riding it, for that means happiness in love. To see a horse

running promises you a handsome husband.

House. If you are living in a strange house, it foretells a hasty marriage, but if the house shakes, there will be scandal.

Hunger. A good dream. Your pathway through life will be peaceful.

Hunting. There are those who wish you ill.

Husband. Not a lucky dream for a girl who is courting, since it signifies a quarrel with her sweetheart.

Husks. A " contrary " dream, for it denotes plenty.

Hyacinth. In bloom, a happy marriage; withered, loss by fire.

Hyena. Your secret is not so closely guarded as you imagine.

Hymns. To sing them, foretells a loss; to hear them sung, the help of a friend in time of need.

Ice. Someone is going to break a promise made to you.

Illness. You are in danger of being cheated.

Imp. If you fly into a temper, you will deeply regret it.

Incense. You will marry your true love.

Ink. You will shortly receive a love letter.

Insects. These are lucky in dreams, and foretell presents, though, perhaps, not very large ones.

Introduction. If you dream you are being introduced to a stranger, you will meet an old friend unexpectedly.

Invitation. If you have fallen out with a friend, hasten to become reconciled, or the breach may be serious.

Iron. This denotes a loss in business.

Ivory. Your sweetheart cannot make up his mind.

Ivy. You may trust your judgment of your friend.

Jam. If you are making jam, pleasure is coming to you, but if you are eating it, do not be too hasty in forming a new friendship. To see jars of jam foretells a present.

Jay. Seen in a dream, this bird signifies loss.

Jealousy. To dream you are jealous of your sweetheart is a sign you have no cause for it.

Jessamine. Your sweetheart is thinking tenderly of you.

Jilted. If you dream that you are jilted, take care to give your sweetheart no cause for jealousy.

Jockey. You will receive an invitation that will give you much pleasure.

Joke. Someone is going to make a very serious proposal to you.

Journey. You will receive a piece of news which will cause you a great surprise.

Joy. A " contrary " dream, for you will hear of a mishap to a friend.

Judge. Someone is cheating you, but you will discover your loss.

Jug. If you are drinking out of this, someone will fail in an effort to part you from your sweetheart.

Jumping. If you jump up, your position will improve ; if down, you will incur a loss, but if you fall on your feet the loss will be made good.

Jungle. There is a tangle in your love affairs.

Jury. Think well over your intentions, for your family may not approve.

Kangaroo. You will quarrel with another girl over a love affair.

Keepsake. If you dream you are given a keepsake, someone you care for is going over the water.

Kennel. News about a boy friend is going to surprise you.

Kettle. You will marry for love, not riches.

Key. To lose one means money ; to find one, that you will succeed in your endeavour.

Kick. If you do this in a dream, beware of making up your mind too quickly.

Kill. This is a " money " dream, and to see or to take part in the killing of anyone foretells a legacy.

Kilt. You will receive a present of clothing.

King. A good omen. Success will crown your efforts.

Kitchen. Someone is in love with you, and will become serious in their intentions.

Kite. Hasty words may lead you into trouble.

Kitten. Lucky only if it is black.

Knapsack. You will be asked to go on a journey, but do not decide in a hurry.

Knife. Not a good dream, for it signifies disputes with someone near and dear to you.

Knight. To see a knight in armour is lucky, but if you put on his armour be careful, for danger threatens you.

Knitting. This signifies there may be a tangle in your love affairs before you reach the happy ending.

Knot. If you dream of this, think carefully over any decision you are going to make, or it may be the wrong one.

Lace. This is a lucky dream, for you will receive a piece of very good news.

Ladder. If you are ascending, there is money for you ; if coming down, there is hard work in front of you.

Lake. If the water is clear, there is some pleasure for you, but if it is muddy, look out for trouble.

Lamb. There is luck coming to a member of your family.

Lamp. If this is not lit, you are neglecting an opportunity ; if it is lighted, a romantic new friendship is in store for you.

Lark. A lucky dream, and happiness is in store for you.

Laurel. Some unexpected advancement is coming to you.

Lawyer. You will hear of a quarrel.

Leaves. You will have a gift of money.

Leek. If you dream you are eating these, beware of a family quarrel.

Lemons. Someone bears you a grudge.

Leopard. A fair man is going to have some influence in your life.

Letters. Both good and bad news is promised you.

Lettuce. You will receive an invitation that will please you.

Light. Should you be carrying one, it signifies that you will triumph over someone who is trying to harm you.

Lighthouse. You have a secret admirer.

Lightning. A very important event is near to you.

Lilac. An unexpected pleasure.

Lily. Marriage is much nearer than you imagine.

Lion. Have courage and you will overcome a difficulty.

Lizard. You have a secret enemy.

Lobster. You will hear of the illness of a friend.

Locks. A good husband is promised you.

Logs. Unexpected visitors are coming to the house soon.

Looking-glass. Not a lucky dream. Trouble will come to you through your own fault.

Loss. Should you dream you have lost something, it foretells a present for you.

Love. To dream you are in love, shows that your affairs will take a turn for the better.

Machine. If you dream you are working one, it foretells that there is some difficulty before you.

Mackerel. You are going to be introduced to a friend who will make a change in your life.

Madness. Should you dream you encounter a madman, think well over any advice that is given you before you follow it.

Magpie. Take care, or your secret will be discovered !

Man. To dream of a strange man foretells that you may lose a friend.

Manger. You will hear news concerning a child.

Mansion. You will marry a man in a better position than yourself.

Map. There are many changes ahead of you.

Marching. To dream you are marching shows that you will receive a very pressing invitation.

Market. If you are shopping in one, you will soon attend a party, and someone very interesting will be introduced to you.

Marriage. Not a good dream, for you will hear of illness.

Mat. You will love the man you marry more than he loves you.

Mattress. There is a change of residence for you.

Meat. Take care, or you will lose something you value.

Medicine. If you are taking it, your judgment of a friend is at fault.

Mice. Lucky if you see them run, but unlucky should they be caught in a trap.

Milk. You will receive a most unexpected proposal.

Mill. To dream you are working in one foretells a difficulty it will need resolution to overcome.

Mine. To descend into a mine promises you long life.

Minister. You will hear bad news of a friend far away.

Moles. You will never lack affection.

Money. Beware or you will give pain to a friend.

Monkey. Someone is trying to make mischief.

Monster. You are worrying needlessly over a small difficulty.

Moon. A lucky month is before you.

Mother. A good dream, while if your mother has passed away, to dream of her foretells happiness in the near future.

Motor-car. You will very shortly attend a wedding.

Mountains. To climb one signifies there is an obstacle before you, but you will overcome it. To come down a mountain, a small success will be yours.

Mulberries. A lucky dream, signifying affection.

Mule. There is an acquaintance you should not trust.

Music. Your doubts of your sweetheart's affection are unfounded.

Musk. You will become reconciled with an old friend.

Mustard. Beware of scandal.

Myrtle. A good dream, for it signifies that you will receive a declaration of love.

Nails. If you dream that your finger-nails are long, there is money coming to you, but to dream you cut them shows a family dispute. To see others cut them, you will hear of a quarrel. If you are hammering nails, your perseverance will overcome a difficulty.

Naked. If you dream of seeing anyone naked, watch your speech carefully or you may quarrel with one you love.

Necklace. A present of gold will be offered you.

Needle. This is a warning not to mistake the motives of one who cares for you.

Negro. Someone who is paying you attention is not to be trusted.

Nest. If the nest be empty, you will have a disappointment, but if there are eggs in it, you will have as many strokes of good fortune as there are eggs.

Nettles. You will have to strive hard to obtain your wish.

Newspaper. Should you dream that you are reading one, you will have news that will give you an unpleasant surprise, but if one is being read to you, a pleasant letter is coming to you.

Night. To walk at night foretells sorrow, but if the moon shines during your journey, happiness will come later.

Night Birds. To dream you hear the cry of any night-bird is a warning to you not to start anything fresh on the day following your dream.

Nightingale. A very lucky dream, and one which foretells happiness in love.

Noise. If you make the noise, it is lucky, but if you hear it, look out for a quarrel.

Nosegay. Should one be offered you, there is a proposal coming to you, but should you be gathering one, take care that you do not lose money.

Numbers. To dream you see any number over ninety is lucky, and foretells success in a business undertaking. Dream interpreters in olden times considered " number " dreams prophetic, and a sign that the particular number dreamed of would be lucky in all matters of chance.

Nun. You will receive a legacy.

Nurse. You will make a change, but do nothing rashly.

Nutmegs. You will travel in far lands.

Nuts. A very good dream, for you may be sure that your sweetheart is all you believe him to be.

Oak Tree. To see it standing, indicates prosperity. Should it be felled, there will be a parting with a friend, while if there are acorns on the tree, you are going to have a slight illness.

Oar. To dream you are rowing with an oar foretells a temporary parting with your sweetheart.

Oats. Always a good dream, for if the oats are standing it means money, while should they be cut down it promises pleasure.

Ocean. To dream that you are on the ocean is a sign that one in whom you have placed your trust is not worthy of it. Should you be swimming in the ocean, perseverance will bring you your wish.

Office. There is a prospect of advancement for you.

Oil. A little foresight will avert a lot of trouble.

Old People. Be careful to do nothing that will give rise to scandal.

Olives. There is a new friend for you.

Omnibus. Should you ride in a crowded bus, you will receive an invitation to a large gathering. Should you be the only occupant, an unexpected honour will be offered you.

Onions. To peel them means a family misfortune, but to eat them is a sign of abundance.

Opal. Your way is not as smooth as you suppose.

Opera. A pleasure is to be offered you, but it may cost you dear.

Operation. To dream that you are undergoing an operation signifies that your affairs will take a turn for the better.

Oranges. To dream you are eating them is a sign of prosperity.

Orange Blossom. You will hear of a wedding in your family.

Orchard. A lucky dream which foretells success in the near future.

Organ. You will hear of sickness.

Orphans. To dream you are an orphan foretells a very unexpected gift of money.

Ostrich. This is a warning to guard your secrets more carefully in future.

Oven. There is a home of your own for you very soon.

Owl. An older friend will give you advice, which you will do well to take.

Ox. This is not a good dream, especially if the oxen be white, but should you dream you see an ox asleep, there is a happy love affair coming your way.

Oysters. You will shortly make a change, and it will prove to be for the better.

Package. If you dream you receive one, look out for some startling news.

Packing. You will be disappointed over a plan you have been making.

Paddling. A warning not to interfere in what does not concern you.

Pail. To carry one indicates that a secret will be confided to you.

Painting. To dream you are painting, or watching anyone else doing so, foretells that you will be asked to share in an adventure.

Palace. You will marry above your station.

Palm Tree. You will have beautiful children.

Pancakes. To eat them, warns you that you will repent of an indulgence.

Pansy. Your lover will be faithful, but in humble circumstances.

Pantomime. To dream you are seeing a pantomime bids you take special care on your next journey.

Paper-hanging. To see a room newly papered foretells a parting with your sweetheart.

Parasol. If open, you have a false friend; if shut, some surprising news will be told you.

Parrot. Beware of gossips.

Party. To dream that you are asked to one foretells that you will be requested to come to the assistance of a friend in distress.

Pastry. To dream you are eating it signifies that you will be offered a present of jewellery.

Patches. If you dream you are patching garments, each patch represents a present you will receive.

Paths. A " contrary " dream, for smooth paths indicate trouble, and rough, rocky ones a peaceful future.

Peaches. A very good dream, for it signifies happiness to you and to those dear to you.

Peacock. Pride will cause a fall.

Pearls. You will shed a few tears.

Pears. To eat them shows you will hear of sickness, but if you gather them there is a pleasant surprise in store for you.

Peas. A very good dream, showing success in an undertaking, with much profit.

Pepper. Be watchful, or someone will slander you.

Perfume. Your husband will be good-natured but not ambitious.

Pet. To dream you have a pet of any kind indicates that you will make a sincere friend of your own sex.

Petticoat. Should you dream you lose it, this is a warning to beware of false friends.

Pheasant. You will receive promotion.

Photograph. To see the photograph of a friend foretells a separation.

Pickles. If you dream you are eating these, it is a sign that you have an admirer much older than yourself.

Picnic. A flirtation you will be advised not to take seriously.

Pictures. A good dream, showing that a worry will soon be over.

Pies. Good news is coming to you.

Pigeon. A white one means a wish gratified, a black one a disappointment.

Pigs. These are a warning to be content with what you have.

Pine Wood. You will have a dispute with an old friend.

Pinks. You will have a present of something to wear.

Pipe. If you smoke it, you will triumph over an enemy.

Pit. To dream you fall into one is lucky.

Ploughing. A dream which bids you hope.

Plums. If these are ripe, you will have an easy future; if green, there are difficulties in your path.

Poison. You will have an admirer, but your family and friends will not approve of him.

Policeman. A family dispute which will be settled to the satisfaction of everyone concerned.

Pomegranate. An omen of success in the near future.

Poplar Tree. There is some way for you to travel before you reach happiness.

Porter. A friend will come to your aid in time of need.

Postman. You will receive news you have been awaiting.

Poverty. A " contrary " dream. You will receive money.

Powder. To dream you are using this indicates that your sweetheart is sincere.

Prayers. To dream that you are praying indicates that you must rely on your own efforts to bring you success.

Precipice. A warning dream; be careful what you do on the day after it.

Present. If a girl dreams that her sweetheart is giving her a present, she will see him when she least expects it.

Prick. To dream you prick your finger is a lucky omen, and if, on awaking, you put the finger in your mouth and wish, your wish will come true within a month.

Prince. A good omen. Someone will leave you money.

Printer. To dream you see a printer is a sign that your husband, or future husband, will make money.

Prison. There is a period of great enjoyment before you.

Prunes. Health and happiness for you.

Psalm. To be singing a psalm is a sign that you will be asked to be a bridesmaid.

Pudding. To dream you are eating one, bids you expect a visitor.

Purse. To find one indicates you will lose a friend ; to lose one, that you will form a new tie.

Quarrel. An affection you thought lost will be yours again.

Quay. To dream you are on a quay is a sign you will be reunited to a friend.

Queen. A good omen, promising you success.

Queue. Should you dream you are standing in a queue, you will meet an old admirer.

Quicksand. This is a warning to do nothing without careful consideration. Special care should be taken on a journey.

Quicksilver. Your sweetheart finds it difficult to make up his mind.

Quoits. You will be asked to do something displeasing to you, but which will turn out better than you think.

Rabbits. If you consent to something that is going to be asked of you, you will regret it.

Race. If you dream that you are running one, it is a sign that you have a rival in love.

Radishes. To dream you are eating these is a sign of profit.

Rags. A lucky dream, foretelling a rise in the world.

Railway. This foretells difficulties, but if you enter a train you will overcome them.

Rain. To dream you are caught in a shower promises you several admirers.

Rainbow. In the east it is lucky, but if in the west, take care you do not quarrel with a friend, while if it is overhead, you may hear of illness.

Raisins. A good dream, signifying you will triumph over one who is trying to harm you.

Ram. To dream a ram butts you foretells a surprise.

Rambling. You will have a quarrel, but it will soon be over.

Raspberries. To pick them is good but to eat them foretells a disappointment.

Rats. These are a warning against enemies. Should they be white rats, it is a sign that you will triumph over those who try to work you harm.

Raven. Not a good omen. Beware of doing anything you would not like known.

Razor. A quarrel, unless you are very careful.

Reaping. A very lucky dream, for it signifies that you will always have abundance.

Red. To dream of anything this colour is a warning of danger ahead.

Reptiles. Secret enemies.

Rhubarb. This is a sign of prosperity.

Ribbons. A warning against extravagance.

Rice. You will receive a proposal, but not the one you desire.

Ring. Always a good sign. If you are wearing one, your love affair will have a happy ending ; if you are already engaged, then your marriage is nearer than you imagine.

River. A good dream, indicating a turn for the better in your affairs, but should you fall in, trouble will be caused by an envious rival.

Robber. You are in danger of losing your heart to someone whom you will meet shortly.

Rocks. There are difficulties ahead, but with courage you will overcome them.

Rook. This is a sign that something which is worrying you will soon be over.

Room. To dream you are in a strange room shows you will accomplish your desires.

Rope. Unless you are very careful you will be drawn into a quarrel.

Roses. Always a good dream. If you gather them full blown, there is happiness coming to you. If they are withered, you must dare all to win all.

Rouge. There is falseness where you least expect it.

Rug. There will be family discord.

Ruin. A " contrary " dream, for it signifies increased good fortune.

Rust. This is not a good dream. Your plans will not fall out according to your wishes.

Sack. A surprise, but it may not be an altogether pleasant one.

Saddle. You will meet with opposition.

Saffron. Gather this, and you will gather gold.

Sailor. To dream of a sailor indicates that you will receive news from overseas.

Saint. Do not come to a hasty decision, or you will repent it.

Salad. To dream you are making a salad denotes that you will hear of the recovery of a sick friend.

Sale. To dream that you attend a sale shows that someone has a deep admiration for you, but is too shy to express it.

Salmon. There will be family squabbles.

Salt. You have treacherous friends.

Salve. To use lip-salve in a dream is a warning to watch your words with special care.

Sand. A good dream, foretelling a happy married life.

Sardines. To dream you are eating these foretells some slight disagreement.

Satin. To dream you are dressed in satin signifies a rise in the world.

Sausages. You will become involved in a dispute, but you will be the victor.

Savages. You will be invited to a party.

Saw. There will be sickness in the house.

Scaffold. To dream of scaffolding shows that there is danger in the way you are thinking of taking.

Scandal. To dream that people are talking scandal about you is the sign of a coming legacy.

School. If you dream you are at school, you will meet an admirer you had almost forgotten.

Scissors. This dream foretells marriage, but if you are cutting out with scissors, someone will try to part you from your sweetheart.

Sea. If it is calm and clear, happiness awaits you, but if it is rough, you will have to overcome difficulties before you attain your wish.

Seed. A very good dream, and your plans will be carried out to your satisfaction.

Servant. Should you dream that you are giving instructions to one, your plans will miscarry.

Sewing. This means good news for you. If you are watching someone sew, you will have an industrious husband.

Shamrock. You will cross the water.

Shawl. There is money for you, but should the shawl be ragged, you will be disappointed in the amount you receive.

Sheep. You will be consoled for a loss.

Shells. If you see them, you will be surprised at a piece of news, but should you be gathering them, beware of treachery.

Shepherd. Not a good dream. You will hear bad news.

Ship. To be sailing in one is a sign that your hopes will be realised, but should you see one sink, beware of a false friend.

Shoes. You will be lucky in your enterprise ; if you lose your shoes there is a small trouble ahead.

Shrimps. Not a good omen. You will be worried about someone dear to you.

Shroud. A very lucky dream.

Silver. A good omen, unless you are selling silverware, and then your wish will be delayed.

Singing. Should you dream you are singing, it is a sign that trouble is coming, but it will be over very soon.

Sisters. To dream of your sisters is a sign of long life.

Skating. You will be offered a more responsible position, but do not be in a hurry to accept.

Skeleton. A very good omen.

Sky. A clear sky indicates happiness, but if there are many clouds you will be vexed before long.

Sliding. If you are sliding alone, it is lucky, while if a young man is helping you, you will shortly have an admirer. Should you both fall over together, you will marry him.

Slippers. You will have comfort in your married life.

Smoke. You will get your wish, but it will bring you little satisfaction.

Snakes. To see these means a quarrel.

Snow. You will be successful in what you are about to undertake. If you are walking in the snow, you are going a long journey.

Soap. If you are in difficulty, to dream of soap is a sign that there is a way out.

Soldier. Family wrangles.

Soot. You will travel.

Soup. A small misfortune may be expected.

Sovereign. A lucky omen, foretelling a rise in the world.

Sowing. Be very careful in starting a new venture.

Spade. Should you dream you are using one, take care to do nothing you wish to hide.

Sparrow. Some slight trouble is indicated.

Spectacles. Someone is trying to deceive you.

Spice. You will be asked a favour you do not wish to grant.

Spider. A lucky dream ; to see the web as well, means much pleasure coming to you. Should you dream that you kill a spider, however, you will hear of an illness.

Spinning. You will receive a legacy.

Sponge. Beware of a false friend.

Spoons. Should you share a spoon in your dream, you should guard against quarrelling with a friend.

Squirrel. You will be told a secret.

Stable. A dear friend will pay you an unexpected visit.

Stag. Someone will make a proposition to you to which it will be to your interest to listen.

Stain. Should you dream you are rubbing out a stain, you will have an opportunity of righting a wrong you have done.

Stairs. If you dream you are ascending, this is lucky, but to descend means a disappointment.

Star. To dream you see one signifies happiness in love, but should it fall from the sky, be prepared for bad news.

Starching. To dream you are starching indicates a prosperous marriage.

Stocking. If they are of silk, you will be offered advancement; if of cotton, unexpected news.

Stones. To see many of these denotes worries.

Storks. To see two promises marriage.

Storm. You are in danger.

Stove. If there is a fire in it, money; if cold, a loss of money.

Stranger. News of a lost friend.

Straw. Your husband will be affectionate, but not very prosperous.

Strawberries. Unhoped-for success.

String. You may expect good news.

Sun. Should you see it rise, it is lucky, but if it is setting, you will meet with vexation.

Supper. You will receive news of a child.

Swallow. Be careful to whom you tell your secrets.

Swan. A good omen.

Sweep. Should you dream you see a sweep, you will hear of an accident, but if you are sweeping you will receive money.

Swimming. You will rise in life through your own efforts.

Sword. An unexpected piece of news.

Table. A sign of prosperity in marriage.

Taffeta. You will spend money without profit.

Tailor. You will pass through sorrow to joy.

Tar. Look before you leap, or you will regret it.

Tea. You will receive an invitation which will give you great pleasure.

Tears. A " contrary " dream, for it signifies joy.

Telegram. To dream you receive this denotes a hasty marriage.

Theatre. A warning against flirting.

Thimble. You will change your occupation for the better.

Thistle. You must be more energetic if you wish to obtain your wish.

Thorn. Difficulties will beset you.

Thread. There will be complications in your romance.

Throne. Not a good dream. You will hear of illness.

Thrush. If you hear one singing in your dream you will listen to a proposition you have long wished to hear.

Thunder. You will hear a piece of news which will greatly surprise you.

Tickle. To dream someone is tickling you indicates pleasure in the future.

Tide. An unlucky omen.

Tiger. Take care, or you will receive a scolding.

Tinker. Your troubles will mend.

Toads. A friend will do you a very good turn.

Toast. To dream you are making toast indicates that you will receive good news; if you are eating it, that happiness is coming to you.

Tobacco. You have a jealous sweetheart.

Toilet. To dream you are making your toilet is a sign that you may have to go into mourning.

Tombs. A very lucky dream.

Tongs. A friend is in difficulties.

Tools. You must work hard to win your reward.

Top. To dream you are spinning a top signifies that you must make up your mind to stick to one friend.

Topaz. A man in uniform will cause trouble.

Tortoise. Your plan will be successful, but do not grow impatient.

Tower. You will be given promotion ; but should you see it fall, you will have a setback.

Tramp. A well-to-do suitor will offer you marriage.

Traps. Should you set one, the attentions being paid you are not sincere.

Travelling. A lucky dream, for there is money in store for you.

Treasure. A " contrary " dream, for it foretells loss.

Trees. You must expect disappointment, but there will be happiness in the future.

Tripe. Be careful, or you will become entangled with an undesirable friend.

Trouble. There is pleasure in store for you.

Trout. To dream of this fish signifies adventure.

Trunk. You must work hard if you wish to succeed.

Tulips. A very lucky dream, for it promises abundance.

Tumbler. To drink from a tumbler denotes that you will hear of a friend recovering from an illness.

Tunnel. Trouble, but it will very soon pass.

Turkeys. Your admirer may be intemperate.

Turnips. An unlucky omen.

Turtle. A very easy-going husband for you.

Turtle-dove. You are in danger of losing your heart.

Twins. You will have news from overseas.

Ugly. A " contrary " dream, for it promises you a handsome sweetheart.

Umbrella. Someone is hiding a secret from you.

Uncle. To dream of an uncle foretells a visit from a friend who will bring you pleasant news.

Unconscious. Should you dream you are unconscious, be careful when you take a journey.

Underground. You are going to share a romantic secret.

Undertaker. A lucky omen, indicating that marriage is to be offered you.

Unemployed. To dream that you are unemployed indicates that you will be asked to undertake a difficult task.

Unfaithful. Should you dream that your lover is unfaithful, it denotes the contrary.

Uniform. If you dream you are wearing uniform, an unexpected honour is to be offered you.

Untidy. If you are in untidy surroundings it is a warning to you not to give offence to a friend.

Upholster. To dream that you are upholstering anything denotes that there will be sickness in the house.

Urn. You will receive news of a birth.

Vaccinate. Should you dream you are being vaccinated, you will receive news of an absent member of the family.

Valentine. Someone admires you, but is too shy to tell you so.

Valley. To dream you are walking through a valley is a sign that you will have an illness from which you will speedily recover.

Van. You will have a piece of unexpected good luck.

Vault. You have found your way to someone's heart.

Veal. To dream you are cooking, or eating, veal promises you good news.

Vegetables. You will work without reward for your labour.

Veil. You will receive news of a wedding.

Velvet. You should make a happy and prosperous marriage.

Village. You will hear a piece of news which concerns your family.

Vine. A good omen, signifying abundance.

Vinegar. Be careful what you do, or you may repent it.

Violets. Romance is coming your way.

Violin. To dream you are playing one promises you happiness in love.

Visit. Should you dream you are going away, then you may expect a visitor, but should you dream you are receiving a visitor, you will go on a journey.

Voice. To dream you hear a strange voice is a sign that your sweetheart has news for you.

Vow. Should you dream you have made one, you may have reason for jealousy.

Vulture. Someone wishes you harm, but you will triumph.

Wading. In clear water it is good ; in muddy water you will have trouble.

Wagon. Not a lucky dream, for you may have a disappointment.

Waiter. Control your temper, or you may say something you will have cause to regret.

Walking. Should you dream you are walking, you will meet with some difficulty in connection with your work.

Wall. Should one stand in your way, you are in danger of doing something you will regret, but if you jump down from one, you will get a wish.

Wallet. You will receive an invitation to a merry gathering.

Walnuts. A very good omen. Your heart's desire will be granted you.

Want. A " contrary " dream, for to dream you are in want signifies riches.

War. A family argument.

Warts. Should you dream you have these on your hands it is a warning to be careful in your dealings with strangers.

Wash. If you dream you are washing yourself, this is lucky, but should you be washing clothes, then you will hear bad news.

Wasp. Someone is spreading unkind tales about you.

Watch. You will take an unexpected journey.

Water. Clear water is good ; dirty water, bad. To dream you are carrying it means bad news, but should you see another person carrying it, you will receive a pleasant surprise.

Water-lily. Your sweetheart will have a fine, upright character.

Waves. Do not believe all that is said to you.

Wax. Your sweetheart has great difficulty in making up his mind.

Wealth. You may lose money.

Weasel. A warning to remember that all is not gold that glitters.

Wedding. You may hear of one soon.

Weeping. You will have cause for laughter.

Well. Should you draw water from it, marriage will be offered you ; if the well is dry, you will fall in love, but not marry.

Whale. There is danger ahead.

Wheat. A very lucky omen.

Whip. To dream of this indicates that you will receive a reproof.

Widow. You will hear of an engagement.

Wilderness. To dream you are wandering in a wilderness promises you many friends.

Willow. You will hear of illness.

Wind. You will be drawn into a quarrel unless you are careful.

Window. There is gossip about you.

Wine. To dream you are drinking this is always a good omen.

Winter. To dream of winter in summer is a sign of illness.

Wireless. To dream you are listening-in foretells startling news.

Witch. You will have a friend when you most need one.

Wolf. You have a dark-haired enemy.

Wood. To dream you are walking in a wood promises you joy after sorrow.

Wool. Your affairs may become entangled.

Work. To dream you are at work foretells a period of idleness.

Workhouse. Money is coming to you.

Worm. Think well over what you are going to do, or you may regret it.

Wreath. You will hear of a wedding.

Wreck. Should you dream you see one, it is a sign that your confidence is misplaced.

Wren. A very lucky omen.

Wrestle. To dream you are wrestling with someone shows that you will require all your courage to overcome a difficulty.

Wrinkles. Someone admires you very much.

Writing. You will receive most unexpected news.

Wrong. To dream you are doing something wrong is a warning to look before you leap.

Yacht. You are in danger of losing your heart.

Yard. To dream you are in a yard promises you a holiday.

Yarn. A very puzzling question will be asked you ; think well before you answer it.

Yawn. Should you dream you are yawning, it is a sign that you must work hard to get your wish.

Yeast. You are going to be vexed.

Yellow. A lucky dream, promising money.

Yew Tree. You will rise in the world through the influence of a friend.

Yolk. To dream of the yolk of an egg foretells a happy year.

Young. To dream that you are younger than you are, promises you a time of pleasure.

Zebra. You will meet with ingratitude.

Zoo. To dream of a visit to a zoo indicates a very eventful life.

KEY TO PLATES

EYES. PLATE 1 :
(1) The Duchess of York. (2) Lady Diana Manners. (3) The Prince of Wales. (4) Amy Mollison. (5) Gladys Cooper.

PLATE 2 :
(6) Ronald Colman. (7) Greta Garbo. (8) Charles Laughton. (9) Anna Sten. (10) George Arliss.

PLATE 3 :
(11) Victoria Hopper. (12) Maurice Chevalier. (13) the late Marie Dressler. (14) Warner Baxter. (15) Katharine Hepburn.

PLATE 4 :
(16) Clark Gable. (17) Marlene Dietrich. (18) Lewis Stone. (19) Gracie Fields. (20) Ralph Lynn.

PLATE 5 :
(21) Janet Gaynor. (22) Jack Hulbert. (23) Mary Brough. (24) Ann Harding. (25) Wallace Beery.

PLATE 6 :
(26) Jack Buchanan. (27) Alison Skipworth. (28) Buster Keaton. (29) Constance Bennett. (30) Jack Holt.

PLATE 7 :
(31) Tallulah Bankhead. (32) Leslie Howard. (33) Kay Francis. (34) Tom Walls. (35) Cicely Courtneidge.

PLATE 8 :
(36) Ruth Chatterton. (37) Clive Brook. (38) Edna May Oliver. (39) Lionel Barrymore. (40) Norma Shearer.

MOUTHS. PLATE 9 :
(41) Ralph Lynn. (42) the late Marie Dressler. (43) Janet Gaynor. (44) Jack Hulbert. (45) Jack Holt. (46) Anna Sten. (47) Gracie Fields. (48) George Arliss.

PLATE 10 :
(49) Mary Brough. (50) Charles Laughton. (51) Wallace Beery. (52) Cicely Courtneidge. (53) Edna May Oliver. (54) Ronald Colman. (55) Jack Buchanan. (56) Greta Garbo.

NOSES. PLATE 11 :
(57) Tom Walls. (58) Ronald Colman. (59) Greta Garbo. (60) Warner Baxter. (61) Gary Cooper. (62) Mary Brough. (63) Ralph Lynn. (64) Kay Francis. (65) Buster Keaton. (66) Marlene Dietrich. (67) Charles Laughton. (68) George Arliss.

PLATE 12 :
(69) Wallace Beery. (70) Norma Shearer. (71) Lewis Stone. (72) Clive Brook. (73) Janet Gaynor. (74) Charles Farrell. (75) Lionel Barrymore. (76) Gracie Fields. (77) Jack Buchanan. (78) Jean Harlow. (79) Leslie Howard. (80) Jack Holt.

CHINS. PLATE 13 :
(81) Tom Walls. (82) Norma Shearer. (83) Lewis Stone. (84) Warner Baxter. (85) Janet Gaynor. (86) Jack Holt. (87) Greta Garbo. (88) Jack Hulbert. (89) Gracie Fields. (90) Ralph Lynn. (91) Charles Farrell. (92) Buster Keaton.

PLATE 14 :
(93) Ronald Colman. (94) Jack Buchanan. (95) Jean Harlow. (96) Lionel Barrymore. (97) Clive Brook. (98) Leslie Howard. (99) Kay Francis. (100) Wallace Beery. (101) Mary Brough. (102) Gary Cooper. (103) Marlene Dietrich. (104) George Arliss.

EARS. PLATE 15 :
(105) Wallace Beery. (106) Charles Laughton. (107) Norma Shearer. (108) Kay Francis. (109) Jack Hulbert. (110) Katharine Hepburn. (111) Warner Baxter. (112) Buster Keaton. (113) Lionel Barrymore. (114) Ronald Colman. (115) Greta Garbo. (116) Jack Holt. (117) Tallulah Bankhead. (118) George Arliss. (119) Ralph Lynn. (120) Clark Gable. (121) Lewis Stone. (122) Mary Brough. (123) Jack Buchanan. (124) Maurice Chevalier. (125) Jean Harlow. (126) Leslie Howard. (127) Charles Farrell. (128) Clive Brook.

HANDS. PLATE 16 :
(129) Gracie Fields. (130) Tom Walls. (131) Leslie Howard. (132) Edna May Oliver. (133) Oliver Hardy. (134) Victoria Hopper. (135) Jack Holt. (136) Ralph Lynn. (137) Norma Shearer. (138) George Arliss. (139) Alison Skipworth. (140) Ruth Chatterton.